ENNIS AND NANCY HAM LIBRARY
ROCHESTER COLLEGE
800 WEST AVON ROAD
ROCHESTER HILLS, MI 48307

YALE HISTORICAL PUBLICATIONS
Leonard Woods Labaree · Editor
MISCELLANY
XLVII

THE TWENTY-NINTH VOLUME
PUBLISHED UNDER THE DIRECTION OF
THE DEPARTMENT OF HISTORY ON THE
KINGSLEY TRUST ASSOCIATION PUBLICATION FUND
ESTABLISHED BY
THE SCROLL AND KEY SOCIETY
OF YALE COLLEGE

THE
COURT OF THE CONNÉTABLIE

A STUDY OF A
FRENCH ADMINISTRATIVE TRIBUNAL
DURING THE REIGN OF
HENRY IV

BY

JOHN HEWITT MITCHELL

INSTRUCTOR IN HISTORY IN
WELLESLEY COLLEGE

NEW HAVEN
YALE UNIVERSITY PRESS

LONDON · GEOFFREY CUMBERLEGE · OXFORD UNIVERSITY PRESS

1947

COPYRIGHT, 1947, BY YALE UNIVERSITY PRESS

Printed in the United States of America

All rights reserved. This book may not be reproduced, in whole or in part, in any form (except by reviewers for the public press), without written permission from the publishers.

To F. F. M.

PREFACE

THE present work is a study of the tribunal of the *Connétablie et Maréchaussée de France* during the reign of Henry IV. M. Georges Guichard and especially M. Gabriel Le Barrois d'Orgeval have already dealt with the subject at some length. This book is not intended to replace either of their works, but is designed to supplement their investigations. These two volumes have been utilized extensively in the preparation of Chapter I and have been referred to frequently throughout the remainder of the present work.

For this study of the *Connétablie* the court records have been used almost exclusively and from them a picture of the court as it actually functioned has been derived. These cases are typical of the work done by the tribunal. Since the court records are summaries rather than stenographic reports, some cases are treated by the clerk more fully than others. These have, naturally, been used more than the briefer ones, but the others, which are cited in the footnotes, confirm the conclusions. In order to facilitate reading I have modernized part of the seventeenth-century spelling in the appendixes and have inserted punctuation.

I wish first of all to thank the officials of Yale University, through whose kindness I was permitted to use a camera belonging to the Sterling Memorial Library. I was thus able, during the period prior to the war, to photograph in full the court records, which I found in the Archives Nationales in Paris. I wish especially to express my great appreciation and my indebtedness to the late Professor John M. S. Allison, of Yale University, and to Professor Leonard W. Labaree, of Yale University, editor of the Yale Historical Series. This work was originally written as my doctoral dissertation under the guidance of Professor Allison. His wide and accurate knowledge, both at that time and since I undertook its revision, was always freely placed at my disposal. Professor Labaree has spent uncounted hours over the manuscript and has done much to bring it to its present form. The comments and suggestions of Professor William H. Dunham, Jr., of Yale University, have been of immeasurable aid. He has analyzed the manuscript carefully and has helped greatly. Professors Lewis P.

Curtis and Hajo Holborn, also of Yale University, have contributed valuable suggestions. Finally, my thanks are due the officials of the Archives Nationales, Paris, who permitted me to bring in the camera and to photograph my material.

J. H. M.

Wellesley, Massachusetts,
October 1, 1946.

CONTENTS

Preface	VII
I. The Historical Background of the Court	1
II. The Court at the End of the Wars of Religion	22
III. The Jurisdiction of the Court	39
IV. The Procedure of the Court	63
V. The Offices of the Court	98
VI. General Conclusions and Summary	118
Appendixes	123
Bibliographical Note	155
Index	161

I

THE HISTORICAL BACKGROUND OF THE COURT

THE work of the tribunal of the *Connétablie et Maréchaussée* was in part military in character, in part civilian. In order to understand this combination of military and civilian cases a brief consideration of the historical background of the court and of the judicial system of the Old Régime is essential. The tribunal originated from a delegation of judicial power by the early military commanders and so the question of leadership of the military forces should first be considered.

The basic reason for the eventual establishment of the tribunal of the *Connétablie* was the simultaneous possession by one official of the powers of military command and the power to dispense military justice. Under the Carolingians and early Capetians military command entailed the concurrent exercise of the judicial aspects of military discipline and the maintenance of public order in territories where soldiers were located. Thus was established a principle which was always observed thereafter in theory, although not in practice. This disciplinary authority was exercised in the manner which the commander deemed necessary. No precise rules for the administration and procedure of justice were laid down, and the accused was completely at the mercy of the judge who was at the same time his immediate military commander.[1] The command of the entire army was often delegated by the king, who was at the same time commander-in-chief and the fountainhead of all justice. The king or his delegate exercised this dual power directly over the royal troops and at times also judged occasional appeals from the decisions of the subordinate commanders, who were royal vassals or rear-vassals. This practice was therefore simply the regular procedure of the feudal hierarchy transplanted to the military sphere.[2] It also laid the basis for the later appellate jurisdiction of the tribunal of the *Connétablie*. The regular exercise of military justice was divided, however, among the

---

1. Georges Guichard, *La Juridiction des prévôts du connétable et des maréchaux de France*, p. 77 (hereafter cited as Guichard, *Prévôts*).
2. *Ibid.*, p. 90.

royal vassals and rear-vassals, who kept the command of their own contingents.[3] In any discussion of the origin of the officers who later reached high military rank, it must be remembered that in early times the command of the royal forces had not the importance which it later acquired. The army was a gathering of motley and often rival bands, each of which acknowledged the direct authority of none but its own commander, who was a vassal or rear-vassal of the king. The king himself was in fact not very different from these great lords. Although he had the nominal command of the entire army of the Crown, his actual authority usually did not extend beyond his personal contingent.

The Merovingian and Carolingian kings either took personal command of the army or delegated that task to someone who enjoyed their confidence. That person was usually one of the several palace officials. He enjoyed a strictly temporary delegation of power, for the exercise of which no definite rules were laid down.[4] No particular official had the exclusive right of command of military affairs. This power was therefore not necessarily a prerogative of any single royal officer, but depended rather on the personal qualities of the holder or on his favor with the king.[5] As the palace officials at that time combined public functions with domestic duties, it is not surprising that later the *comes stabuli* or the *marescallus* should be in command of armies.[6]

The kings of the late eleventh and twelfth centuries retained in appearance the Merovingian and Carolingian officials, but in reality they wrought a transformation in the character of the central administrative organization. A degree of specialization ultimately grew out of the former confusion and resulted in the division of major governmental duties among the *chancelier, bouteiller, connétable, chambrier,* and *sénéchal*.[7] These five were thenceforth known as the *grands officiers de la couronne*. Included in this specialization was the command and discipline of the armed forces, which finally was given exclusively to the *sénéchal*.

3. *Ibid.*, pp. 79–80.
4. *Ibid.*, pp. 80–81.
5. Jacques Flach, *Les Origines de l'ancienne France: x^e et xie siècles*, III, 468 (hereafter cited as Flach, *Origines*).
6. Numa-Denis Fustel de Coulanges, *Histoire des institutions politiques de l'ancienne France*, VI, 336 (hereafter cited as Fustel, *Institutions*).
7. Guichard, *Prévôts*, p. 86; Achille Luchaire, *Histoire des institutions monarchiques de la France sous les premiers Capétiens, 987–1180*, I, 167–171 (hereafter cited as Luchaire, *Capétiens*).

During the Merovingian period the *sénéchal* was the director of the service of the king's table.[8] Although he continued these purely domestic duties after the advent of the Carolingians, the *sénéchal* also began to play a military rôle.[9] This period marks the beginning of his rise to the first rank, since he also inherited part of the judicial powers of the *comte du palais* after the suppression of that office.[10] After an interval of obscurity during the tenth century, the *sénéchal* forged rapidly to the front and by the early twelfth century had in fact, although not in law, become a viceroy. Henry I (1031–1060) added to the *sénéchal's* political strength by conferring on him the exclusive right of military command.[11] The *sénéchal* was at this time the superintendent of the king's household, the commander of the royal army, with the responsibility for summoning the royal vassals for military expeditions and for the direction of military operations, the head of the local administration with responsibility for the surveillance and the direction of the *prévôts*, and the supreme head of justice (shared with the *chancelier*).[12] As army commander and head of the judicial system, the *sénéchal* pronounced on appeals from judgments rendered by dukes and counts in positions of subordinate army command.[13] This usage strengthened the principle of the union of military command and the exercise of military justice, whose origin lay in the Merovingian period.

At the opening of the reign of Louis VI (1108–1137), the king was in very real danger of becoming a shadow monarch, similar to the later Merovingians. The power and ambition of the Rochefort family, who had held the *sénéchalat* since 1091, made the

8. Guichard, *Prévôts*, pp. 82, 87.
9. In 786, for instance, he commanded an expedition against the Bretons. Fustel, *Institutions*, VI, 335.
10. Ernest Glasson, *Histoire du droit et des institutions de la France*, V, 359 (hereafter cited as Glasson, *Droit*).
11. Flach, *Origines*, III, 466; Guichard, *Prévôts*, pp. 86–87.
12. Luchaire, *Capétiens*, I, 177–180; Flach, *Origines*, III, 465–466; Paul Viollet, *Histoire des institutions politiques et administratives de la France*, II, 109–110 (hereafter cited as Viollet, *Histoire*); A. Chéruel, *Histoire de l'administration monarchique en France, depuis l'avènement de Philippe-Auguste jusqu'à la mort de Louis XIV*, I, 9 (hereafter cited as Chéruel, *Administration*); Edgard Boutaric, *Institutions militaires de la France avant les armées permanentes*, p. 268 (hereafter cited as Boutaric, *Institutions militaires*); A. Esmein, *Cours élémentaire d'histoire du droit français*, 15ᵉ éd., p. 431 (hereafter cited as Esmein, *Cours*); Glasson, *Droit*, V, 361; Guichard, *Prévôts*, p. 87; A. Luchaire, *Manuel des institutions françaises; période des Capétiens directs*, pp. 521–522 (hereafter cited as Luchaire, *Manuel*).
13. Guichard, *Prévôts*, p. 90.

peril more acute. Louis VI finally defeated the Rocheforts in a civil war and deprived them of the *sénéchalat* which he then conferred on a member of the equally ambitious Garlande family.[14] The only result was a second civil war in which the *sénéchal* was once more humbled. The other kings of the twelfth century kept a strict control over the office and Philip II (1180–1223), at the death of the incumbent in 1191, simply suppressed the position in practice by leaving it vacant. Not until the fourteenth century, however, was it abolished in name. Part of the powers of the *sénéchal* devolved upon the *connétable*, the cavalry commander.[15]

The office of *sénéchal* joined in one person the two functions of military command and exercise of military justice and discipline. The feudal procedure of appeals from vassal to lord was observed in judicial matters in the feudal royal army and paved the way for the establishment of appellate jurisdiction in later times for the tribunal of the *Connétablie*. Knowledge of these facts is essential for an understanding of the history and the operation of the tribunal of the *Connétablie et Maréchaussée de France*.

Although there is some disagreement among the authorities on the date of the origin of the *connétable*, all are agreed that under the Merovingians and Carolingians this officer was of high rank in the royal domestic service and that on occasion, by means of temporary royal commission, he commanded military expeditions.[16] He was the manager of the royal stables, a position which became more important after the eighth century, when cavalry became the driving force of the armies.[17] With the advent of the Capetians the *connétable* took his place among the five *grands officiers* and to his earlier duties and judicial powers added the command of the cavalry.[18]

14. Luchaire, *Capétiens*, I, 181–183.
15. *Ibid.*, I, 184–185; A. Chéruel, *Dictionnaire historique des institutions, moeurs et coutumes de la France*, II, 1148 (hereafter cited as Chéruel, *Dictionnaire*); Chéruel, *Administration*, I, 9–10; Glasson, *Droit*, V, 362, 370; Esmein, *Cours*, p. 431; Guichard, *Prévôts*, pp. 87–88; Boutaric, *Institutions militaires*, pp. 268–269; Viollet, *Histoire*, II, 110–111.
16. Paul Guérin, "Recherches sur l'office de connétable," *Positions des thèses* (*Ecole des Chartes*), 1867–1868, pp. 31–32 (hereafter cited as Guérin, "Recherches"); Gabriel Le Barrois d'Orgeval, *Le Maréchalat de France des origines à nos jours*, I, 11 (hereafter cited as Orgeval, *Maréchalat*); Guichard, *Prévôts*, p. 91; Luchaire, *Capétiens*, I, 171; Luchaire, *Manuel*, p. 526; Fustel, *Institutions*, VI, 327, 335; Esmein, *Cours*, p. 431; Glasson, *Droit*, II, 307.
17. Flach, *Origines*, III, 467–468.
18. Chéruel, *Dictionnaire*, I, 209; Guérin, "Recherches," p. 33.

Although the suppression of the *sénéchal* resulted in an increase in the power of the *connétable*, his rise to supreme military command was not immediate. The *sénéchalat*, with its right of supreme command, was still in existence and might at any time be filled.[19] Though the *connétable* in the thirteenth century often led military expeditions, he did so not by any prerogative, but by virtue of a temporary royal commission. The rise in prestige of the office was due primarily to the personal qualities of three illustrious soldiers: Raoul de Clermont, Dreux de Mello, and Mathieu II de Montmorency, *connétable* from 1218 until his death in 1230.[20]

As part of his general policy of centralization and institutional development, Philip IV (1285–1314) began the practice of appointing members of the royal family, princes of the blood, great vassals, and high officials as his *lieutenants-généraux* in the provinces, especially when there was a state of war or a danger thereof. He granted to these new officials extensive civil and military powers. The first example of this was in 1294, when Languedoc was menaced by the Emperor.[21] Since the *connétable* was frequently at the same time a provincial *lieutenant-général*, he gradually acquired the prerogatives of the latter position.[22] The final result of this dual impetus of personal prestige and additional powers was the elevation of the *connétable*, by the middle of the fourteenth century, to the permanent supreme command of the army. The seal was set on this development by the events of the Hundred Years' War and by the prestige and ability of the *connétables* Du Guesclin (1370–1380) and Olivier de Clisson (1380–1392).

The prerogatives of the *connétable*, besides the supreme command of the army and numerous other rights and privileges, included the following judicial powers: exclusive jurisdiction over all members of his personal suite; jurisdiction over all crimes and misdemeanors of soldiers in time of war; jurisdiction over all personal suits in which soldiers were defendants; and jurisdiction

---

19. Guérin, "Recherches," p. 33.
20. Chéruel, *Dictionnaire*, I, 209; Guichard, *Prévôts*, pp. 94–95; Guérin, "Recherches," p. 34; Luchaire, *Manuel*, p. 526.
21. Boutaric, *Institutions militaires*, pp. 272–273; Guérin, "Recherches," p. 34; Luchaire, *Manuel*, pp. 526–527.
22. Boutaric, *Institutions militaires*, pp. 272–273; Guérin, "Recherches," p. 34; Luchaire, *Manuel*, pp. 526–527.

over the administration of the army.[23] As in the case of the *sénéchal* during his period of power, the supreme direction of military operations was combined in the person of the *connétable* with absolute jurisdiction over criminal, civil, and administrative cases arising within the armed forces. The vesting of these diverse powers in one officer was the basis of the later composition of the tribunal which bore the name of the *connétable*.

In the fourteenth and fifteenth centuries the *connétable* was at the height of his glory, possessed the right to be addressed as "cousin" by the king, and took precedence only after the monarch himself. The tenure of the *connétable* de Saint-Pol (1465–1475) marks the beginning of the decline in the glory of the *connétable*. When Saint-Pol betrayed Louis XI, the power of his position availed him nothing, for the king caused him to be executed, with scant regard for previous relationships.[24] Thenceforth, and particularly after the treason of the *connétable* de Bourbon, the office was held in extreme distrust by the kings and in the sixteenth century remained vacant for many years. In 1627, Louis XIII (1610–1643) suppressed it permanently. The mantle of military command then fell upon the *maréchaux de France*.

Although the *maréchaux de France* were the most brilliant military figures of the last three centuries of the Old Régime and survive today in modified form, their origin, like that of the two earlier military commanders, was in domestic employment in the palaces of the early kings of France. *Maréchaux* are mentioned in the laws of the barbarians. Most authorities agree that under the Merovingians and Carolingians the *maréchaux* were subordinate officers, concerned with the service of the royal stables and directly dependent on the *connétable*.[25] Throughout this period they apparently possessed neither the right to command troops nor to dispense military justice.[26] Until sometime during the thirteenth century there was but one *maréchal*. The burden of duties, however, necessitated the creation of a second. From the four-

23. Chéruel, *Dictionnaire*, I, 209; Boutaric, *Institutions militaires*, pp. 269–271; Viollet, *Histoire*, II, 114–115; Guérin, "Recherches," pp. 35–37; Glasson, *Droit*, V, 371; Marcel Marion, *Dictionnaire des institutions de la France au xviie et xviiie siècles*, pp. 129–130 (hereafter cited as Marion, *Dictionnaire*); Guichard, *Prévôts*, pp. 95–97.

24. Viollet, *Histoire*, I, 116.

25. Chéruel, *Dictionnaire*, II, 733; Fustel, *Institutions*, VI, 327; Guichard, *Prévôts*, p. 104; Orgeval, *Maréchalat*, I, 10–11.

26. Guichard, *Prévôts*, pp. 105–106.

teenth century until the reign of Francis I (1515–1547) there were in theory but two, although in practice there were often three or more.[27]

The *maréchaux* were never permitted to acquire the extensive rights and privileges previously enjoyed by both the *connétable* and the *sénéchal*. The position was never hereditary nor, prior to the sixteenth century, given for life. There are several examples of forced or voluntary resignation.[28] Clearly the royal policy was to prevent the development of another viceroy. The *maréchaux*, although still subordinate to the *connétable*, had acquired by the late twelfth century military duties and a certain importance.[29] This rise seems to be the logical consequence of the increase in importance of the *connétable*. There is, however, no proof for the contention that the *maréchaux* held military command before the *connétable* acquired that power.[30] A charter of 1209 reveals that at about this time the *maréchaux* began to command armies.[31] It must always be remembered that during this period a *maréchal* exercised military command, like the *connétable*, more because of personal merit than because of any prerogative attached to the office.[32] Under Philip IV the *maréchaux* shared in the appointments to the civil and military government of provinces with the title of *lieutenant-général* and later permanently acquired some of the prerogatives of that position.

As the duties of the *maréchaux* developed during the thirteenth and fourteenth centuries, they included more than the command of part of the army under the supreme direction of the *connétable*. The *maréchaux* also had disciplinary and administrative tasks and were responsible for the proper arrangement of camps, the maintenance of good administration of the combat units, the protection of the civil population from the excesses and depredations of the soldiers, the exercise by delegation from the *connétable* of the judicial powers inherent in the above duties, the

27. See the following authorities for their divergent conclusions regarding the number of *maréchaux*: Boutaric, *Institutions militaires*, p. 271; Chéruel, *Dictionnaire*, II, 733–734; Glasson, *Droit*, V, 372; Guichard, *Prévôts*, p. 113; Orgeval, *Maréchalat*, I, 13–15, 30–31.
28. Chéruel, *Dictionnaire*, II, 733; Orgeval, *Maréchalat*, I, 30–37. Bernard de Moreuil and others.
29. Glasson, *Droit*, V, 365, 372; Marion, *Dictionnaire*, p. 362; Luchaire, *Manuel*, p. 526.
30. Guichard, *Prévôts*, pp. 107–110.
31. Orgeval, *Maréchalat*, I, 17.
32. *Ibid.*, I, 18.

presence in the army of the correct quotas of soldiers of each vassal, the supervision and management of the payment of the troops, after verification of the quotas, and the supervision of marches.[33] As the number of troops and the extent of territory grew, the *maréchaux* were obliged to appoint assistants, whose task it was to help them in their duties of inspection and administration. These assistants enjoyed at first temporary delegations of power and later evolved into permanent officials. In 1567, the royal offices[34] of *commissaires des guerres* and *contrôleurs des guerres* were created. These were the institutional descendants of the appointees who helped the *maréchaux* determine that the quotas of soldiers were all filled.[35] By the same process the assistants in the preparation of camps evolved into the royal offices of *maréchaux de camp*.[36] Similarly, the powers of discipline held by the *maréchaux* were delegated to the *prévôts des maréchaux*. Since the latter occupied a prominent place in the business of the tribunal of the *Connétablie et Maréchaussée*, they merit further attention.

The origin of the *prévôts* probably lies somewhere between 1240 (the date of the creation of a second *maréchal* by Louis IX) and 1357.[37] The *maréchaux*, due to the pressure of their military duties, began to delegate their power of discipline over the army to a *lieutenant des maréchaux*, later called the *prévôt des maréchaux*. At the outset this officer simultaneously fulfilled the duties of policing the army and of presiding over the court of the *maréchaux*, thus freeing the latter from all except strictly military work.[38] Embodied in this officer are the origins of an organized military justice. Though the *lieutenant* and the *prévôt* were at first identical, they later separated and formed two distinct jurisdictions: the *Connétablie et Maréchaussée*, under the direction of the *lieutenant*, and the *justice prévôtale*, administered by the *prévôt*, which was a more strictly military justice.[39] The date

33. *Ibid.*, I, 199–201; Boutaric, *Institutions militaires*, pp. 273–275; Glasson, *Droit*, V, 372–373; Guichard, *Prévôts*, pp. 106–107.
34. The term "royal office" signifies that the position was purchased. The candidate was inducted into office after his capabilities had been ascertained.
35. Boutaric, *Institutions militaires*, p. 277; Orgeval, *Maréchalat*, I, 201–202.
36. Orgeval, *Maréchalat*, I, 204–205. These officers were also, in the sixteenth and seventeenth centuries, called *maréchaux des logis*.
37. Guichard, *Prévôts*, pp. 40–41, 183.
38. *Ibid.*, pp. 98, 119–120.
39. *Ibid.*, pp. 122–126.

of this transformation cannot be exactly determined, but it occurred sometime in the later fourteenth century.

One of the responsibilities of the *maréchaux* was the protection of the civil population from the excesses and depredations of the soldiery. Troops of archers, led by *prévôts*, were created at about the same time to discharge this duty. These subordinate *prévôts des maréchaux* were chosen by the central *prévôt* and were the agents of justice, by delegation through him, of the *connétable* and the *maréchaux* and of their respective courts.[40] Let it not be imagined that this system sprang immediately into full maturity. Its origin lay in the increase in the number of soldiers, which accompanied the gradual change from feudal levies to a royal standing army, and appeared first in the frontier provinces, where most of the troops were concentrated. Not until the fifteenth century, with the arrival of the standing army, did the jurisdiction of these subordinate *prévôts* pass from the qualification of exceptional to that of ordinary. During this century they were gradually extended from the frontier provinces throughout the kingdom.[41] At the end of the fifteenth century the *prévôts des maréchaux* began to change from simple temporary delegates of a central officer into royal officials and began to purchase their offices. This practice was sanctioned by decree in 1500 and freed them in fact, though not in theory, from the tutelage of the *maréchaux* and their court.[42] Thereupon, the central *prévôt*, deprived of any *raison d'être*, disappeared.[43] The *prévôts des maréchaux* at once began to extend their jurisdiction by a systematic policy of competition with the powers of the ordinary civil judges. The result was the development of a *prévôtal* jurisdiction, somewhat military in character, but in greater part completely divorced from military affairs.[44]

The sixteenth century saw the stabilization of the hitherto fluid organization of the *prévôts des maréchaux*. Besides those in the provinces, there was one attached to the suite of each *maréchal* and called *prévôt à la suite*. In order to increase efficiency,

40. Esmein, *Cours*, p. 386; Glasson, *Droit*, VI, 434; Guichard, *Prévôts*, pp. 27–28, 182; Marion, *Dictionnaire*, p. 362.
41. Esmein, *Cours*, p. 387; Glasson, *Droit*, VI, 434; Paul Viollet, *Le Roi et ses ministres pendant les trois derniers siècles de la monarchie*, p. 308 (hereafter cited as Viollet, *Le Roi*).
42. Guichard, *Prévôts*, p. 28.
43. *Ibid.*, p. 51.
44. Esmein, *Cours*, pp. 386–387.

Henry II (1547–1559) decreed in 1547 that each *maréchal* should be responsible for the maintenance of military discipline in a particular group of provinces.[45] They were soon released from this duty, but their *prévôts à la suite* were retained with the title of *prévôts généraux des maréchaux*. Those already established in the individual provinces then became known as *prévôts provinciaux des maréchaux*. Below these were the *prévôts particuliers des maréchaux*, who had evolved from the fifteenth-century practice of sending a *prévôt* to a particular locality, smaller than a province, when requested by the inhabitants.[46] The *prévôts particuliers* were found only in some places. There was a vague sort of hierarchy, sporadically enforced, at the head of which were the *prévôts généraux*.

In 1554 Henry II first suspended and then suppressed the *prévôts provinciaux*.[47] Greater unification of the varied elements composing the *maréchaussée* was needed. There was also a desire to bring all public offices firmly under royal control. Finally, there was a need to improve the quality of the *prévôts*, of whom there had been constant complaint. By virtue of the edicts of suppression, the *lieutenants criminels de robe longue* of the *présidiaux*, *bailliages*, and *sénéchaussées* assumed the duties of the former *prévôts*.[48] These judges protested vigorously, however, asserting that police work was beneath them and that in any case they already had enough work to do. A second edict therefore created for this purpose officers called *lieutenants criminels de robe courte*. Subsequently those *lieutenants* attached to the *bailliages* and *sénéchaussées* became known as *vice-baillis* and *vice-sénéchaux* respectively, while those attached to the *présidiaux* retained their original title. Furthermore, despite the edicts of suppression, most of the *prévôts* soon re-appeared by the sides of those who had in theory replaced them. The sixteenth century also marked the completion of the transformation of the jurisdiction of the *justice prévôtale*. Although Francis I and his immediate successors[49] issued edicts restricting the *prévôts* to their original disciplinary power over the troops, they and their brother officials resumed the old practice of extending their au-

45. Guichard, *Prévôts*, p. 197; Viollet, *Le Roi*, p. 306.
46. Guichard, *Prévôts*, pp. 29, 57–59, 197.
47. *Ibid.*, pp. 29–30, 244–245; Marion, *Dictionnaire*, p. 454; Viollet, *Le Roi*, pp. 309–310.
48. Guichard, *Prévôts*, pp. 245–247.
49. Viollet, *Le Roi*, p. 309; Guichard, *Prévôts*, pp. 221–231.

thority at the expense of the ordinary courts. Hence, the *maréchaussée* by the end of the sixteenth century had changed from an agency of military justice into one for the maintenance of internal tranquillity. These changes did much to divorce that body in fact from its dependence upon the *maréchaux* and their tribunal.

The *maréchaux*, by the creation of the *commissaires* and *contrôleurs des guerres*, the *maréchaux de camp*, the *prévôts des maréchaux*, the *lieutenants criminels de robe courte*, the *vice-baillis*, and the *vice-sénéchaux*, lost all but their strictly military duties. They still retained, however, the supervision of all these newer officers. Although the latter purchased their offices and were in fact responsible to no one but the king, in theory they were exercising their powers only by delegation from the *maréchaux* and hence were their subordinates. By a further process of delegation, these newer officers were also the subordinates of the court of the *maréchaux* and that of the *connétable*, later known as the *Connétablie et Maréchaussée de France*.

To implement their judicial powers the *connétable* and the *maréchaux* each had a court. Any attempt to fix the date of origin of these bodies is futile. They were not created by decree, but evolved over a considerable period. Furthermore, early writers, most of whom were officers of the tribunal, are most unreliable. Some of their works are memoranda addressed to the higher judicial authorities in defense of their jurisdictional rights in disputes with other courts.[50] When not composing such memoranda these officers wrote treatises to prove the extensive and ancient powers of their institution.[51] The old authors asserted that the *Connétablie et Maréchaussée de France*, a single tribunal, had sat at the *Table de Marbre* in the *Grande Salle* of the *Palais de Justice* in Paris from time immemorial. They based their claims to wide jurisdiction and great age upon the alleged "Twelve Ancient Articles," which enumerate in great detail the specific powers of the tribunal, and were said to have been issued as an ordinance by the Estates General in 1356. Locked in struggles with rival bodies, the court constantly put them forward as justification for its own extravagant claims. Most modern authorities deny that

50. Guichard, *Prévôts*, p. 100.
51. Complete bibliographies of these works are to be found in Guichard, *Prévôts*, and Gabriel Le Barrois d'Orgeval, *Le Tribunal de la Connétablie de France* (hereafter cited as Orgeval, *Connétablie*).

the articles were issued in the fourteenth century. They maintain, on the contrary, that the articles were a fabrication of the sixteenth century and were issued in an effort to bolster the tribunal in its contests over jurisdiction with other courts. In support of this claim, the modern writers point out that there is no mention of the articles in any connection before the sixteenth century and that the ordinances of the mid-fourteenth century contain no hint of any such decree.[52] The articles finally assumed an air of pseudo-legality, however, due to the practice by officers of the *Connétablie et Maréchaussée* of proclaiming them at every turn and of extorting, whenever possible, confirmatory declarations from the government. Thus, the declaration of August 3, 1573, based the jurisdiction of the tribunal on the articles, without, however, dating them. Similar declarations followed in 1617, 1618, and 1660.

No modern writer denies that before their union as the *Connétablie et Maréchaussée de France* the two courts functioned independently of each other.[53] They originally had no fixed seat, but followed the *connétable* and the *maréchaux* on their tours of duty about the country. Not until the middle of the fourteenth century did their place of business become the *Table de Marbre*, where the court, with but three changes during the sixteenth century, remained until its suppression during the Revolution.[54] It is probable that the two originally ambulatory courts merely fell into the habit of conducting their business there, gradually became permanently installed, and finally fused into one body.[55]

At the beginning of the fifteenth century it was still possible to distinguish clearly between the *curia marescallorum* (court of the

---

52. As this work is not primarily a history of the antecedents of the *Connétablie*, but a study of its operation at a much later date, and is not based on early documents, it seems sufficient to refer those interested in this question to the following works: Guérin, "Recherches," p. 38, believes that the content, if not the form, of the "Articles" is genuine; Guichard, *Prévôts,* pp. 97, 128–129, Orgeval, *Connétablie,* pp. 8–14, 47–49, and R. Delachenal, "Journal des états généraux réunis à Paris au mois d'octobre 1356," *Nouvelle revue historique de droit français et étranger,* XXIV (July–August, 1900), 442–443, reject the possibility of authenticity of the "Articles" in that particular form. They also doubt that they were ever issued as an edict. The text of the proceedings, as edited by Delachenal, shows no trace of any such document. The present author, on the basis of the available evidence, agrees with the latter school of thought.

53. Guérin, "Recherches," p. 37; Guichard, *Prévôts,* pp. 115–118, 136–137.

54. Guérin, "Recherches," p. 37; Guichard, *Prévôts,* pp. 138, 142, 143; Orgeval, *Connétablie,* p. 42; Viollet, *Le Roi,* pp. 306–307.

55. Guichard, *Prévôts,* p. 138.

maréchaux) and the *audiencia constabularii Franciae* (court of the *connétable*).[56] Texts of the period show that although the two tribunals met in the same place they worked independently. In principle, the military command of the *maréchaux* was subordinate to that of the *connétable*. Their judicial functions in general, however, were exercised in a parallel and sometimes in an overlapping fashion. The earliest account of a trial dates from 1317. The document speaks distinctly of the *curia* and omits mention of the *connétable*. It seems doubtful, especially as there was a *connétable* in office that year, that if there was but one court the clerk should omit any mention of him or his representative. A manuscript of 1321 shows that the *connétable* on the other hand had his own court. The *chambre des comptes* challenged his jurisdiction in a case and began a long investigation. The king then intervened and assigned the trial to the *bailli* of Vermandois. The text omits any mention of the *maréchaux* or their representative. Decrees of the *parlement* of Paris refer now to one, now to the other, but never do they mention a single tribunal. There are in existence many letters patent issued by the two courts, which differ not only in forms of expression but also in the types of cases considered. Many of these letters still bear their original seals, which are likewise very different. Texts prove that at the time of the *connétable* de Richemont (1424–1458) there were still two distinct courts and that this condition lasted until well into the reign of Louis XI.

The jurisdiction of the two tribunals was very similar. The long separation cannot, therefore, be explained on the basis of differing jurisdictions, nor on the other hand can it be maintained that, due to that similarity, they were not separate bodies, or that independence of each other was but a legal fiction. During the Old Régime there were many institutions which performed nearly identical duties and yet remained entirely independent of each other. The feudal origin of this judicial power is a partial explanation of the continued separation.

The fusion of the two earlier institutions into the *Tribunal de la Connétablie et Maréchaussée de France* took place sometime in

56. *Ibid.,* pp. 115–118, 137; Orgeval, *Connétablie,* pp. 32–36, 40, 43–45, 51, 57–60, 65–66. Nearly all the material for the discussion of the development of the courts and their ultimate union is taken from these two monographs. The other works utilized in this chapter are of so general a nature that only brief accounts are given. Since their conclusions differ in no way from those of Guichard and Orgeval, they will be referred to only incidentally.

the reign of Louis XI, in all probability shortly after the death of the *connétable* de Saint-Pol (1475).[57] The probable reasons were the diminution in the number of cases, due to the rise of other judicial agencies, the decline of the *audiencia,* caused by the loss of prestige by the office of *connétable,* the union in one person of the offices of *lieutenant* of the *connétable* and *lieutenant* of the *maréchaux* about 1475, the common use of the *Table de Marbre* by both courts, and the similarity of the duties performed by the two tribunals. The fusion was thus a natural movement and was not the result of a royal edict. The similarity of their duties was probably the most important single factor. The work of the *audiencia* was of a more general disciplinary nature than that of the *curia.*[58] The former had jurisdiction over personal cases in which soldiers were defendants and had a disciplinary power over the entire army. The latter, on the other hand, had a more administrative jurisdiction. To it were referred petitions for payment of salaries, disputes over prisoners of war, questions concerning reviews of troops and cases of excesses of soldiers towards the civilian population. The duplication of work, therefore, is obvious. The *audiencia,* with its more general powers, often tried cases which with equal justice might have been referred to the *curia.* The latter, on the other hand, with its more specific prerogatives in many instances claimed the right to try cases which in a general way might have been the property of the *audiencia.*

The formation of the new court marked the final and definitive breakdown in practice of the theory of union in one officer of the powers of military command and the exercise of military justice. In theory, the commanders retained their judicial powers, but in practice had delegated them to the *audiencia* and *curia.* When these were joined, their prerogatives devolved upon the new, single tribunal whose jurisdiction was therefore extensive at the outset. It included crimes and misdemeanors of soldiers, lawsuits in which soldiers were concerned, appeals from the courts of the *prévôts des maréchaux,* and the right to remove, on demand, a case from the courts of the *prévôts des maréchaux* and try it. The new court also dealt with nobles who refused military service and considered questions relative to the muster and payment of troops and excesses of the *prévôts des maréchaux.* It had the right to approve the appointments of the following officers and to administer

---

57. Guichard, *Prévôts,* pp. 117–118; Orgeval, *Connétablie,* pp. 65–66.
58. Guichard, *Prévôts,* p. 116; Orgeval, *Connétablie,* pp. 56–57.

to them their oath of office: *connétable, maréchaux, commissaires* and *contrôleurs des guerres, prévôts des maréchaux, vice-baillis, vice-sénéchaux, lieutenants criminels de robe courte*. The tribunal also had the duty of enforcing edicts against duels, illegal carrying of arms, and illegal assemblage, and of registering royal letters of pardon for any of the above crimes.[59] The tribunal of the *Connétablie* thus formed for a time an important part of the French judicial system. In order to place the *Connétablie* in its proper setting, the character and component parts of that system must be understood.

The judicial system of the Old Régime was divided into two parts. The ordinary law courts, on the one hand, included the *parlements*, the presidial courts (*cours présidiaux*), the *bailliages* and *sénéchaussées*, and the *prévôtés*, all of which had emerged either from the *curia regis* or from the local representatives of the king in the royal domain. The ordinary local law courts developed out of the original institution of *prévôt*, the chief representative of the crown in the royal domain. As the size of the domain increased and as the institutions of government grew more complex, the *bailliages, sénéchaussées*, and the presidial courts appeared and supplemented the work of the original officer. These courts all had civil and criminal jurisdiction and appeal went ultimately to one of the *parlements*. These courts possessed the right to judge in original and in appellate jurisdiction all civil and criminal cases not specifically denied to them. They were the backbone and the oldest parts of the French judicial system. On the other hand the *tribunaux d'exception*, or special tribunals, of which the *Connétablie* and the *justice prévôtale* were part, began their development later. As the governmental machinery grew more complex, there arose the need for tribunals to handle particular types of cases. For this reason there were created these special courts, whose jurisdiction was limited by law to certain specific fields.

Until the end of the twelfth century the *prévôts* were the only local royal judges in civil and criminal jurisdiction; they were under the general supervision of the *sénéchal*. The practice of granting the *prévôté* as a fief and the constantly increasing size of the royal domain made the *sénéchal's* task of supervision and control very difficult. Furthermore, the *prévôts* were very power-

---

59. Chéruel, *Dictionnaire*, I, 210–211; Glasson, *Droit*, VI, 434; Guichard, *Prévôts*, pp. 133–134; Marion, *Dictionnaire*, p. 130; Viollet, *Le Roi*, p. 315.

ful in their own districts. Not only were they the royal judges, but they also performed the local royal administrative, military, and financial duties. Finally, the disappearance of the *sénéchal* at the end of the twelfth century left the *prévôts* virtually free from supervision. These factors and the constant development and increasing complexity of the royal administration at the end of the twelfth century led to the creation of the *baillis* and the *sénéchaux*.[60] Each of the new officials became the supervisor of several *prévôtés*, replacing the *sénéchal* in that capacity, and also performed military, administrative, financial, and judicial services. They became the trial judges of the "royal cases" and began to hear appeals in civil and criminal matters from the decisions of the *prévôts*. The court of the *bailli* also served sometimes as a court of original jurisdiction for all the inhabitants of the *bailliage*. In part, therefore, the *bailli's* duties duplicated those of the *prévôt*.

Henry II further elaborated the system of local courts. The edict of 1551 transformed a number of *bailliages* and *sénéchaussées* into presidial courts (*cours présidiaux*), each of which was to serve as a court of appeals for several *bailliages*. This reform remedied in part one of the greatest defects in the development of the judicial system. The greatest source of delay in the settlement of cases had been the almost unlimited right of appeal. Neither the number of trials already held nor the monetary evaluation of the case (in all civil and in some criminal matters) had served as a limitation on the right of appeal. Trials thus often lasted interminably and minor litigations were frequently carried from the court of the *prévôt* to one of the *parlements*. The latter were, therefore, constantly overburdened with minor affairs and far behind in their work. The edict of 1551 provided that the presidial courts should serve as the highest court of appeal for civil and criminal cases which were evaluated at not more than 250 livres. The presidial also retained its old character of *bailliage*. If, therefore, the presidial court sat as a *bailliage* and heard appeals from the decisions of the *prévôts* within the *bailliage*, one court of appeals was thereby eliminated. If it sat as a presidial and heard appeals from the other *bailliages* in its presidial dis-

60. These two officers performed identical duties. The term *sénéchal* appears generally in the southern part of the country, while *bailli* is the name employed in the remainder of France. The *sénéchal* as a local judge must be distinguished from the *sénéchal* described above as the military commander and head of the judiciary.

trict, cases of less than 250 livres' value were decided there and not carried to one of the *parlements*. This reform of the judiciary was most successful. The authority of the *parlements* was diminished, their work was greatly lightened, and the course of justice made cheaper and more efficient.

The *parlement* of Paris and the provincial *parlements* formed the central judicial organization. The king was the source and fountainhead of all justice and the Capetian monarchs began very early, therefore, to dispense justice in person. The crown officers and various of the king's lay and clerical vassals formed the *curia regis*, which met at irregular intervals, advised the king, and transacted judicial and other types of business. The members of the *curia* served merely in an advisory capacity, however, and had no authority of their own. The direct authority of the king as sovereign was limited to the territorial boundaries of the royal domain. The direct jurisdiction of the *curia* as a royal (as opposed to a feudal) court of justice, therefore, was likewise limited and did not extend over the domains of the great feudatories. As the central royal court of justice, the *curia* judged cases within the limits of the royal domain. With the creation of the *prévôts* (and later that of the *baillis*), however, the direct jurisdiction of the *curia* declined in importance and virtually disappeared. The *curia* then became principally a court of appeals from the decisions of the *baillis*, just as the latter served as courts of appeal from the decisions of the *prévôts*. At the same time, with the development of the study and use of Roman law, there grew up a class of professional lawyers who replaced the original members of the *curia* in their judicial functions. From this permanent and professional group emerged in the thirteenth and fourteenth centuries the *parlement* of Paris which now no longer formed a part of the *curia regis*. At the same time, the king, except on special occasions, ceased to administer justice in person. The *parlement* was his delegate and became the supreme court of justice for about half of what is modern France, an area representing the approximate limits of the royal domain before the creation of the first provincial *parlement* (Toulouse) and before the great annexations of the fifteenth and later centuries.

The *parlement* of Paris had been originally the only judicial body above the courts of the *baillis*, since its immediate predecessor, the *curia regis*, had been the only central royal court. When the royal authority had extended merely over the old royal domain such an arrangement had been sufficient for the administration of justice. But with the progressive territorial extension of the domain in the thirteenth and subsequent centuries such a system led to inefficiency and delay. The creation of new courts became imperative. A single central court was no longer sufficient to handle the ever-increasing number of cases. Journeys to Paris were long, costly, and often dangerous. As long as the king dispensed justice in person there could be only one central court. The erection of new courts was facilitated by the divorce of the person of the king from the administration of justice and by the emergence of the *parlement* of Paris as a body with an independent existence which rendered judgment in its own name.[61] There was now nothing to prevent the king from creating other courts in the image of the *parlement* of Paris. The latter had become merely a court and was no longer the sole embodiment of the king as the fountainhead of justice.[62] The period after the reign of Philip the Fair witnessed the creation of provincial *parlements*. These courts, contrary to the often-expressed claim of the *parlement* of Paris, were in no way related to or dependent on that body, but were independent creations, erected by royal prerogative. The provincial *parlement* was often the former supreme court of a fief transformed into a royal court of justice after the annexation of the territory. For instance, the high court of the dukes of Normandy became the royal *parlement* of Rouen. Just as the *parlement* of Paris was supreme in its territory, so were the provincial *parlements* supreme in theirs, with the right of appeal in civil and criminal cases from their *bailliages* or *sénéchaussés*.[63]

The royal judicial machinery also included numerous tribunals with jurisdiction over special types of case and usually having no contact with the ordinary courts. As the royal government became more complex there arose the need for tribunals to settle administrative cases. The majority of these new and special courts were

61. The formula of judgment of the *parlement* was *"la cour ordonne," "la cour condamne."* The council of the king, however, although it too developed from the old *curia regis*, issued decrees in the name of the king: *"par le roi en son conseil."*

62. The personal intervention of the king was, however, still possible and was used not infrequently. The *lit de justice* was the best-known example of this intervention. A discussion of this subject will be found in Esmein, *Cours*, pp. 421–429, 513–514.

63. The reader will find in Esmein, *Cours*, pp. 342–429, a full account of the development of royal justice and the royal judiciary. The foregoing pages are a brief summary of the principal features of that development.

administrative tribunals; they possessed civil and criminal jurisdiction in their particular fields of activity, and judged nothing but those matters specifically referred to them by edict. Sometimes there was no appeal from their decisions, but more often appeal could be carried to the *parlement* of Paris. To some of these bodies decisions were appealed from lower courts. There was a continual rivalry between the ordinary and special courts, for the work of the latter was often closely akin to the ordinary types of civil and criminal cases. The most important of these special courts were the *chambres des comptes*. The *chambre des comptes* of Paris was virtually as old as the *parlement* of Paris itself. Provincial *chambres des comptes* were soon established, each with final jurisdiction in its particular locality. These bodies audited the royal accounts and settled all disputes arising from their administration. The *cours des aides* were established to decide in civil and criminal jurisdiction all cases dealing with the assessment and collection of taxes. They also served as final courts of appeal from the local courts of the *élections* and the *greniers à sel*.[64] The admiralty courts judged all matters concerning the royal navy and maritime commerce. The *juges consuls* handled cases involving land commerce.

The *Connétablie et Maréchaussée* and the courts of the *prévôts des maréchaux* were among the special courts. Their evolution has been traced from the original power of the military commander to exercise military justice and discipline down to the creation of the *prévôts des maréchaux*, the establishment of the court of the *Connétablie*, and the elaboration of a special jurisdiction for matters of military discipline and the maintenance of public order. The interpretation of the term "military discipline" and the steady expansion of the concept to include many matters not germane to disciplinary problems furnished material for the constant disputes between the *Connétablie*, the *justice prévôtale*, and the ordinary courts. The *parlement* of Paris, as the chief representative of the ordinary courts, particularly resented the constant extension of the jurisdiction of the *justice prévôtale* which went on during the sixteenth century.

The jurisdiction of the *Connétablie*, the result of hundreds of years of development in the field of military administrative and disciplinary problems, contained within itself the seeds of its own

64. The *élections* were the local tax districts and the *greniers à sel* the local warehouses where the salt tax was collected.

dissolution. As the extent of territory and the number of troops grew, the tribunal, a single, sedentary body, could not possibly handle by itself the many and varied problems presented by its original powers and prerogatives. Many of the *Connétablie's* powers therefore gradually slipped from its grasp into hands better fitted to wield them. This process was greatly accelerated during the sixteenth century. The disciplinary powers fell for the most part to the new special agencies which sprang up in the sixteenth century, the *prévôts des bandes* and the *conseils de guerre*. The *commissaires* and *contrôleurs des guerres* assumed the responsibility for the muster and payment of the armed forces, and themselves handled many of the questions and disputes which arose concerning these matters. By the end of the sixteenth century virtually the only link remaining between the court and the officers just mentioned was the power of registration of their letters of appointment, a rather tenuous right of supervision of their activities, and the prerogative of hearing appeals in some cases from the decisions of the *prévôts des maréchaux, vice-baillis, vice-sénéchaux,* and *lieutenants criminels de robe courte*. These rights, of course, had their origin in the delegation of their powers by the *maréchaux* to the officers concerned and in a simultaneous delegation of general power to the *Connétablie et Maréchaussée* as their direct representatives in general affairs.

Until about the mid-fourteenth century, the *connétable* and the *maréchaux* personally conducted the business of their courts. As the scope of military operations grew, however, the commanders were no longer able to devote time to the performance of their judicial duties. The result was the rise of a body of professional lawyers and clerks, who replaced them and substituted an organized procedure for the informal methods of earlier days. The *connétable* and the *maréchaux* were supplanted by a *lieutenant*, who conducted business in their names.[65] By the time of Richemont (1393–1458) this officer had assumed the title of *lieutenant-général*, which he retained until the suppression of the court during the Revolution. Sometime after 1500 a *lieutenant particulier* was added, to assist the *lieutenant-général*.[66] In their private capacity as great lords, the two military commanders had the

---

65. Guérin, "Recherches," p. 37; Guichard, *Prévôts,* pp. 100, 115–116, 143; Orgeval, *Connétablie,* pp. 34, 41, 46, 51–52; Viollet, *Histoire,* II, 114; Viollet, *Le Roi,* p. 307.

66. Guérin, "Recherches," p. 37; Viollet, *Le Roi,* p. 307.

right, as did all the members of the higher aristocracy, to maintain their own permanent *procureurs*, whose duty it was to look after their interests. These officers represented their employers at the sessions of their courts. By the end of the fourteenth century a *procureur* first appeared as part of the permanent staff of both the *curia* and the *audiencia*.[67] The two posts later merged and became the *procureur du roi*, a permanent royal officer rather than the representative of the *connétable* and the *maréchaux* as private persons. By the addition of lesser officials the civilian personnel of the *Connétablie et Maréchaussée* was completed. At the end of the sixteenth century it included the *lieutenant-général*, the *lieutenant particulier*, the *procureur du roi*, the *greffier* (clerk), and the *commis greffier* (assistant clerk).[68] The minor duties, such as message-carrying and the serving of summonses, were handled by bailiffs.

This account of the background of the tribunal has revealed several significant facts. In the feudal era the right of military command brought with it the concomitant right to the exercise of military justice. As the size of the armed forces grew, the military officers were no longer able to attend in person to their judicial duties. The result was the rise of a body of professional lawyers who subsequently formed a court known as the *Connétablie et Maréchaussée de France*. The military commanders delegated their administrative duties to officers created especially for that purpose. The latter, through the power of delegation enjoyed by the *Connétablie*, were under the nominal control of that body, but in the main they retained a *de facto* independence. The final result was that while the *Connétablie* was never abolished under the Old Régime, its functions, after the fifteenth century, were greatly curtailed and changed in character. The tribunal ceased to be a military court and became primarily a body in charge of the agencies responsible for the maintenance of internal order and for the good administration of the army.

67. Guérin, "Recherches," p. 37; Orgeval, *Connétablie*, pp. 39, 46, 52; Viollet, *Le Roi*, p. 307.
68. Chéruel, *Dictionnaire*, I, 211; Guérin, "Recherches," p. 37; Marion, *Dictionnaire*, p. 130; Viollet, *Le Roi*, p. 307.

II

THE COURT AT THE END OF THE WARS OF RELIGION

AT THE end of the sixteenth century France was facing one of the great crises in her history. Since 1560 a series of civil wars had torn the kingdom asunder. At first predominantly religious in character, these wars later became political as well and threatened to destroy the very structure and unity of the country and undo the work of centuries of Capetian and Valois effort. The toll of human life was appalling. The conflict had been so prolonged and so general that almost all the elements of the population had fought at one time or another, either for the sake of their religious or political convictions and ambitions or simply in self-defense. The material destruction was tremendous. For forty years the land had suffered from sieges, passages of troops accompanied by frightful depredations, pillaging by private robber bands, and destruction of property and productive facilities. Roads, bridges, harbors, and dikes all lay in ruins. Commerce, industry, and agriculture in many places almost completely ceased.[1] The first task of Henry IV after the pacification of the country by 1598 was therefore a physical one, to rebuild the country's productive powers. Material damage, given a period of reasonable security, can be repaired in a relatively short time. The great strides towards prosperity made in France between 1598 and the death of Henry IV in 1610 illustrate this truth. The greatest danger to the crown lay rather in the political and constitutional fields and manifested itself by the habits of disregard for the process of law and the general contempt for the authority of the central government which had developed during half a century of strife and unrest. The second and far more difficult task of Henry IV was therefore a moral and spiritual one, to rebuild the power and prestige of the crown,

1. J.-H. Mariéjol, *Henri IV et Louis XIII (1598–1643)*, pp. 1–47. (Volume VI, part 2, in Ernest Lavisse, ed., *Histoire de France illustrée, depuis les origines jusqu'à la Révolution.*) Hereafter cited as Lavisse. These pages give a comprehensive account of conditions at the end of the Wars of Religion, and describe the process of the restoration of royal authority.

to revive respect for the central government and its actions, and to restore and carry on the traditional constitutional centralization.

The centuries since the accession of Hugh Capet had witnessed the gradual triumph of the crown over the forces of feudalism and decentralization. Royal authority had spread over all France and a centralized constitution, wherein all authority emanated from the crown, had developed. Philip II had struggled with the most dangerous of the great barons, the kings of England. Philip IV had greatly increased the power of the crown within the country. Charles VII had at last driven the English from France. Louis XI had triumphed over apanaged feudalism and had finally made the king the chief authority in the state. This struggle had occupied several centuries and by 1560 had been but lately completed. At the outbreak of the Wars of Religion the *connétable* of Bourbon had been dead but thirty years. The wars, beginning as they did so soon after the defeat of feudalism and the forces of decentralization, re-opened the question. The feeble royal leadership of the last half of the sixteenth century aggravated the danger to the authority of the crown.

During the wars the central administration almost completely broke down. In the provinces the Protestant forces, the adherents of the Catholic League, and the local royal officials vied with one another for mastery and agreed only to flout the authority of the crown. The concern of the Huguenots and of the League was primarily that of religion, but their resistance to the crown on that account gave to the local royal officials the chance to increase their political power and to entrench themselves in their positions. Furthermore, religious and political motives were combined in those officials who were Huguenot extremists or members of the Catholic League. The portion of France under the direct rule of the king was at one time confined to the area about Paris. The feebleness of the central authority, added to the latent forces of feudalism and decentralization, brought about a situation which threatened to undo the work of centuries. A new feudalism, based on the virtually independent power of the local royal officials, seemed at hand.

The most dangerous of these local authorities were the powerful royal provincial governors. As representatives of the king in the provinces they possessed vast military, civil, and administrative powers. During the sixteenth century they usurped in addition some of the prerogatives of the crown. They rendered justice in their own names; they levied taxes on their own authority and recruited their own troops; they authorized the establishment of fairs and regulated the export of grain from the kingdom; and they issued in their own names letters of naturalization. They considered their positions as hereditary. Governmental families arose in many provinces. The Montmorency family in Languedoc allied itself with the Huguenots and successfully resisted the authority of Charles IX. The Duke of Epernon, governor of Provence, negotiated as an independent sovereign with Philip II of Spain. The Duke of Mercoeur ruled Brittany. Minor officialdom in general zealously imitated the royal governors in their efforts to free themselves from the authority of the central government. There was a very real danger that the work of previous kings would be lost and that the king of France would once more have only the shadowy authority of his Carolingian and early Capetian ancestors.

This universal disregard for the crown was the most serious menace to the king, since its continued existence made impossible any real material recovery or constitutional development. The records of the tribunal of the *Connétablie* provide specific illustrations of the truth of these general statements about the administrative condition of the country. The registers are full of accounts of crime, neglect, and intrigue on the part of officials of the *maréchaussée* and private persons in general. Officials of the *maréchaussée* neglected their duties and engaged in sharp practices. People used violence increasingly in their daily relations. The holding of civilians for ransom proved lucrative and was used increasingly by all. Since judicial authority was so feeble, citizens often took justice into their own hands.

Examples of neglect of duty and disputes over the possession of offices abound. Here the authority of the *Connétablie* had failed to maintain order among its subordinates and to ensure good administration. At Joinville, for example, the king had established a *procureur du roi*, a clerk, and six archers who were to reside there and exterminate the thieves and robbers who were infesting the neighborhood. Pierre Martinet, the commander of the archers, had decamped with the salaries of his men. The archers were left without any money and were obliged to try by their own efforts to apprehend the malefactors.[2] Despite all their efforts to get

---

2. Archives Nationales, Série Z^{1c}, Connétablie et Maréchaussée de France, Volume 44, folio 110 recto. (Hereafter cited as Z^{1c} 44, etc. The words "recto"

him back, Martinet persistently refused to make his headquarters at Joinville. The administration of justice was therefore neglected and evil-doers remained unpunished because of Martinet's disregard for his responsibilities.[3]

A long litigation concerning the payment of salaries between Eustache de Jouy, *lieutenant* and paymaster of the company of the *prévôt des maréchaux* of the Ile de France, and some of his archers reflects the hardships of the time, the breakdown of the discipline of the *maréchaussée*, and the partial collapse of the financial administration responsible for the payment of its personnel. The passions engendered by this dispute evidently rose on one occasion to the boiling point, for in court the archers begged Jouy to forget what had happened in his house and to realize that if they had acted with disrespect it was because they had not received their salaries for a long time. The judges, however, did not take such a casual view of the matter. They ordered the culprits "in the future to maintain honor and respect towards the said *lieutenant* and forbade them any more to use frightful and insulting words to him, and for the blasphemies uttered by them" they imposed a fine.[4] The archers reiterated that not only had Jouy not paid them for the previous year but also that he had made no serious efforts to get the money from the financial officials. Instead, they maintained, he had gone to the neighborhood of Corbeil, where he had bought a great quantity of grain at a very low price from some soldiers encamped there. He had then returned to Paris and had sold it at a huge profit.[5] Also, in return for large sums of money, he had engineered the release of the financial officials who had been arrested for non-payment of the salaries in question. After he had procured their release, he had crowned his infamy by charging them exorbitant prices for the delivery of their letters of discharge.[6] They insisted that he had not been satisfied with this exploit and other crimes, but had taken good care to collect his own salary. They also stated that he had persistently replied to their inquiries that he had no funds with which to pay them.[7]

Jouy replied to these charges of negligence and crime that the

and "verso" are hereafter rendered as "r" (recto) and "v" (verso) respectively. Thus, this reference would read: Z^{1c} 44, f. 110r.)

3. Z^{1c} 44, f. 110rv.
4. Z^{1c} 44, f. 6v. See also Z^{1c} 44, f. 5v.
5. Z^{1c} 44, f. 14v.
6. Z^{1c} 44, f. 6r, 14v.
7. Z^{1c} 44, f. 14v, 15r.

edict creating the position of paymaster required him only to come to Paris and ask the receiver of the *tailles* to give him the funds for the payment of salaries. If the latter refused, he was under the obligation to protest, but he was not required to go out and collect the money from the taxpayers. Concerning the specific charge that he had not paid the salaries of the year 1590, Jouy declared that his chief, the *prévôt des maréchaux*, had obtained the payment rolls from the receiver of the *tailles* and had asked him to go and collect the money, since he himself was sick. This Jouy did as a special favor, for he was not required by law to do so. He went with only five unmounted archers and was compelled to return empty-handed, "because of the danger there was on the roads." Subsequently he stated that he had returned later with "ten of the said archers and having received some money in their presence at once distributed it to them." [8] Jouy denied that he had profiteered in grain and bluntly stated that to his knowledge "there was no law which forbade those for whom it was necessary to take care of their households and stock their homes with food . . . , as he had done." [9] He also categorically denied the archers' claim that he had released and gouged the collectors of the *taille*.[10] The archers then charged that it was illegal for Jouy to hold simultaneously the positions of *lieutenant* and paymaster. The defendant replied that there was no reason for prosecuting him on that basis, since the *prévôt des maréchaux* of the Ile de France was himself notorious for his disregard of the law in that respect. He was at the same time councillor of the Treasury and *prévôt des maréchaux* and had always appropriated for his own use the salaries of two archers who had never reported for duty.[11]

The administrative breakdown was also characterized by defiance of the *Connétablie* by subordinate officials and by their bickering among themselves. In 1597 the *procureur du roi* protested that in the past the *Connétablie* had always possessed the right to hold the musters of the *prévôts des maréchaux, vice-baillis*, and *vice-sénéchaux*. This power had been delegated to commissioners, except in the *généralité* of Paris. A recent royal edict had created thirty new commissioners and thirty new councillors to hold musters of the personnel of the *maréchaussée* throughout the kingdom. Using this edict as a pretext, many

8. Z^{1c} 44, f. 15rv.
9. Z^{1c} 44, f. 15v.
10. Z^{1c} 44, f. 16r.
11. Z^{1c} 44, f. 15r.

persons had obtained by fraud the right to hold musters in the *généralité* of Paris. Furthermore, the new decree had expressly reiterated that the *prévôts des maréchaux* of the *généralité* of Paris should come to the *Connétablie* for their musters and that the sixty new commissioners and councillors should also appear and be inducted into office. The *procureur* insisted that many had not satisfied this requirement, were therefore not legally a part of the administrative staff of the *maréchaussée*, and hence could not function. He requested that the receiver general be ordered to withhold the salaries of the new commissioners and councillors and also those of the *prévôts, lieutenants,* clerks, and archers of the *généralité* of Paris who for the past year had not come to muster, until they should have observed the requirements of the edict.[12]

The court received complaints from the archers of the *prévôt des maréchaux* of the Ile de France that on his own authority their chief had imprisoned members of his company. The offender was questioned and replied that whenever his men were negligent in the performance of their duties he would punish them in any way he might choose and that the *Connétablie* had no right to interfere with his actions. The tribunal thereupon forbade him to discipline his archers "by any means other than those which are prescribed for him by the ordinances, which are suspension of their salaries and dismissal, . . . and for the insolence and irreverence committed by him condemned him" to a large fine.[13] A jurisdictional quarrel caused the lawsuit between Michel Le Gallois and Thibault de Vausselles, *lieutenant* of the *prévôt provincial* of Picardy. Le Gallois maintained that while he was investigating the murder of a sergeant and other soldiers by a certain Antoine de Séricours and others, he had imprisoned Séricours at Montdidier, intending later to take him to Paris. Vausselles was not concerned in the affair, but, on the pretext that Le Gallois was encroaching on his jurisdiction, he had released Séricours and had confiscated and disposed of Le Gallois's clothes, baggage, gold, silver, and other belongings.[14]

Officials frequently used their power to help their friends at the expense of others. Jean Robbe, an archer of Adrien Chartier, *prévôt des maréchaux* of Blois, sued his chief for illegal use of his authority. Robbe alleged that in 1598, after having faithfully served the king as a soldier during the "late disturbances," he

12. Z^{1c} 46, f. 72rv.   13. Z^{1c} 47, f. 77rv.   14. Z^{1c} 47, f. 77v, 78r.

was appointed archer in Chartier's company. He was stationed at Vendôme and had always done his duty faithfully. Shortly after his own appointment a royal edict had placed one Huldebert in a legal post at Vendôme. For purposes of economy, the edict also required the dismissal of one archer at Vendôme, either the newest member of the company or the least diligent. In June, 1599, therefore, Chartier dismissed a certain Verneuil who had already resigned his position in favor of one du Montier. The *prévôt*, however, was unwilling to have du Montier in his company and declared that he had previously prevailed upon Verneuil to sign a statement that he could not resign his post in favor of someone else. He thus removed both Verneuil and du Montier from the scene and then gave that position to someone else. Then, simply because of his alleged desire to enforce the economy edict at Robbe's expense, Chartier dismissed him. He thus gave the position to a friend and got rid of Robbe, Verneuil, and du Montier. Since the plaintiff was not the newest member of the company and since he maintained his colleagues' testimony would show that he was not the least diligent, he asserted that the provision for the reduction in the number of archers could not possibly apply to him. Robbe maintained that Chartier had fulfilled the terms of the edict by his original dismissal of Verneuil, that his later actions were therefore illegal and entirely in his own private interest, and that he was motivated solely by personal prejudices.[15] In 1599 the *procureur du roi* protested that although royal decrees had provided that clerkships in the *maréchaussée* should be held as royal offices,[16] many of the *prévôts des maréchaux* continued to appoint to these posts their relatives, or people over whom they had a hold. The appointees were therefore completely at the mercy of their benefactors who were thus enabled to "dispense justice at their will," to indulge with impunity in all kinds of illegal activities, and to frustrate all efforts to maintain and conduct a strong and honest judicial administration in the provinces.[17]

The misdirection of funds was often a cause of litigation and shows the lack of concern with which some officials regarded their obligations. The *procureur du roi* protested that in 1575 Henry III had granted to the personnel of the tribunal the sum of 200

---

15. Z^{1c} 47, f. 267v, 268r.
16. *Royal offices:* This means that positions were to be purchased by qualified candidates. Chéruel, *Dictionnaire*, II, 883–884.
17. Z^{1c} 47, f. 121v.

livres to be employed for miscellaneous purposes. The money was to be taken periodically from forfeited salaries. He declared that there were seven archers who had not appeared for muster and whose salaries were in consequence forfeited, and demanded that Louis Trudelle, receiver of the *tailles* in the *élection* of Paris, be compelled to surrender the money so that the terms of Henry III's gift might be fulfilled.[18]

Failure to register letters of appointment to positions in the *maréchaussée* was frequent. This condition shows the laxity in fulfilling the requirements of the law and illustrates the general administrative weakness in the last years of the sixteenth century. By edict, all such appointments were to be registered with the clerk of the tribunal of the *Connétablie*, but in 1595 the *procureur du roi* remonstrated that the *prévôt des maréchaux* of Soissons had a number of archers who had never complied with the law. The court ordered that unless at the next muster they produced their letters of appointment and swore the required oath, their salaries would be declared forfeit.[19] On another occasion the *procureur* reminded the court that by law the clerk of any *prévôt des maréchaux* could not hold office without letters of appointment signed by the king and without taking the required oath. He then requested that a certain Pierre Bellot be forbidden to act as clerk to the *prévôt à la suite* of Marshal Boisdaulphin until he should have presented his credentials.[20] Nicolas Breton, the commissioner for musters of the *prévôt des maréchaux* of Orléans, was suspended, his salary stopped, and all his acts declared void because he had failed to obtain proper credentials and to have the required investigation made of his habits and religion.[21]

The foregoing examples have shown briefly that conditions in the *maréchaussée* were far from satisfactory. The tribunal of the *Connétablie* was charged with the administration of the *maréchaussée* and with the supervision and discipline of its members. In this organization the tradition of centralization which characterized all other phases of French constitutional development is found. In the *maréchaussée*, as in other branches of the administration, the central authority had been seriously weakened by the

18. Z^{1c} 44, f. 149v.
19. Z^{1c} 45, f. 1v, 2r.
20. Z^{1c} 46, f. 234r.
21. Z^{1c} 47, f. 60rv. See also a similar order to the *prévôt des maréchaux* of Brittany in Z^{1c} 47, f. 21rv. Cases of this type are the most numerous among the court records. Their prevalence reflects the administrative weakness of the period. The above are but a few examples.

long Wars of Religion. The unsatisfactory condition of the *maréchaussée* reflects the general conclusions already stated about the condition of the country. Indifference, neglect, corruption, intrigue, and usurpation of authority were the order of the day and extended down into the lower reaches of the administration.

The principle of centralization of authority was threatened from still another direction. Attempts by courts to encroach on the jurisdiction of other courts are everywhere far from uncommon, even in times of internal tranquillity. The constant rivalry in France between the ordinary and the special courts has already been discussed. Because of the chaos in the administration of public affairs during the last half of the sixteenth century, this chronic ill-feeling was greatly intensified. The weakening of the central power made it more difficult to confine the rival tribunals to their particular spheres of activity. Although the *Connétablie* had already lost much of its original control over military cases in fact, no definite limits to its jurisdiction had ever been laid down. The court, therefore, could still and did press its claims to jurisdiction over all cases concerned at all with military affairs. A single body such as this tribunal could not hope, however, to handle by itself the problems of troops in all parts of the country, and so it began to lose these powers in practice to other courts. The disorganization due to the wars helped to accelerate the process. Furthermore, the ordinary local courts took advantage of the situation to widen the limits of their jurisdiction at the expense of the *Connétablie*. This situation had become aggravated by the end of the century and illustrates once again the contemporary feebleness in the traditional centralized constitution of France.

In September, 1600, the *procureur du roi* protested that by law military justice had always been distinguished from ordinary justice. It possessed jurisdiction over the "privileges and differences" of soldiers and had the exclusive right "to judge concerning booty, ransom, captures of cities, châteaux, violations of passports and safeguards, and concerning all acts of hostility taking place during and on account of war and other cases specified by the ordinances." The *procureur* had, however, ascertained that many men who had fought in the Wars of Religion were being prosecuted against their will before the ordinary courts for their acts while under arms. Many others were not sure where to appeal, nor where such suits should be tried. They were thus being deprived of their rights "to the injury of themselves and of our authority and jurisdiction, which thus remains . . . without effect and vigor." He therefore requested authority to serve notice on all those who were at litigation before lower courts for these causes and to forbid the prosecution of such cases except before the *Connétablie* on pain of imposition of a fine and of nullification of the proceedings. He also obtained authority to serve notice on those who were about to begin actions that such cases must be tried before the *Connétablie*, "to the exclusion of all other judges." [22]

The collapse of authority was not confined to administrative operations and to the relationships among the various parts of the governmental machinery. Private persons became accustomed in many cases to become a law unto themselves. The records of the *Connétablie* show that violations of contracts were frequent. Although not as spectacular as other forms of lawlessness, they reflect contemporary conditions. Just as the administrative weakness of the time permitted disobedience of laws against robbery and murder, so did that weakness encourage the disregard of other laws and obligations. People took advantage of the opportunity and often violated the provisions of agreements they had made. In 1600, for instance, Mathurin de Saint-Frais brought suit against several of the inhabitants of Chéron. He alleged that in November, 1595, the military authorities had ordered the town to receive in billets the company of soldiers of the Sieur de Foisseux. The townspeople had refused to obey, whereupon the captain of the company had gone to Chéron and ordered immediate compliance with his instructions. The inhabitants had then bargained with him and agreed to pay him 200 écus, in return for which he was to billet the soldiers elsewhere. Unable to raise the money, they had borrowed it from a certain Jacques Dupuy and had repaid part of the loan. Dupuy had then ceded his claims for the remainder to the plaintiff. Saint-Frais had succeeded in collecting all but 90 écus which he had been demanding in vain for a long time. Although the defendants insisted that they had met in full their obligations, the tribunal ordered them to pay the 90 écus, less what they had already paid.[23]

In June, 1592, Georges Nodot sued Guillaume Rousseau for breach of contract. Nodot asserted that Jacques Rousseau, brother

---

22. Z^{1c} 47, f. 297rv.
23. Z^{1c} 47, f. 218rv, 219rv. See also Z^{1c} 47, f. 223 bis rv, 224r for the suit brought by Clément Girard, a merchant, against the Duke of Montpensier for the failure of the latter to pay for war supplies which he had ordered and received.

of the defendant, had been taken prisoner and thrown into the château of Héméry, under the guard of the Sieur de Chantrast. Guillaume Rousseau had begged Nodot to help secure the release of the prisoner and had promised him an unspecified reward. Nodot, after considerable trouble, had persuaded Chantrast to free the prisoner in return for a consideration. Since then he had been trying in vain to force Rousseau to keep his part of the contract and finally brought suit to compel him to do so, in order that Chantrast might be recompensed.[24] Rousseau admitted the existence of the contract, but maintained that Nodot had not fulfilled his part of the bargain, which was to procure Jacques Rousseau's release and bring him to Paris. He had not even gone to the château and seen the prisoner, who had escaped and come to Paris entirely through his own efforts.[25] Jacques Rousseau was called for questioning and denied that he had gained his freedom through any efforts of Nodot.[26] Despite this damaging testimony, Nodot was apparently able to prove his assertions, for the court "condemned Guillaume Rousseau, according to his promise," to reimburse Nodot for his part in the ransoming of Jacques Rousseau.[27]

The weakness of the crown and the general chaos in governmental affairs during the Wars of Religion brought about a vast increase in the practice of seizing people and forcing them to pay ransom for their release. This was not confined, as in earlier times, to soldiers captured in battle, but was extended to civilians and proved to be a good source of revenue. The holding of soldiers for ransom had long been an established custom. The broadening of the concept to include civilian non-combatants was a product of the chaos of the Wars of Religion. Many civilians spent much time in the hands of soldiers, who often bled them white. It is of interest to note that virtually all ransom cases tried are concerned with the aftermath, rather than with the original capture. The weakness in the authority of the government is further demonstrated, since the arrest and prosecution of the perpetrators of such acts were rare. It was evidently extremely difficult to bring the latter to justice. Only when something went wrong with the arrangements for payment did the victims appeal to the *Connétablie*, and then usually to prosecute a companion who had refused to pay his share of the sum demanded.

Three Paris merchants sued Pierre Ollivier, the *procureur*

24. Z^{1c} 44, f. 60rv.
25. Z^{1c} 44, f. 60v.
26. Z^{1c} 44, f. 61rv.
27. Z^{1c} 44, f. 77v.

fiscal [28] of the seigneurie of Meudon and a candle merchant in the same town. The plaintiffs stated that the garrison of Poissy had taken them and Ollivier prisoners and that in order to collect money for their ransoms Ollivier had been permitted to go to Paris. He promised to return within three days with 200 écus, which had been settled on as his ransom. He and the three other prisoners then agreed that they should act as guarantors for him during his absence. In return, he would lend them the money to pay for their own ransoms. The soldiers had agreed to this arrangement. Ollivier, however, had remained in Paris and had failed to carry out his promise, leaving the rest, despite all their pleas and threats, at their captors' mercy.[29] They had remained in prison for several months, after which, "having sold all that remained to them," [30] they were released. Consequently, reminding the court of the "poverty, want, and evil which the poor imprisoned plaintiffs are enduring, whose wives are burdened with small children who are dying of hunger," [31] the three asked that Ollivier be forced to pay them the 150 écus remaining from his ransom of 200 écus which they had paid, that he reimburse them for expenses incurred to buy food and other items from their captors while in prison, and demanded that Ollivier be ordered to pay the fourth of all sums spent by them for trips from Paris to Poissy and return.[32]

In March, 1600, Gabriel de Montboucher brought suit against Jean Maurault, alleging breach of contract. The plaintiff, a follower of the Duke of Mercoeur, asserted that in July, 1597, he was taken prisoner in Brittany by the Sieur de la Tremblaie, a commander in the service of the king. He was taken to Rennes and compelled to agree to a ransom of 2000 écus. As Montboucher was unable to pay that sum, he had had recourse to the Duke of Mercoeur and had begged for assistance in his predicament. Mercoeur accordingly freed Maurault, one of his prisoners, on condition that he procure Montboucher's unconditional release. Although Maurault agreed to this and gave his word, he had failed to abide by his promise. Montboucher therefore had been held prisoner for more than three months and at last was forced to pay

---

28. The representative of the king's interests in the seigneurial courts. Chéruel, *Dictionnaire*, II, 1028.

29. Z¹ᶜ 44, f. 28v. See also Z¹ᶜ 44, f. 83rv, 84r. This is another ransom case, between Philippe du Resnel and Adrien Barat.

30. Z¹ᶜ 44, f. 47v.

31. Z¹ᶜ 44, f. 28v.   32. Z¹ᶜ 44, f. 47v.

half the ransom in cash and assume the obligation to pay the remainder.[33]

Perhaps the most obvious and oft-mentioned characteristic of the late sixteenth century was the use of physical violence. Force went far in supplanting legal procedure as a method of settling disputes. Not only was this tendency manifested by the increase in ransom and kidnapping, but also, and in even more convincing fashion, by plunder, robbery, and murder. The courts and administration were usually unable to deal with the situation.

Pierre Rousseau and Charles Vallois, merchants of Chastres-sous-Montlhéry, sued Jean Gonau, alleging that they and others had, during the siege of Paris, risked their lives and property to bring food and supplies to the city. On Monday, June 17, 1591, they and several other merchants of Chastres, were proceeding towards Paris with some cows when they were attacked near the bridge of Vaux at about midnight by robbers, whom, on account of the darkness, they were unable to recognize. Some of the merchants fled, but the rest were captured and together with the cattle were taken to the château of Savigny. While they were attempting to recover the cows, the plaintiffs were warned that someone was about to bring the animals to Paris. They therefore came into the city on Monday, June 24, 1591, to identify and claim the cattle. One of the plaintiffs followed Gonau and his associates as far as the main gate of the Mathurin monastery, stopped them, and claimed one of the cows in their herd. The archers of the *prévôt des maréchaux* of the Ile de France arrived on the scene, attracted by the noise of the crowd which had gathered, and took the disputants to the prisons of the Petit Châtelet, whence they came before the *Connétablie*. Gonau then admitted that the cattle had been stolen and offered to return the cow and six écus, on condition that the plaintiffs drop all action against him.[34]

Pierre de Miraulmont, *prévôt des maréchaux* of the Ile de France, sued Arnoul Citart for damages to himself and his family resulting from acts of violence committed on his property. Miraulmont asserted that during the siege of Paris, he, like the rest of the population, was reduced to want. Shortly before the end of the siege, therefore, he sent his wife and family to his house at Soisy-sur-Seine. A few days later, Citart, asserting that the

33. Z^{1c} 47, f. 216v, 217r. See also Z^{1c} 47, f. 217v, 218r.
34. Z^{1c} 44, f. 33rv, 34r.

garrison of the château of Soisy had stolen some wine from him, came to Miraulmont and showed him an order from the Duke of Nemours, governor of Paris, for the return of the wine. Citart was unwilling to await a peaceful settlement of the matter and took a number of Walloons and other foreign soldiers to Soisy. He swore that he and his men would do no harm and asked to be admitted. No sooner had they entered, however, than they seized Madame de Miraulmont, took her clothes, jewels, and money, and pillaged and ravaged the château. Citart treated his prisoner harshly, handed her over to the soldiers, and compelled her to pay 400 écus' ransom. He then went to Paris and begged the Duke of Nemours to confiscate the château and give it to him, alleging that Madame de Miraulmont was a supporter of the king (rather than of the Catholic League) and had refused him admittance. By means of this falsehood he succeeded in obtaining permission from Nemours to occupy the building. He then also appropriated the property, including the grain and all the revenue of the lands, and excluded Miraulmont, whom he prevented from collecting the dues from his lands.[35]

Violence frequently masqueraded under the guise of legal repressive actions. Pierre Le Mareschal brought suit on behalf of his father, Julien Le Mareschal, against Joachim Le Vasseur. Le Mareschal alleged that in October, 1599, Le Vasseur maintained headquarters at the seigneurial mansion of Avoince and commanded a band of soldiers, all of evil life and habits. This unsavory group, "decked out with pistols, arquebuses, and other arms, and some of them in armor," came to the home of the elder Le Mareschal, "a simple cultivator," plundered it, took the old man to Avoince, and demanded that he pay ransom. When the plaintiff said that he was not one of those who should pay ransom, but a simple farmer who had never borne arms, the defendant threatened his life if he did not pay. As he had been warned of the cruelties

---

35. Z^{1c} 44, f. 18v, 19rv, 20r. See also Z^{1c} 47, f. 293v, 294rv, in which is related the story of Jonathan Petit and François de La Vergne. Petit had killed La Vergne and had obtained royal letters of pardon on the grounds of provocation and self-defense. For some time La Vergne had been publicly insulting Petit, asserting among other things that he was the son of a hangman and a swindler, and uttering threats against his life. One day Petit and a party met La Vergne and a group of his cronies. After a tirade La Vergne and his companions fell upon Petit and his group with drawn swords. During the ensuing melee Petit fatally wounded La Vergne. Incidents such as this, pitched battles between armed bands and between individuals, are legion. People like La Vergne (and presumably Petit) were numerous at that time.

and outrages of Le Vasseur, he paid 250 écus and was thereupon sent home. He had up to the present, for fear of his life, not dared to complain, but after order had been restored he gave to his son his claims to the 250 écus. The son therefore caused Le Vasseur to be summoned before the *prévôt* of Paris, in order to obtain the return of the sum "thus taken and extorted." [36] Le Vasseur in his defense asserted that in 1589 the king had appointed him commander of the garrison at Thouars and Avoince, in order to "carry on war against the said rebels . . . who were occupying several fortresses in the environs." There were frequent skirmishes between the parties, during one of which the father of the plaintiff, who was one of the rebels, was captured and taken to Avoince to be tried. Le Vasseur, as commander, heard in the presence of Le Mareschal several witnesses who testified that both he and his son were rebels. Thereupon Le Vasseur declared that the elder Le Mareschal was a legitimate capture and turned him over to the soldiers. The latter held him for ransom, which the prisoner's son finally paid. The defendant maintained that he had but done his duty. His treatment of Le Mareschal "was an act of war, . . . by the edicts and ordinances of the King." [37] Irrespective of the actual guilt in this particular case, the commander who exceeded his authority and the lawless inhabitant of the countryside were common during the Wars of Religion.

The court records present a gloomy enough picture of conditions at the end of the century. In the trial of Eustache de Jouy the *prévôt des maréchaux* of the Ile de France is shown illegally holding two offices at once, prosecuting his paymaster for doing the same thing, and retaining for his own use the salaries of several archers. Jouy himself was more than negligent in the discharge of his duties. The archers felt free to invade the paymaster's house and threaten him with violence. Jouy's description of his difficulties in obtaining funds for the salaries of his men shows the condition into which the financial organization had fallen. The receivers of the *taille* themselves had been unable to pry any money out of the population. Since Pierre Martinet had absconded with the funds for the salaries of his company of archers, justice was neglected at Joinville. Robbers and murderers flourished in

---

36. Z¹ᶜ 47, f. 255v, 256r.
37. Z¹ᶜ 47, f. 256r. The dates 1589 and 1599 both appear in this account. The former is presumably correct, since Le Vasseur refers to his actions "at the beginning of the disturbances."

that region. The provincial branches of the *maréchaussée* seethed with intrigue and corruption. In some localities, the *prévôts* placed their henchmen in office and so freed themselves from control. In others, they used their authority to favor their friends and settle old scores, and usurpations of authority were common. Civilians were seized, forced to pay large ransoms, and were totally unable to bring their captors to justice. They therefore spent their energies in prosecuting each other for violations of the arrangements for payment. Contracts and other agreements were broken daily with scant regard for the consequences, which, it is true, generally were not forthcoming. Eustache de Jouy, with five armed companions, was forced to abandon his efforts to collect money for the payment of his men, because of the dangers of travel on the highways. Armed bands, such as that of Arnoul Citart, invaded and plundered houses and estates and generally succeeded in getting some kind of legal approval for their actions. Such activities and many others fill the pages of the court records and are treated always as perfectly ordinary and commonplace happenings. No particular notice is paid them by any of the parties involved.

France thus faced at the end of the Wars of Religion a most serious situation. Her centralized constitution, the result of centuries of effort, was in grave danger of collapse; a new feudalism seemed at hand. Disorder and insecurity were the condition of the day, and authority was badly weakened. It might seem that the study of any contemporary judicial institution would be futile; yet this is incorrect, for the very existence of these judicial records in such profusion brings to light an important feature of the age. Although the period was in many respects one of near-anarchy, there remained among some of the officials and people a strong current of resistance to the processes of disintegration. The number of cases dealing with the administration of the *maréchaussée* shows a chaotic condition, but it also shows that many members of the *maréchaussée* did regard the *Connétablie* as the source of authority and appealed to it for settlement of disputes. Force was therefore not always employed. The *procureur du roi* worked hard and on numberless occasions came before the judges to protest against the existence of fraudulent practices in the ranks and among the officers of the *maréchaussée*. The judges strove as best they could to maintain the authority of the court over its subordinates. Furthermore, the numerous suits brought by provincial officials indicates that among them existed a strong sense of duty and order. Many of the cases handled by the tribunal were of such a character that their settlement might easily have been managed by unscrupulous local authorities. A further proof that respect for the central government was not entirely dead is the registration by the court of the appointments to office of archers and other subordinate officials. Finally, although the victims of kidnapping and robbery were rarely able to prosecute their attackers, they at least regarded due process of law as the proper method for settlement of their own quarrels.

These facts compel a modification of the prevalent view that France at the end of the Wars of Religion was a land in which all law and order had been submerged beneath the tide of anarchy and violence. They show that from below as well as from above, there was an active, fundamental desire, perhaps unconsciously expressed, for a revival of the authority of the crown and an end to violence. The rapidity with which France recovered from the Wars of Religion illustrates the truth of this statement. Given a period of relative tranquillity, the country made great strides in material recovery. That the power of the crown revived so rapidly after the disruptive effects of forty years of strife and ineptitude demonstrates further this desire for an end to violence and for a restoration of the traditional position and rôle of the crown. Had the events of those years made any really permanent impression, or had the writings and activities against the crown really been subscribed to by any substantial element of the population the constitutional and material recovery of France would have been slight and would have taken place only after a long delay. Henry IV, a great leader, was the moving force in the material rehabilitation of his country. He was also chiefly responsible for the revival of the authority of the crown. By his efforts he surmounted the constitutional crisis and resumed the traditional course of constitutional development. But he did not accomplish this task alone. He was aided by this general desire for a return to the ways of peace, by the fundamental dependence of the general population on the traditional institutions and practices, and by the determination of most of the judges and other officials to maintain their authority. The established institutions of France, such as the *Connétablie*, by their persistent efforts to maintain their authority, were of significant assistance in the task of constitutional and material recovery.

III

THE JURISDICTION OF THE COURT

ANALYSIS of the jurisdiction of the *Connétablie* will show the place of that court in the judicial and administrative life of France at the end of the sixteenth century. The basic reason for the existence of the *Connétablie* was the original union in the person of the military commander of the rights to direct military operations and to exercise military justice. The military commanders subsequently delegated their judicial, disciplinary, and administrative powers to various officials and performed directly and in person only their strictly military duties. In theory, and for a time in fact, the principal rights and duties of the *Connétablie* were to judge all civil suits of soldiers, to exercise disciplinary power over the troops, to maintain order in the countryside where troops were stationed or passing through, and to direct the administrative aspects of army life. As the size of the armed forces increased and as the standing army came into existence, the court delegated in turn some of its powers to subordinates and retained only a supervisory and disciplinary power over them.[1]

The use of the many and varied original prerogatives of the *Connétablie* led to the development of a wide and complex jurisdiction. Civil jurisdiction included all civil suits of soldiers. Criminal jurisdiction gave the tribunal the right to judge crimes committed by or against soldiers. The administrative and disciplinary powers of the court gave it in practice the supervision of the activities of its subordinate agencies and in theory the right to enforce military discipline. Finally, litigants appealed from decisions of the *prévôts des maréchaux* and other local bodies to the *Connétablie* and gave to that body its appellate jurisdiction.

Despite its delegations of power the court at the end of the sixteenth century retained in theory all of its original prerogatives and could in theory take a direct part in their operation. But various factors militated against its full use of them and gradually most of these original jurisdictional rights were all but lost in

1. See Chapter I.

practice. A single body, permanently located in Paris, could not possibly handle cases arising in all parts of France. Furthermore, the *Connétablie*, one of the special courts, suffered heavily in the constant struggle for power between these bodies and the ordinary tribunals. In practice, therefore, the work of the tribunal had by 1600 changed a good deal in character from that of the fourteenth and fifteenth centuries. Civil and criminal jurisdiction had declined greatly in importance, and cases of this type were more and more tried before other courts. Civil jurisdiction was confined virtually to ransom cases and disputes over contracts to supply the army. Criminal jurisdiction was even less important and consisted of little more than an occasional murder or robbery case. Although in theory the *Connétablie* had the power to try *cas prévôtaux*, very few of these cases actually came before it. The power of military discipline had been lost to other agencies, and it is probable that by the end of the sixteenth century the *Connétablie* had ceased to put forth any serious claims to it. Appellate jurisdiction was but seldom used and was of slight importance. The court exercised its direct disciplinary and administrative powers almost exclusively over the members of the *maréchaussée*. These prerogatives emerged by 1600 as the most vital and important of the original duties of the court and were the principal ones remaining to it in practice. It was in fact no longer a military court but an administrative tribunal, and in the administrative field it performed useful tasks.

The most important remaining element of the tribunal's civil jurisdiction was the right to settle questions of ransom.[2] During the Wars of Religion this practice flourished in connection with military operations and was, in addition, extended for reasons of financial gain to civilians. Such cases were relatively numerous, since ransom was a legally recognized military practice and since the disruptive effects of the wars had weakened the agencies of law enforcement.

2. For their conclusions on jurisdiction see Guichard, *Prévôts*, pp. 145–177, and Orgeval, *Connétablie*, pp. 149–215. The court records in general support the theories and conclusions advanced by both these authors. The following pages, therefore, will in the main be devoted, by reference to specific cases, to the illustration of their statements. There are two important differences. First, as will be shown, there were certain phases of jurisdiction which were far more important than other elements and occupied a great portion of the court's time and efforts. These elements have in general not been stressed by Guichard and Orgeval. Second, it must be pointed out that while these authors base their conclusions in the main upon ordinances and treatises, the present analysis is derived directly and solely from the court registers.

The nature of the case, rather than the military or non-military status of the litigants, determined the jurisdiction of the *Connétablie* over ransoms. This point is illustrated in the case of Jean Dumoulin who claimed from Charlotte de Luppe reimbursement of his ransom money. He alleged that Charlotte's late husband, Guillaume Noblet, had sent him as a substitute to serve in the trenches during the siege of Paris in 1589. There he had been captured and compelled to pay a ransom of 100 écus. As Noblet had since died, Dumoulin brought suit against the widow, asserting that since he had taken Noblet's place in the army, the ultimate responsibility for the payment of the ransom rested on his employer.[3] Noblet had been a lawyer at the Châtelet, Charlotte was his widow, and Dumoulin his clerk. The jurisdiction of the *Connétablie* could not have been decided on the grounds that the parties were military figures. It was determined rather by the connection of ransom with the military operations around Paris. The trial between Nicolas Baguereau, a lawyer attached to the *parlement* of Paris, and Captain Saint-Bernard de Maisonneuve, former commandant of the château of Aulinville, gave rise to an interesting bit of jurisdictional by-play. Baguereau had been captured by one of Maisonneuve's soldiers during a quarrel over a promissory note allegedly signed by the lawyer. The cause for the trial was, as in so many instances, not the detention of Baguereau, but his refusal to honor the note. Strangely enough, it was Maisonneuve, the soldier, who did not wish to have the case tried before the *Connétablie*. He argued that the holder of the note was a soldier under the ultimate authority of the military governor of Paris, and insisted that that official should try the case. Baguereau maintained that since a ransom was under discussion, the *Connétablie* had jurisdiction and the court not unnaturally agreed with him.[4] The type of case, rather than military status, decided the court to which the litigation should go.

The civil jurisdiction of the *Connétablie* also embraced the entire field of money disputes, including quarrels over the fulfilment of contracts. Here the professional calling of the litigants and the nature of the case played parts of equal importance. In the case of ordinary money payments, the former was dominant,

3. Z^{1c} 44, f. 10v, 11r. See also for similar cases Z^{1c} 44, f. 28v, 29rv, 60rv, 61r, 63rv, 80rv, 81rv, 105rv, 106r.
4. Z^{1c} 44, f. 108rv. See also Z^{1c} 44, f. 4rv, 5r, 11rv, 12rv, 13r, 24rv, 25rv, 26rv, 27rv, 28rv, 31r.

one or both of the parties being either soldiers, officials connected with the military administration, or members of the *maréchaussée*. In order to force Ives Magistrey, a hanger-on of the army of the Duke of Mayenne, to acknowledge the validity of a promissory note, François Chauvel, a supply merchant, used his position as an army contractor to compel his opponent to come before the *Connétablie*.[5] Louis Travère, archer of the guard of the Duke of Mayenne, and later the *maréchal général des logis* of the Duke of Aumale, caused Michel Tamponnet, former private secretary to the late Duke of Anjou, to be summoned to court. During the campaigns in Normandy, Travère asserted, he had rented a horse to the defendant and in addition had for some time paid for the upkeep of the animal and had also supported Tamponnet. Since then the latter had refused to pay any rent for the horse and had neglected to reimburse Travère for his expenses.[6] François Frou, a Paris hotelkeeper, sued for payment of a bill for the lodging of Jacques Le Hardy, his soldiers, and their horses.[7] In each of these cases the dispute was a purely personal one with no military aspects. Since one or both of the parties was either a soldier or otherwise connected with the army, the *Connétablie* succeeded in establishing its jurisdiction. The professional calling of the litigants was the determining factor.

Concerning contracts, on the other hand, the nature of the quarrel determined the jurisdiction of the *Connétablie*. The dispute between Perrette de Fontenay and Pierre du Castel arose out of the interpretation of their contract to coöperate in supplying the army of the Catholic League, then besieging Corbeil. The connection with military affairs lay not in the personal status of the litigants, who were civilians, but in the nature of their contract.[8] Similarly, the Duke of Montpensier, a Prince of the Blood, was sued by one Clément Girard, a Breton merchant. In fulfilment of the terms of their written agreement, the plaintiff had duly delivered the military supplies desired, but had never received anything but evasions in payment. Since the magistrates of the *Connétablie* insisted that they were the "true judges to decide the said case," Girard brought his troubles thither.[9]

---

5. Z^{1c} 44, f. 40v, 41r. See also Z^{1c} 44, f. 4rv, 5r, 11rv, 12rv, 13r, 24rv, 25rv, 26rv, 27rv, 28rv, 31r.
6. Z^{1c} 44, f. 109r, 121rv.
7. Z^{1c} 44, f. 126rv, 127r. See also Z^{1c} 44, f. 141v, 142r, 148rv; Z^{1c} 47, f. 206v, 207r, 218rv, 219r.
8. Z^{1c} 44, f. 1rv, 2r.   9. Z^{1c} 47, f. 223 bis v.

The foregoing examples have shown that in disputes over money the personal status of the parties determined whether or not the *Connétablie* should have jurisdiction. A glance at them will show that never was the case anything that possibly could be termed military, since personal loans, payments for goods purchased, hotel bills, and payments of rent comprised the reasons for the quarrels. In every instance, on the other hand, one or both of the litigants was in some way connected with the military administration. With regard to contracts, however, the reverse was true. While the personal element inevitably played a part, the dominant factor was the terms of the contract. In the examples cited the contract provided that civilians should supply the armed forces. That this, rather than the personal element, was dominant is shown by the case of Perrette de Fontenay, in which two merchants brought their dispute to the *Connétablie*.[10]

The third sphere of civil jurisdiction of the *Connétablie* was the settlement of cases dealing with booty. Denis Mahon, *lieutenant* of the *prévôt des maréchaux* of the Ile de France, Guillaume Hue, his clerk, and several archers brought suit against three other archers and asserted that the defendants had stolen from them a large quantity of fine clothes, furs, and expensive robes.[11] Jean de La Croix, a Paris merchant, sued Marguerite de Marsilly, wife of the governor of the château of Ham, alleging that her husband and his soldiers had left a great quantity of war booty in the merchant's house. Since the loot had remained there for a long time, La Croix had been forced to spend a considerable sum to maintain it in good condition. So long a period had elapsed, however, that the goods were rapidly deteriorating. La Croix therefore petitioned the court to let him dispose of them, so as to avoid a large financial loss.[12] Maclou Bongarçon, a Paris hotelkeeper, Michel Catif, captain of a company of cavalry in the army of the Duke of Mayenne, and Louis Le Cousturier, archer of the *grand prévôt de la Connétablie*, became involved in a quarrel over the possession of a horse. Bongarçon and Catif alleged that the animal was in reality their property and that Le

---

10. Orgeval maintains that by the beginning of the eighteenth century the number of lawsuits dealing with contracts for military supplies had diminished considerably, due to the increasing importance of the *juges consuls*. The scarcity of such cases in the records of the *Connétablie* indicates that even during the reign of Henry IV the tendency was beginning to be manifest.
11. Z^{1c} 44, f. 36rv, 37rv.
12. Z^{1c} 44, f. 44v, 88rv, 89r.

Cousturier had illegally made off with it.[13] Quarrels concerned with war booty should be considered as distinct from those dealing with disputes over money. Whereas in the latter case the issues at stake were purely civil and, but for the personal status of the parties involved, might with equal right have been tried in an ordinary civil court, the quarrels in the former possessed a further complicating factor, that of seizure under war-time conditions. Because of the nature of the case jurisdiction over disputes concerning booty of war had always been one of the prerogatives of the court.

The civil activities of the tribunal, as distinguished from the administrative duties, were determined in some cases, notably money disputes, by the subject matter, and in others, such as ransoms, contracts, and booty, by the military status of the parties. The difference is often difficult to perceive, since at times both concepts are found in the same trial. Nevertheless, it must always be kept in mind. These criteria in later times separated more and more, due to the constantly decreasing importance of the tribunal. Emphasis was increasingly placed on the personal element as a method of attracting the largest possible number of cases to the *Connétablie*.[14] By the end of the sixteenth century the importance of the civil jurisdiction was in a state of decline. The competition of the ordinary law courts was too stiff and the disadvantages of the *Connétablie* in the struggle too great. Ransom cases are virtually the only type of civil action found in quantity.

With the rise of the *prévôts des maréchaux* most of the responsibility for the maintenance of order within the kingdom was transferred to them from the *Connétablie*. Since the parent body was established permanently in Paris, it obviously could not, save within a very limited radius, maintain order by its own unaided efforts. The responsibility for internal peace did not, however, pass entirely out of its hands. Under certain circumstances the *Connétablie* could and did exercise criminal jurisdiction. It must be emphasized, however, that the criminal jurisdiction of the court was declining just as fast as the civil jurisdiction and for the same reason. The first element of criminal jurisdiction was derived from the very cases which since the reign of Francis I, under

---

13. Z^{1c} 44, f. 55rv, 56r. See also Z^{1c} 44, f. 49v, 50rv, 51r, 52r, 53v, 81v, 82r, 119v, 120rv, 121r.

14. See Guichard, *Prévôts*, p. 147; Orgeval, *Connétablie*, pp. 158–159.

the name of *cas prévôtaux*, had been the property of the *prévôts des maréchaux*.[15] The tribunal was, by the power of delegation from the *connétable* and the *maréchaux de France*, the head of the entire *maréchaussée* and exercised the power of discipline over that group. It therefore also possessed the jurisdiction which had been granted by the ordinances to the *prévôts des maréchaux*.[16] Thus, the power of delegation, which had obtained for the *Connétablie* first the exercise of military justice and then the supervision of the *prévôts des maréchaux* and other officials operated once again and gave to it the power to judge *cas prévôtaux*.[17] This prerogative was not, however, usually exercised in direct fashion. The court seems to have lost much of the power to begin by its own efforts the prosecution of such cases, and was forced rather to accept them only after they had first passed through the hands of the *prévôts des maréchaux*. The latter were obliged by law to allow either the nearest *bailliage* or the *Connétablie* itself to decide whether they might be allowed to proceed with the trial of a case.[18] The second method by which the tribunal entered upon *cas prévôtaux* was through the exercise of the right of *prévention*. This principle provided that if a *prévôt des maréchaux* were negligent in the discharge of his duties, the *Connétablie* might transfer the case to its own court.[19]

The criminal cases which in theory came under the jurisdiction of the *Connétablie* were divided into several categories and were determined both by personal status and by the nature of the case.[20] Persons with no legal domicile and criminals who had previously been convicted were subject to the criminal jurisdiction of the tribunal. The following crimes were also included:[21] robbery and murder at any time on the highways,[22] counterfeiting, and rape. In addition, the trial of certain other crimes was by ordinance assigned exclusively to the *Connétablie*. These included

15. See Chapter I for an account of the *cas prévôtaux*.
16. Guichard, *Prévôts*, p. 162; Orgeval, *Connétablie*, p. 179.
17. See Chapter I.
18. Orgeval, *Connétablie*, p. 181. The *grand prévôt de la connétablie* was always obliged to refer to the *Connétablie* for this purpose if the crime had taken place within the limits of the Ile de France. Guichard, *Prévôts*, p. 164; Orgeval, *Connétablie*, p. 181.
19. Orgeval, *Connétablie*, pp. 181–182. See also Guichard, *Prévôts*, p. 164.
20. Orgeval, *Connétablie*, p. 180.
21. All persons, domiciled or not, were subject to this classification.
22. Committed by armed bands.

duels, sodomy, incest, bigamy, atheism and sacrilege, blasphemy, and witchcraft.[23]

Although in theory all the foregoing types of cases might be tried by the *Connétablie*, the *cas prévôtaux* most commonly heard were murder and robbery. And these are not found in numbers which correspond to the generally disturbed state of the country. These facts testify again to the great decline in the importance of the criminal jurisdiction of the court. Denis Maillet, a lawyer, "deposited in the office of the clerk of this court the investigations made against Nicolas Uger, surgeon, defendant, . . . because of the homicide committed upon the person of Louis Bernard." The *bailli* of Lyon had begun the trial by performing the investigations.[24] The tribunal dealt with the quarrel between Laurens Plantel, a farmer, and Jean de Compiègne, a miller living near Senlis. Plantel charged that the defendant was one of a band who had stolen his horses.[25] The trial had not originated in the *Connétablie* but, as in the case of the trial of Nicolas Uger, had been brought there by Plantel from another judicial body. The Plantel case had been undertaken by the Paris consular court. It is distinctly a *cas prévôtal*, since neither of the parties was connected in any way with the military forces and since the robbery had been committed by an armed band. The dispute between Jean Bigot, a Norman farmer, and Nicolas Baguet was taken from a lower tribunal to the *Connétablie*, for the latter deliberated upon Bigot's petition, which stated that he had lodged a complaint before the *bailli* of Longueville "against a certain Nicolas Baguet, soldier, because of several excesses, ransomings, and robberies committed against his person and his children by . . . Baguet, who appealed the said sentence before us."[26] Here indeed is a *cas prévôtal*. The defendant, a soldier, had plundered and robbed Bigot, the case had originated in a lower court, and had finally been taken before the *Connétablie* after the *bailli* of Longueville had ruled on the jurisdictional issues involved.

The second category of criminal jurisdiction consisted of *faits de guerre*, or acts of war. Many of these were very similar to the murder and robbery cases and the other *cas prévôtaux* and might conceivably have been classed with them had not a different prin-

---

23. Guichard, *Prévôts*, pp. 163–164; Orgeval, *Connétablie*, pp. 183–185.
24. Z^{1c} 45, f. 262v. See also Z^{1c} 45, f. 8v, 9r, 52v, 53r; Z^{1c} 47, f. 88v, 89rv, 90rv.
25. Z^{1c} 45, f. 250rv.
26. Z^{1c} 47, f. 219v.

ciple been invoked either by the tribunal or by the parties. Whereas murder and robbery were patently *cas prévôtaux* and were treated as such both by the litigants and the court, the cases regarded as *faits de guerre* were of no single type and included ransom, kidnapping, disregard of treaties, and various other actions not specifically listed. They were brought to the *Connétablie* solely by virtue of their connection with war. The connection in question was frequently tenuous. That one party to a dispute had some vague connection with the army caused the application of the principle of *faits de guerre*. It was actually a weapon which the *Connétablie* used in its jurisdictional struggles with other courts rather than a genuine legal principle.

François de Malbernard was held for the death of François de Saint-Avid, who was murdered while their regiment was on the march.[27] The circumstance of murder on the highroad made the matter a *cas prévôtal* and put the case clearly under the jurisdiction of a *prévôt des maréchaux*. In fact, the *sénéchal* of Périgord, in accordance with the laws dealing with the *cas prévôtaux*, was investigating the murder at the time. In order to get hold of the case, however, the *Connétablie* invoked the principle of "acts of war" in the following terms. Jurisdiction belonged to this tribunal, it maintained, because the crime was "an act committed . . . by soldiers . . . in the service of the King." [28] Two royal letters patent, which ordered all other courts to end any connection with the case, supported the *Connétablie* in this stand. The judges and the king thus invoked this relatively new principle of "acts of war." This maintained that since the court was the delegated representative of the heads of the army all acts which had any relation, however remote, to war should come under its jurisdiction. The use of this new concept in connection with the Malbernard case is of interest. Both parties were soldiers. From the earliest times the military commanders and their courts had had jurisdiction over the crimes of soldiers. The *Connétablie* in its early days had inherited this element of criminal jurisdiction. And yet, in the midst of a clearly defined case, the court and king both suddenly invoke a new principle, for the purpose of trying the Malbernard case, which, on the basis of the court's powers, really belonged to the *Connétablie* in the first place. This appeal to a new principle in such a clear-cut case demonstrates at the

27. Z^{1c} 44, f. 156rv, 157r.
28. Z^{1c} 44, 156r.

same time the greatly diminished importance of the *Connétablie's* criminal jurisdiction and the efforts to bolster it. As the *Connétablie* progressively declined in importance, its judges came more and more to rely upon this theory. In order to do away with the possibility that the Malbernard case might be tried before a *prévôt des maréchaux* the judges by this method circumvented the laws dealing with the *cas prévôtaux*.

The principle of acts of war was invoked by Henry IV himself in letters patent addressed to the court in 1594, shortly after his entry into Paris. Asked to settle a jurisdictional dispute, the king referred to his letters patent issued in late 1593 in which he "had ordered that if it seemed to you [the *Connétablie*] that the . . . murder inhumanely committed [by Martin Heurdebourg] upon the person of the late René Le Maître in our city of Alençon, and on account of which the *bailli* of . . . Alençon . . . had investigated and judged, were dependent on *faits militaires* and consequently on your jurisdiction, you should in that case, according to our edicts and ordinances, judge and decide them." [29] The Sieur de Biragues had been imprisoned in the Conciergerie by order of the *Connétablie*. The court cited the principle of *faits de guerre* when it attempted to question him. When the chief judge visited Biragues in his cell and ordered him to take the oath before submitting to questioning, the prisoner replied that the king, by edict and by his agreement with the Duke of Guise, had pardoned his crimes and wished that the investigation be dropped. The magistrate thereupon reminded the prisoner that "the ordinances" gave the *Connétablie* jurisdiction "over plunder and other affairs concerning war." [30] Although the court register does not always specify the charge against the defendant, in view of the examples in which it does, the *fait de guerre*, or *fait militaire*, appears to be one of several types of criminal action. Many of the cases so listed had but little connection with military affairs. Invocation of this principle bears out with regard to criminal jurisdiction the statement which Orgeval has made. He pointed out that certain civil cases in which neither the parties involved nor the subject of their dispute had the slightest connection with the army were tried by the *Connétablie*.[31] The tendency of the court in its struggle with

29. Z^{1c} 92, f. 63v. See also Z^{1c} 47, f. 256r.
30. Z^{1c} 45, f. 39rv. See also Z^{1c} 47, f. 57r, 215v, 244r.
31. Orgeval, *Connétablie*, pp. 158–159. He is here speaking of the eighteenth century.

other courts to attempt to drag before it on the flimsiest of grounds as many cases as possible has already been noted. The vague principle of the *fait de guerre* furnishes as early as 1600 one more example of this tendency. This general trend reflects a decline both in the prestige of the tribunal and in the importance of its criminal jurisdiction.

The final category of the *Connétablie's* criminal jurisdiction was rebellion and resistance to the *maréchaussée* and other judicial authorities or to the army. The tribunal's jurisdiction over such cases was derived from the ancient prerogative of maintaining order in territories where soldiers were located. The *cas prévôtaux* originated in the same manner. Suzanne Hillert asked for action with regard to the murder of her husband Samuel Moreau, clerk of the *vice-sénéchal* of Saintonge, who had been killed in the line of duty. She charged that he had been brutally murdered by Pierre Chastaigner and four other men as he was attempting to arrest Pierre. All of the assailants were men of evil habits and were charged at the time with several robberies and murders, according to the plaintiff. Suzanne stated that it was impossible under present conditions to do anything with regard to the criminals and obtained an order from the court that the *vice-sénéchal* of Saintonge and all his men should help the bearer of the court's decree to put it into force.[32] Julien Le Fort demanded assistance in the arrest of a band who had ambushed him. His petition stated that "because of an armed attack from ambush and a robbery committed against his person" by Isaac Turcault and three other ruffians he had appealed to the *prévôt* of Chinon, who investigated the matter and issued a warrant for their arrest. Only Turcault was arrested, but the officers were prevented from holding him prisoner by a great number of women and several "unmarried girls, who started several armed riots . . . so that they caused the prisoner to escape." The *prévôt* then "in the name of the king" ordered a group of local men to help him put down the riot. They refused, however, and "on the contrary they incited and encouraged the said women to continue . . . their violence and rebellions, by means of which he was unable to deal with the said robbery and murder, and the said *prévôt* does not wish to commit himself further to the execution of his decree."[33]

The criminal jurisdiction of the *Connétablie* depended in part,

32. Z^{1c} 47, f. 199rv, 200r.
33. Z^{1c} 47, f. 264v, 265r.

especially in cases of robbery and murder, first upon the action taken by the *prévôts des maréchaux* and then upon the subsequent rulings of the *bailliages* and *presidiaux*. Although the tribunal had the power to hear *cas prévôtaux* in first instance, the right was seldom used. The *Connétablie* evidently realized that its rôle was diminishing in importance, for it regularly invoked the principle of the *faits de guerre*, a legalistic concept of dubious validity but of considerable aid in attracting an increased number of criminal cases. It has often been emphasized that the rise of other institutions and its chronic struggle with the ordinary courts caused the *Connétablie* to lose many of its former powers. This process began as early as 1500 and was well advanced at the end of the sixteenth century. The effect was particularly noticeable in the civil and criminal work of the *Connétablie*. By 1600 these types of work formed but a small and unimportant part of the labors of the tribunal.

The decline in importance of the civil and criminal work of the *Connétablie* was in part compensated by the increasing burden and significance of administrative work. During the reign of Henry IV the bulk of the court's activity dealt with administrative affairs. Since the court was the head of the *maréchaussée* by delegation from the *maréchaux* it was responsible in theory for the smooth functioning of that organization and succeeded to a fair degree in imposing its authority in practice.

The first category of administrative jurisdiction was the right to register the appointments to office of the *connétable* and the *maréchaux* and to receive into office all officers of the *maréchaussée* and some of the administrative officials of the army. The relations of the *Connétablie* with the *commissaires des guerres* and the other administrative officials of the army whose jobs (like that of the *maréchaussée*) had originally been part of the duties of the *maréchaux* were confined largely to the registration of their letters patent of appointment. The tribunal had in practice no supervisory functions over them similar to those it had over the members of the *maréchaussée*. The *maréchaussée* was in need of supervision and management and the *Connétablie* was the logical body to fill that need, both from the point of view of theory and of practical considerations. The *commissaires* and the rest, on the other hand, despite the origins of their jobs, were in constant touch with the military authorities rather than with the *Connétablie* and so were supervised and managed primarily by the former.

On December 8, 1593, Henry, Duke of Montmorency, was appointed *connétable de France*. He took an oath of personal loyalty to the king and was received into office by the *parlement* of Paris, after which the appointment was recorded in the registers of the *Connétablie*.[34] By royal letters patent of March 30, 1594, Charles de Cossé, Count of Brissac, was chosen *maréchal de France*. On April 2 Brissac swore his oath of loyalty to the king in the presence of the chancellor and one of the secretaries of state and on April 5 was received into office by the *parlement* of Paris. On September 3 his letters of appointment were registered at the office of the clerk of the *Connétablie*.[35]

It was a relatively rare thing to register the appointment of a *connétable* or a *maréchal*, but the tribunal spent an enormous amount of time receiving into office the members of the *maréchaussée*. Philippe de Bresle presented his letters of appointment as archer of the *prévôt des maréchaux* of Paris and the Ile de France and petitioned for induction into office. The judges reviewed "the said letters, the investigation made by the said *prévôt* of the life, habits, conversation, and Catholic . . . religion of the said Bresle, together with the conclusions of the *procureur du roi*, to whom . . . everything has been communicated, and after having taken the oath required and accustomed in such a circumstance from the said Bresle" confirmed the appointment, "in witness whereof we have caused the seal of our court to be attached to these presents."[36] On November 4, 1592, Louis Bernard, Sieur du Plessis, *commissaire ordinaire des guerres*, appeared at the office of the court clerk in order to register his appointment.[37] An ordinance of 1573 had ordered all administrative officials of the army and *maréchaussée* to register their letters of appointment at the clerk's office of the *Connétablie*, on pain of dismissal from the service. In late 1593 and early 1594 there was therefore a great rush to comply with the law, probably for protection against a victorious and potentially resentful Henry IV.

Appointments made by the Duke of Mayenne during his *de facto* rule over Paris and those sections of the country faithful to the League were usually annulled by the king and then revived as

34. Z^{1c} 93, f. 14rv, 15r. See Appendix 1.
35. Z^{1c} 92, f. 73v, 74rv. See Appendix 2.
36. Z^{1c} 44, f. 136r. See also Z^{1c} 44, f. 5v, 6r, 18v, 106v, 107r, 109rv, 116v, 123v, 124r, 138v, 139r, 140r, 143r, 145v, 146v, 148v, 149r, 150r, 151r; Z^{1c} 46, f. 131r.
37. Z^{1c} 44, f. 103v. See also Z^{1c} 44, f. 107r, 116v, 117r, 121v, 122r, 124v, 127r, 139v, 140r, 142r, 147r, 159rv.

royal appointments. The records of the *Connétablie* contain some of these ducal choices. Laurens de Rouvre, for example, had been chosen *contrôleur provincial des guerres* in Anjou, Berry, Blésois, Maine, Touraine and other regions and appeared for the registration of his letters, which would make him a royal, as well as a ducal, appointee.[38]

The second phase of the tribunal's administrative jurisdiction included the settlement of all administrative problems of the *maréchaussée*.[39] The disturbed state of the country and the consequent laxity and confusion in the *maréchaussée* (as in all branches of the administrative machinery) caused this phase of the court's activity to be virtually the most important. During the periodic muster of the company of archers of the *prévôt des maréchaux* at Meaux, held before the *Connétablie*, the *prévôt* protested to the tribunal that Quantin Bernard, one of his archers, had presented a decree of the *parlement* of Paris, exempting him from active service, due to wounds received in the line of duty. The *prévôt* maintained that, while it was true that the injuries had resulted from service in the *maréchaussée*, Bernard had been completely recovered for the past ten years. He complained that Bernard refused to do any active work, but that he insisted on collecting his full salary. The *prévôt* then cited the small number of archers at his disposal and asked that the tribunal either command Bernard to return to active service or permit his dismissal and replacement.[40] Bernard insisted that the injury had incapacitated him permanently and then produced, in addition to the decree of the *parlement*, letters patent from the king ordering that he should be exempted from active service and continue to receive full salary. The judges finally complied with the royal order "that the said suppliant shall be included in the [muster] rolls" and ordered that he should be paid his full salary.[41] Michel Du Bois, one of the two *lieutenants* in the *maréchaussée* of Orléans, had received letters patent from the Duke of Mayenne stating that the office of the other *lieutenant*, vacant at the time, should not be filled. He petitioned successfully that the letters should be registered at the office of the clerk of the tribunal.[42]

38. Z^{1c} 44, f. 141r. See also Z^{1c} 44, f. 124v, 126r, 130r.
39. Orgeval, *Connétablie*, pp. 159–164.
40. Z^{1c} 44, f. 123r.
41. Z^{1c} 44, f. 125v, 126r.
42. Z^{1c} 44, f. 53v, 54r.

Some time later Gabriel Sauvage, a lawyer attached to the *parlement* of Paris, and the *procureur du roi* both petitioned for the registration of letters patent of Mayenne ordering the permanent suppression of the post at Orléans.[43] Marc-Antoine Froment, *lieutenant criminel de robe courte* at Amboise, protested that he was without a clerk and that in consequence the administration of justice and rapid suppression of crime was hindered. He therefore asked that pending a permanent appointment he be permitted to name a temporary clerk. The judges, "for the good of justice, temporarily, and until the King should have provided someone with the rank and office of clerk . . . and without setting a precedent, nor prejudicing the rights of the King, permitted . . . the said Froment to appoint . . . a clerk experienced in judicial affairs."[44]

The duties of the *prévôts des maréchaux* included periodic tours of inspection in the areas subject to their control and the preparation of written reports of conditions and remedial measures which should be taken. They then submitted this document to the clerk of the *Connétablie* and in return were given a receipt. The tribunal acknowledged the presentation by Pierre de Miraulmont, *prévôt des maréchaux* of Paris and the Ile de France, of the records of his administration during several of the preceding years.[45] Gabriel Pelost, president of the *élection* of Gien, in the name of the *vice-bailli* of Gien, "brought and deposited at the . . . clerk's office the records of the duties, diligence, and tours made by the said *vice-bailli*, his *lieutenant*, clerk, and archers during the quarter of January, February, and March of the present year 1596, for which he has asked [for] the present certificate." The officers of the *maréchaussée* were likewise obliged to bring their muster rolls periodically to the clerk's office of the *Connétablie* and to have them registered there.[46] These muster rolls and the periodic reports of the activities of the provincial *maréchaussée* officials enabled the *Connétablie* to have a knowledge of local conditions and to discharge more effectively its duties of supervision over the *maréchaussée*.

The final aspect of administrative jurisdiction was the adjust-

---

43. Z^{1c} 44, f. 121v. See also Z^{1c} 44, f. 106rv.
44. Z^{1c} 44, f. 142v. See also Z^{1c} 44, f. 145r, 152r.
45. Z^{1c} 44, f. 128v, 129r.
46. Z^{1c} 45, f. 200r. See also Z^{1c} 44, f. 136r, 143r, 144v, 149rv, 161r, 167r, 179r, 220r, 267v, 268r; Z^{1c} 45, f. 44r; Z^{1c} 47, f. 54v.

ment of all disputes over the possession of offices. The administrative weakness of the period inevitably led to a large number of such quarrels. The great number of cases of this sort also shows that the tribunal was regarded, not only by itself but by the members of the *maréchaussée* as the natural head of that body. Paul Duval became embroiled with Nicolas Jolly over the possession of the office of *lieutenant-général* at Abbeville of the *prévôt des maréchaux* of Picardy. Duval maintained that he had been duly appointed by the "late King Charles" and the Duke of Mayenne.[47] Jolly countered with the assertion that he himself had been installed by the *Connétablie* two years earlier. The court, however, held that the evidence was all in favor of Duval and ordered that Jolly's claims be annulled.[48] The induction into office of François Le Faucheux as counsellor in the jurisdiction of the *lieutenant* of the *prévôt des maréchaux* in Mayenne, "plaintiff, and petitioning to be received . . . into possession . . . of the said . . . office," was opposed by Gilles Richard, *sénéchal* of Bourgnouvel.[49] Richard stated that in his capacity of royal judge of Bourgnouvel he had always had the right to assist the *lieutenant* at Mayenne in the prosecution of criminal cases. He asserted that the appointment of a special counsellor for this purpose would deprive him of part of his own rights and duties and consequently was illegal despite the royal letters patent creating the new post and Le Faucheux's appointment to it.[50] The *procureur du roi* stated in his opinion, however, that he had been unable to find any evidence to prove that the duty of assisting the *lieutenant* was among the prerogatives of the *sénéchal* and declared that he could not support Richard's argument.[51] The judges then threw the case out of court, ordered the induction of Le Faucheux, and sentenced Richard to the payment of the costs of the trial.[52]

The great number of cases which can be classified as administrative jurisdiction indicates that as early as 1600 the *Connétablie* had lost the greater part of its military aspect. It had become

---

47. A reference to the Cardinal of Bourbon, uncle of Henry IV. Bourbon was the League's candidate for king after the death of Henry III. He died in 1590.
48. Z^{1c} 44, f. 61v, 62rv. See also Z^{1c} 44, f. 64rv, 98v, 99r, 104v, 105r, 111rv, 112r, 116r, 127rv, 129rv, 131rv, 136v, 142rv, 143rv, 144v, 145rv, 146r, 147v, 151r, 152v, 157v, 158rv, 159r; Z^{1c} 45, f. 45r, 78rv, 91r, 116v, 117r, 291rv; Z^{1c} 46, f. 141v, 150rv.
49. Z^{1c} 46, f. 173v.
50. Z^{1c} 46, f. 173v.
51. Z^{1c} 46, f. 174r.
52. Z^{1c} 46, f. 174r. See also Z^{1c} 47, f. 205v, 206rv.

primarily an agency for the supervision of the personnel and offices of the *maréchaussée* and administrative cases formed at this time the bulk of its work.

The *Connétablie* had always retained in theory the power of military discipline over the regular army, but by the end of the sixteenth century it had in practice virtually lost this control. Since the armed forces were never concentrated in Paris, Guichard correctly asserts that this was a theory which took little account of practical difficulties.[53] The *Connétablie* was permanently installed at the *Palais de Justice* in Paris and so was at a disadvantage in judging cases in remote parts of the kingdom or, in time of war, beyond the frontiers. In practice the administration of military discipline was divided among three organizations. In time of war the *grand prévôt de la connétablie*, the *conseils de guerre*, and the *prévôts des bandes*, all of whom traveled with the armies, handled the problems of discipline, crimes, and civil suits of soldiers. The only circumstances under which the *Connétablie* took charge were when the accused succeeded in making his escape from the army and in avoiding the clutches of the *prévôts des maréchaux*, or when the campaign ended before the accused was brought to trial. In time of peace cases of discipline were fewer and usually brought before the court only because it had succeeded in wresting them from rival bodies.[54] Guichard[55] maintains, and perusal of the records supports his conclusions, that the power of military discipline of the *Connétablie* was exercised only on rare and exceptional occasions. Such powers normally belonged to the aforementioned officers and, in the provinces, to the *prévôts des maréchaux*. The claims of the *Connétablie* therefore generally remained within the realm of theory.

It seems evident, furthermore, that by the middle of the reign of Henry IV the tribunal had ceased even to put forth serious claims to disciplinary jurisdiction. In 1600 the *procureur du roi* presented a petition in which he dealt with matters of general policy. The document states that military justice had originally been established as a jurisdiction distinct from that of the ordinary courts for the purpose of settling quarrels between soldiers and for judging cases of plunder, ransom, the capture of cities and châteaux, the violation of passports, and in general all acts of

---

53. Guichard, *Prévôts*, pp. 150–151.
54. *Ibid.*, pp. 158–160.
55. *Ibid.*, p. 161.

"hostility" due to war. This statement is a reiteration of the traditional claims of the *Connétablie* in matters of military jurisdiction. The *procureur* then asserted that he had been informed that many professional soldiers and others who had borne arms during the civil wars were being prosecuted before ordinary courts. They seemed unaware of their right to trial before the *Connétablie* and were therefore laboring under a handicap. In addition, the interests of the court itself were jeopardized by this situation. The *procureur* therefore asked for permission to compel the transfer of all such cases to the court of the *Connétablie*, since jurisdiction over them belonged there, "to the exclusion of all other judges." [56]

All the rights named in this petition, and also that of military discipline, had from the beginning been among the prerogatives of the tribunal. It is herein that the oddity of the passage becomes apparent. Although the *procureur du roi* was enumerating the rights which the tribunal had always possessed or to which it had always laid claim and was laying down a general policy for the *Connétablie* to follow with regard to certain cases then being tried in ordinary courts, he neglected even to mention the controversial question of military discipline. Two factors make the omission even more curious. Although the court had for some time past lost in practice its monopoly over the types of cases enumerated in this petition, it still claimed that monopoly over them. Furthermore, the *Connétablie* invariably seized every available opportunity to press even the most extravagant claims. In the light of these two facts, therefore, the failure to mention the question of military discipline can only lead to the conclusion that the tribunal recognized tacitly the loss of the right of disciplinary jurisdiction over soldiers.

The disciplinary rights of the tribunal were therefore confined in practice to supervision over the *maréchaussée* and in theory to some of the administrative officers of the army.[57] Disciplinary action was begun at the request either of the *procureur du roi* or of one of the *prévôts des maréchaux*. It was also undertaken as a result of complaints by outsiders or was initiated against the higher officials of the *maréchaussée* at the behest of their subordinates. Disciplinary cases occur frequently and testify once

56. Z^{1c} 47, f. 297rv.
57. Guichard, *Prévôts*, pp. 160–161.

more to the general laxity of administrative affairs. A good deal of the court's time was occupied by such work.

The *procureur du roi* protested that Henry III had awarded to the tribunal an annual sum of 200 livres, which was to come from forfeited salaries of members of the *maréchaussée*. For the past six years and more, however, no money had been forthcoming. He had recently learned that Louis Trudelle, receiver of the *tailles* in the *élection* of Paris, had on hand surplus funds assigned for the payment of the *lieutenant* of the *prévôt des maréchaux* of the Ile de France and seven of his archers. Since all had been absent at the last muster, their salaries had been declared forfeit. The *procureur* therefore petitioned the court to order Trudelle to turn over to the court clerk the salaries of the eight delinquents under discussion.[58] The *procureur* elsewhere protested that "to the contempt and detriment of our authority" several *prévôts des maréchaux, lieutenants,* and clerks had usurped their posts during the wars without the required royal letters of appointment and without having been investigated, approved, and installed by the *Connétablie*. He therefore petitioned that it might please the court, pending further action, to grant him permission to command all such delinquents to submit their letters of appointment for inspection. In the meantime he urged that they be forbidden to perform their duties, on pain of a fine of 1000 écus, and that payment of their salaries be stopped. The tribunal granted the petition in full.[59]

On another occasion the *procureur* told the court that at the request of the *procureur du roi* in the *maréchaussée* at Orléans investigations had been undertaken of frauds which Augustin Piart and Pierre Fleury, archers of the company at Orléans, had allegedly perpetrated. Although "jurisdiction over it belongs to us to the exclusion of all other judges," one of the *lieutenants* of the *prévôt des maréchaux* at Orléans had already begun the prosecution. Consequently, the *Connétablie* ordered, "at the request of the said *procureur du roi*," the clerk of the *prévôt des maréchaux* at Orléans "to bring or send, within two weeks, to the office of the clerk of our . . . court the charges and investigations, documents and proceedings undertaken against the said Piart and Fleury . . . whom we forbid to proceed anywhere but before us

---

58. Z^{1c} 44, f. 149v. See also Z^{1c} 45, f. 1v, 2r, 4v, 5rv.
59. Z^{1c} 46, f. 94rv. See also Z^{1c} 46, f. 125v, 234rv; Z^{1c} 47, f. 17r, 21rv, 60rv.

for the said frauds and crimes committed by them in their offices." [60]

Complaints of civilians against the members of the *maréchaussée* were frequent. Denise du Chef de La Ville, widow of François Sionnière, a lawyer formerly attached to the *parlement* of Paris, sued François de Bourges and Guillaume Bessaut, respectively clerk and subordinate judge of the *Connétablie*. She asked for payment of some money in the possession of Bourges, claiming that Bessaut owed it for the rent of one of her houses.[61] Michel Le Gallois, captain of an infantry company in the regiment of the Sieur de Saint-Géran, brought suit against Thibaut de Vausselles, *lieutenant* of the *prévôt des maréchaux* of Picardy.[62] The plaintiff asserted that he had arrested one Antoine de Séricours and his accomplices for the murder of several of his soldiers and had placed his prisoners temporarily in the jail at Montdidier. The defendant, entirely on his own authority, had released the culprits, had started judicial proceedings against Le Gallois, and had then seized a large amount of coined and uncoined silver and other goods belonging to the plaintiff.[63]

The unscrupulous actions of some of the officials of the *maréchaussée* led to complaints by their colleagues or subordinates. Isaac de Montfaulcon, recently inducted as *lieutenant de robe courte* of the *prévôt* of Montmorillon, brought suit against the clerk of the *Connétablie*. He asserted that because he had not yet paid the fee to the assistant judge, the clerk consistently refused to give him his certificate of induction. Since the assistant judge was temporarily absent, Montfaulcon maintained that he could not pay him the fee until his return. He asserted that it was not the clerk's prerogative to receive the money and demanded that he should be given his certificate. The court finally ordered the clerk to comply with Montfaulcon's request.[64] The archers of the *maréchaussée* of Paris and the Ile de France appealed to the *Connétablie* for redress against their *prévôt*. They asserted that he had for some time been disciplining them by throwing them in prison. This they maintained was illegal. The *prévôt* readily

60. Z^{1c} 47, f. 60v, 61r. See also Z^{1c} 47, f. 80rv, 84rv, 85r, 121v, 122r, 195v, 196rv, 225r.
61. Z^{1c} 44, f. 39v, 40rv. See also Z^{1c} 44, f. 52r, 78v, 107rv, 170v, 171r.
62. Z^{1c} 47, f. 37v.
63. Z^{1c} 47, f. 77v, 78r. See also Z^{1c} 47, f. 294v, 295r.
64. Z^{1c} 44, f. 96v. See also Z^{1c} 44, f. 109v, 110rv, 111r, 123v, 124r, 129v, 130r, 137v, 138r, 143rv, 147rv, 148rv, 152r; Z^{1c} 47, f. 61v, 62r.

admitted that he had jailed them, asserted that he would continue to do so whenever necessary, and informed the tribunal that his actions with regard to his archers were not in the slightest its concern. The judges then ordered that in the future he should confine his methods of punishment to those prescribed by the royal ordinances on the subject and fined him 20 écus.[65]

The *grand prévôt de la connétablie*[66] was obliged by law to take before the *Connétablie* those of his *cas prévôtaux* which occurred within the limits of the Ile de France.[67] This obligation was in a way a type of appeal. There was also a regular channel of appeal for ordinary civil and criminal cases running from the *grand prévôt* to the higher tribunal. This channel of appeal existed beside the *Connétablie's* regular practice of supervising and occasionally revising the *grand prévôt's* decisions. The case between Perrette de Fontenay and Pierre du Castel began before the *grand prévôt*. The ensuing trial had resulted in an order to Fontenay, a supply merchant following the army of Mayenne, to admit du Castel as a full partner in her business and to render to him a complete account of her transactions. She appealed from this decree to the *Connétablie*. Her opponent obtained from the *grand prévôt* an order for her imprisonment, but shortly thereafter she succeeded in obtaining her provisional freedom.[68] The *Connétablie* finally freed her unconditionally, declared that the sentences of the *grand prévôt* had been "well-appealed," and annulled them.[69] Jean Martin, Pierre Dohin, and Pierre de La Salle secured from the *grand prévôt* an order directing Germain Lamoieux to pay them at once a sum of money which he owed them. Lamoieux thereupon appealed to the *Connétablie*. The court decided, however, that he must comply with the original sentence.[70]

The *Connétablie's* disciplinary jurisdiction over the *prévôts des maréchaux* included the right to receive appeals from their penal decisions against subordinates and also against civilians. Com-

---

65. Z^{1c} 47, f. 77rv. The ordinances provided for suspension of salary or dismissal. See also Z^{1c} 47, f. 196v, 197r, 266r.

66. The *grand prévôt de la connétablie* accompanied the army commanded by the *connétable* and exercised police and disciplinary powers over it. Chéruel, *Dictionnaire*, I, 505.

67. Guichard, *Prévôts*, p. 164.

68. Z^{1c} 44, f. 1rv.

69. Z^{1c} 44, f. 9v, 10r. See also Z^{1c} 44, f. 4v, 5r, 40v, 52v, 53r, 86rv, 87rv, 89v, 90r, 94rv, 95rv, 96r, 99v, 103v, 104rv.

70. Z^{1c} 44, f. 7r. See also Z^{1c} 44, f. 132v, 133rv, 134rv, 135rv.

pleted cases involving civilians, however, were exceptional, for the *Connétablie* usually took these cases from the lower courts after the latter had partly finished trying them. The tribunal, for instance, ordered that Charles de Sonningue, who was accused of the murder of René Chaudet and who had repeatedly failed to answer summonses, should be arrested and that the trial "begun by our *prévôt* of Anjou" should be brought at once to the *Connétablie*.[71]

Decisions of governors and *lieutenants-généraux* of provinces were occasionally appealed to the *Connétablie*. A trial was begun between Julien Pelle, archer of the *prévôt des maréchaux* of Anjou, who appealed from a sentence of dismissal handed down by the *lieutenant-général* of Anjou at the instance of Antoine Desmoulins, archer of the *prévôt des maréchaux* at La Flèche. Since Desmoulins unexpectedly declared through his attorney that he wished to withdraw from the case, the judges "maintained and kept the said appellant in the said rank and place of archer," and prohibited Desmoulins and all others from disturbing him in the exercise of it.[72]

Sentences of *baillis* were sometimes appealed to the *Connétablie*. A trial was begun between Henry Caignart, a merchant of Saint-Quentin, appellant from a sentence rendered against him by the *bailli* of Vermandois, who had thereby confirmed an earlier sentence given by the "mayor, aldermen, and *jurés* of the said city," and Jacques Hochédé, also a merchant of Saint-Quentin. The tribunal denied Caignart's appeal and sentenced him to pay the costs of the trial.[73]

Finally, appeals from decisions of the courts of the *élections* were on occasion heard by the *Connétablie*. Ciret Samyon, *prévôt provincial des maréchaux* at Sens, had obtained from the president of the *élection* of Sens a judgment against two of his archers, Mathurin Diminal and Germain Hodry, which resulted in their dismissal. At once they appealed their case and succeeded in having it heard by the *Connétablie*.[74]

The foregoing review of the jurisdiction of the *Connétablie*

71. Z^{1c} 47, f. 89r.
72. Z^{1c} 46, f. 126v.
73. Z^{1c} 45, f. 108v, 109r.
74. Z^{1c} 44, f. 115rv, 116r. Appeals from the decisions of the *Connétablie* were heard only by the *parlement* of Paris, despite the efforts of the *Grand Conseil* to establish that right for itself. See Orgeval, *Connétablie*, pp. 30, 273 (for the *parlement*), 192–193 (for the *Grand Conseil*); Guichard, *Prévôts*, pp. 167–168.

has revealed the court in the last years of the sixteenth century as a body almost entirely occupied with administrative duties in connection with the *maréchaussée*. Civil jurisdiction, while still in existence, had been greatly reduced in scope. Although cases illustrative of its several phases can be found they form but a minute part of the total amount of business. Many civil trials were lost as a result of the rapid growth of the consular courts whose specialty was commercial cases. Still others were lost to the regular civil tribunals which were usually located much nearer to the homes of the litigants. Ransom cases are the only ones found in quantity. With criminal jurisdiction the story is identical. Murder and robbery cases were usually settled in the courts of the *prévôts des maréchaux* or found their way to other tribunals, especially the *parlement* of Paris. In order to bolster its sagging fortunes and to attract as many clients as possible, the tribunal during the late sixteenth century hit upon the new principle of *faits de guerre*. That this theory enjoyed but partial success at the time of Henry IV is shown by the small number of cases in which it figures. The use of so fictional a concept testifies to the decline in importance of the court's criminal jurisdiction. Riots against the *maréchaussée* and army, while in theory among the prerogatives of the tribunal, evidently were in great part handled by other courts, for the small number of such cases is not proportional to the disturbed condition of the country during this period.

Administrative work formed the bulk of the duties of the *Connétablie*. The rise of the institution of the *prévôts des maréchaux*, who were not renowned for their peaceable habits, made urgent the need for an agency to control them. Since the *prévôts* had originated as holders of temporary delegations of power from the *maréchaux de France*, the *Connétablie*, as judicial representative of the latter, claimed, and succeeded in exercising, supervision over these officials. The greatest part of the court's time was therefore occupied by the registration of their letters of appointment, the settlement of their disputes, and a general supervision of their activities in an effort to force them to perform their duties correctly. The *commissaires* and *contrôleurs des guerres*, regimental paymasters, and certain other army officials had originated in the same manner as the *prévôts des maréchaux*. The tribunal retained in theory similar rights over them, but in practice did little more than receive them into office and register their letters of appointment. Although the prerogative of military discipline had been lost, the tribunal benefited by the existence of the *prévôts des maréchaux*, for it possessed the power of discipline over their actions towards the general public and their own subordinates. This new disciplinary power, together with administrative work, occupied the major portion of the time and energies of the court.

In fact, as opposed to theory, the *Connétablie* had by 1600 become a court engaged principally in the business of supervising and on occasion restraining the *maréchaussée*. It managed to retain in practice but a small part of its originally vast civil and criminal jurisdictional powers. As a military court it was an anachronism; as a civil and criminal court it was unimportant and had little to do. But it had a usefulness, which lay entirely in its administrative work. This distinction between its theoretical and its actual powers must be understood, as well as the new character the court was assuming. Although the name and the theory remained the same, the character of the tribunal changed and adapted itself to new conditions. The *Connétablie* had become entirely an administrative, rather than a military, tribunal and had made for itself a new and different place in the administrative hierarchy.

IV

THE PROCEDURE OF THE COURT

THE *Connétablie* had by the sixteenth century undergone a profound change, which was manifest in all phases of its activity. It was no longer a military tribunal but had become a judicial body in every sense of the term. Its jurisdiction was fundamentally altered in character and was by 1600 chiefly administrative. Its officers were no longer military men, but professional lawyers. In its procedure the *Connétablie* likewise experienced a fundamental change. The summary methods of the original military tribunal had disappeared, and the complex judicial procedure of the ordinary courts had replaced them.

Several reasons explain this change.

The new character of the court had much influence on its procedure. Since the tribunal was no longer a military body, some method of procedure had to be introduced to meet the requirements of a court of civil, criminal, and administrative law. During the course of the sixteenth century the change in the character of the personnel was extended and completed. The military commanders ceased to administer the affairs of the *Connétablie* and were replaced in this task by professional lawyers and court assistants. This advent of a professional legal personnel was also influential, since these men brought gradually to the *Connétablie* the methods in which they had been trained and which they had been accustomed to practice. The procedure of the ordinary royal courts exercised throughout the fourteenth and fifteenth centuries the greatest influence on the development of French jurisprudence in general and determined the character of judicial procedure. Royal ordinances merely confirmed and made more precise the methods which the ordinary courts had evolved by practice and experience. The seigneurial courts which managed to survive showed this influence. The power and prestige of the ordinary courts and the influx of people trained in them led the *Connétablie* to adopt their methods of judicial procedure.

The plaintiff began proceedings before the *Connétablie* by submitting to the judges a petition for the investigation of the charges which he made. The petition also had numerous other uses in the civil and administrative work of the *Connétablie*. The court determined by means of the investigation whether or not the plaintiff's charges warranted further judicial action. Witnesses against the defendant testified during the investigation. In an effort to arrive at a truthful account, the court always compelled witnesses to testify under oath. If the judges decided that further action was desirable they issued a summons to the defendant to appear before them for questioning and in some instances issued a decree of arrest. If either party at any time during the trial refused or neglected to obey court orders, the judges issued a *défaut* against him and imposed a variety of penalties for continued disobedience.[1] In criminal cases the defendant was questioned after his appearance in court. The plaintiff on occasion took the stand. The witnesses again testified. In civil cases the attorneys for both parties then presented their clients' cases and demands for reparation. The court often felt the need of further information in a trial and handed down an *appointement*, or interlocutory decree. This decree gave the litigants additional time in which to make further investigations and produce further evidence in support of their contentions. When the case was ready for final judgment the court turned over all evidence to the *procureur du roi*, who studied it and submitted his recommendations for action.[2] The judges then deliberated on and reviewed the evidence, announced their decision, and imposed a penalty.[3]

The petition was one of the most significant elements in the procedure of the *Connétablie*, for it set in motion the machinery of judicial action. In the ordinary courts the prospective plaintiff

1. The *défaut* was issued to the plaintiff in case of disobedience on the part of the defendant. If the plaintiff was at fault the court granted a *congé* and accompanying penalty to the defendant. Hereafter referred to as "default" and "congé."
2. The *procureur du roi* was the representative of the crown attached permanently to the staff of the *Connétablie* and watched over the king's interests. This officer also acted as prosecutor in criminal and in some civil cases. See Chapter V. Hereafter referred to as *"procureur du roi."* The litigants also had attorneys, who were called *procureurs*. These men represented their clients and protected their interests. Hereafter referred to as "attorneys."
3. See A. Esmein, *Histoire de la procédure criminelle en France*, pp. 135–158, for a discussion of criminal procedure in the ordinary courts during the sixteenth century. A comparison with the procedure of the *Connétablie* will show clearly the influence of the ordinary law courts on that body. Hereafter referred to as Esmein, *Procédure*.

had to obtain the permission of the tribunal to begin an investigation of his complaint.[4] The defendant did not appear until the investigation had been completed and was not to be disturbed without a writ of summons. To obtain this judicial support it was customary for the plaintiff to present a petition to the court. The *Connétablie* adopted these rules of procedure in the ordinary courts for use by its own judges.[5] During the course of a trial, furthermore, all parties employed the petition extensively. They petitioned for certificates showing that they had complied with court orders. They petitioned for permission to introduce new evidence or witnesses. They petitioned for the assistance of the *procureur du roi*. They used the petition in order to ask for delays in which to prepare their cases. The *procureur du roi*, despite his official position, was compelled to use the petition for many of his actions. Finally, the petition had its place in the administrative activities of the *Connétablie*. The petitioner in every case was compelled to present in his petition a full account of the reasons for his recourse to legal action. The tribunal therefore possessed at the outset of the investigation the full story of one side of the argument.

The forms of petitions are in general always the same. First comes the salute to the court, next the exposition of the problem at hand, then the conclusion and recommendation for action, and lastly the final plea and the signature of the petitioner. With regard to word variations there are several general types.[6] Despite superficial variations there are very few fundamental differences in the forms of address and in the bodies of the petitions themselves. Probably no rigidly fixed formula for wording was enforced. There seems to have been a minimum requirement, beyond which the petitioner was more or less free to express himself. There remains the question of whether all petitions were written, or whether some were delivered orally. Many written petitions still exist. All petitions were written and handed to the court as part of the evidence. When a case came up for final judgment, the court always gave a list of all documents studied in the effort to arrive at a decision. In every case, petitions are

---

4. Esmein, *Procédure*, p. 140.
5. Orgeval, *Connétablie*, pp. 217–218, agrees with this.
6. See Appendix 3 for examples of the various types of petitions and their variations in wording.

listed among the evidence "seen and considered," as opposed to pleas, for instance, which are always listed in the review of evidence as "heard."

Plaintiffs who wished to initiate proceedings before the *Connétablie* submitted petitions to begin one of three types of action. They might make charges and petition the court to investigate the matter. The judges reviewed, for instance, the investigation they had conducted "upon the petition of Denis Boulle, ... against the Sieur de Poitrincourt" and several others, who were his "confederates and accomplices." [7] They might present their side of a dispute and demand an immediate decision on the case. Hubert Charpentier and his wife presented a petition in which they demanded permission, "for the reasons therein contained," to seize from the clerk of the *grand prévôt* 100 écus belonging to Louis de La Roche as payment for a horse belonging to them and which La Roche had fraudulently sold.[8] Finally, there was a formal procedure concerning the frequent disputes over offices in the *maréchaussée*. People often maintained that the induction into office of someone else defrauded them of their rightful claims. The procedure in such cases was for the plaintiffs to come to the clerk's office, register their opposition to the appointment, and then petition the court to grant them a certificate showing their compliance with the forms. Action might then begin. René Barre, attorney of Philippa Clément, registered his client's opposition to any appointment as clerk of the *prévôt des maréchaux* at Montargis, where Philippa's late son had been hereditary clerk. His mother was his heir and so opposed any appointment which she did not approve. Barre presented the foregoing facts briefly and then "in her name petitioned [for this] act." [9]

The petition also regulated many phases of procedure during the trial itself. Those who had been summoned to court always petitioned for an official acknowledgment of their obedience. In order to comply with the summons and to choose an attorney, Guillaume Pigneron and several other inhabitants of Argenteuil appeared at the clerk's office. The first act of their attorney,

7. Z^{1c} 45, f. 1r. See also Z^{1c} 46, f. 210rv, 223r; Z^{1c} 47, f. 66r, 73rv, 74r, 88v, 199rv, 204v, 216v, 225r, 234r, 264v, 265r, 282v, 283r, 287r.

8. Z^{1c} 44, f. 23v, 24r, 27v, 28r. See also Z^{1c} 44, f. 5v, 6r, 10v, 11rv, 21v, 22r, 28v, 45rv, 46rv, 48r, 63r, 73rv, 81v, 87v, 88r, 91rv; Z^{1c} 46, f. 169rv; Z^{1c} 47, f. 90r, 196v, 197r, 210r, 215rv, 218rv, 219r, 223 bis v, 224r, 244rv.

9. Z^{1c} 44, f. 127rv. See also Z^{1c} 45, f. 45r, 91r, 116v, 117r, 291rv; Z^{1c} 46, f. 147rv, 148r.

Vincent Raffard, was to petition for "the present act, granted to him." [10] When on the other hand a defendant considered that he had been unjustly summoned to court, he demanded by means of a petition to be cleared of the accusations against him. Etienne Guichard, archer of the *prévôt des maréchaux* at Meaux, had been ordered to appear for questioning as to his absence from musters of his company. He came to court bearing letters patent excusing him from attendance and a petition that he be cleared of all charges against him.[11]

The introduction (and attempts to prevent it) of evidence or witnesses into a trial necessitated the use of the petition. Jean Beau, the *lieutenant* of the *prévôt des maréchaux* of Poitiers, and others sent an attorney to attempt to prevent the reading and publication of an edict creating a *vice-sénéchal* and staff in the *sénéchaussée* of Civray. Jean Sasserye, however, submitted a petition for the publication of the edict and for the confirmation by the court of his appointment as *vice-sénéchal* of Civray.[12] Nicolas Lemaire and Nicolas Lefebvre brought to the *Connétablie* their dispute over the possession of a horse, which Lemaire asserted had been stolen from him. During the trial the horse, which had been left in the custody of one Le Moyne, was stolen by the defense witnesses. Lemaire's attorney at once petitioned the court that Lefebvre be denied the use of those witnesses until the horse should have been returned to the care of Le Moyne.[13] When litigants deposited evidence with the clerk they petitioned for a receipt. Séverin and André Dumont "petitioned for an act" stating that they had complied with the court order and had handed to the defendant copies of receipts for payment of their ransoms and for the expenses incurred "during their long and troublesome detention caused by the negligence of the defendant." [14]

Should litigants desire to have more time to prepare their cases, they petitioned the court for an *appointement*, or time-extension. Nicolas Lespoir, "plaintiff with regard to a petition aiming at renewal of delay," obtained an additional six weeks.[15]

---

10. Z^{1c} 47, f. 12v. See also Z^{1c} 44, f. 163v, 164r; Z^{1c} 46, f. 2rv; Z^{1c} 47, f. 13v, 105r, 229r.
11. Z^{1c} 47, f. 210r. See also Z^{1c} 47, f. 57r, 105v, 281rv, 282v, 283r.
12. Z^{1c} 46, f. 141rv. See also Z^{1c} 47, f. 208r, 288v.
13. Z^{1c} 44, f. 93v. See also Z^{1c} 44, f. 93r; Z^{1c} 47, f. 66r.
14. Z^{1c} 44, f. 46rv. See also Z^{1c} 45, f. 262v; Z^{1c} 47, f. 46r, 272v, 273r, 284r.
15. Z^{1c} 47, f. 260v, 261r. See also Z^{1c} 44, f. 79r; Z^{1c} 47, f. 24r.

When parties had been sentenced to furnish bond their guarantors appeared, signed for the sum involved, and then petitioned for the act which proved their obedience to court orders.[16] If a litigant failed to comply with a court order, his opponent invariably petitioned for a default and penalty against him. René Bodet, a *maréchaussée* official at Angers, had protested the induction into that company of Jean Chitton. Chitton protested that Bodet had failed to comply with the order to come and explain in person the reason for his stand, and petitioned for a default, "by virtue of which it might please us" to disregard Bodet's objections and to impose costs and damages.[17]

Although the *procureur du roi* was an important official of the *Connétablie* he was subject to many of the same rules as ordinary litigants. When he desired action by the court he was obliged to submit a formal and detailed petition to that effect. He might do this on his own initiative or he might add his request to that of a civilian litigant. At the instance of Antoine Jacquart investigations had been started against a certain La Fontayne. After reviewing the charges, the tribunal, "on the petition of the said Jacquart" and of the *procureur du roi*, ordered that La Fontayne be summoned to court for questioning.[18] On the occasion of the induction into office of the *prévôt général* of Marshal Boisdaulphin the *procureur du roi* submitted a petition. The petition stated that it was forbidden by law for anyone to be a clerk of a *prévôt des maréchaux* unless appointed by the king and installed by the *Connétablie* and then asked that the new *prévôt* be forbidden to hire any clerk unless the candidate had fulfilled the necessary requirements.[19] The *procureur* always submitted a petition for investigation of prospective officers of the *maréchaussée*. Upon receiving royal letters patent of appointment the applicant came before the *Connétablie*. At the request of the *procureur du roi* the tribunal then conducted an investigation of the candidate's character, morals, religion, and ability. Should the applicant be found satisfactory induction into office followed.[20]

16. Z^{1c} 44, f. 24v, 25r, 74v, 116v.
17. Z^{1c} 46, f. 150v, 151r. See also Z^{1c} 44, f. 29v, 30r; Z^{1c} 47, f. 200rv, 223 bis rv, 224rv, 246v, 247r, 266r.
18. Z^{1c} 46, f. 210rv.
19. Z^{1c} 46, f. 234rv. See also Z^{1c} 47, f. 60rv, 80rv, 84rv, 121v, 122r, 199r, 268v, 269rv, 297rv.
20. Z^{1c} 282, Oct. 27, 1594. See also Z^{1c} 282, Sept. 17, Oct. 24, Nov. 4, 14, 18, Dec. 20, 1594.

A layman might petition for the assistance of the *procureur du roi*. Jean Robbe appealed to the *Connétablie* from a sentence of dismissal handed down by his chief, Adrien Chartier, *prévôt des maréchaux* of Blois and Vendômois. Robbe claimed that Chartier had used a royal edict for retrenchment in the *maréchaussée* as an excuse to get rid of him. The *prévôt* countered that his action was in perfect harmony with the edict and presented a petition for the assistance of the *procureur du roi*.[21] The latter intervened, but on the basis of his investigations delivered an opinion which led the court to order Robbe's reinstatement with full salary from the day of his dismissal.[22]

The petition also figured largely in the administrative activities of the *Connétablie*. The *prévôts des maréchaux* were required periodically to deposit reports of their actions with the clerk of the *Connétablie*. Gilles de Saint-Yon brought to the clerk's office the records of the actions and tours of inspection done by the *prévôt des maréchaux* of Senlis and petitioned for a receipt from the clerk.[23] During 1593 and early 1594, probably because they feared royal reprisals, officials in the military administration and *maréchaussée* hastened to comply with the law of January 15, 1573, which required registration of their appointments with the clerk of the *Connétablie*. Many of them had never before complied with the law. Upon fulfilling this requirement each officer petitioned for the usual acknowledgment.[24]

The parties in litigation were designated according to the circumstances of the case as plaintiff and defendant at the outset of the trial. If a litigant initiated any action during the trial, or if he sought to oppose any action by his adversary, he automatically became the plaintiff in that action alone and his opponent became the defendant, irrespective of their status at the beginning of the trial. But when the case came up for final judgment both sides were then presented in their original rôles of plaintiff or defendant. Any reversals which might have occurred earlier represented simply a clearer method of identification and did not signify any real change in their status. Great care must therefore be exercised in order to avoid arriving at false conclusions regarding the real designation of the parties in litigation. Charles de

21. Z^{1c} 47, f. 268rv. See also Z^{1c} 47, f. 37v, 38r, 78rv.
22. Z^{1c} 47, f. 268v, 269r. See also Z^{1c} 47, f. 289v.
23. Z^{1c} 45, f. 37v. See also Z^{1c} 44, f. 116v, 117r; Z^{1c} 45, f. 44r, 200r, 211v; Z^{1c} 47, f. 54v.
24. Z^{1c} 44, f. 117r. See also Z^{1c} 44, f. 121v, 126r.

Sonningue was defendant against a charge of murder brought by Jean Chaudet, the plaintiff. At the beginning of the trial Sonningue wished to introduce certain royal letters patent as evidence in his defense. He appeared as petitioner for the introduction of the new evidence and was referred to for this purpose alone as the plaintiff. He was therefore at the same time defendant against the murder charge and plaintiff concerning the introduction of the new evidence. Chaudet opposed the introduction of the royal letters patent as part of Sonningue's case. He is referred to as defendant against Sonningue's petition, but remained plaintiff as far as the original murder charge was concerned. Sonningue therefore appears at the same time as defendant and plaintiff and Chaudet as plaintiff and defendant.[25] In the case of Marin Noury against Jacques Pommereau and Alexandre Daier the parties underwent similar transformations. Pommereau, one of the defendants, entered a plea for removal of the case to another court. He thereby became plaintiff for that single action, but remained defendant in the case as a whole. Noury, the plaintiff, opposed Pommereau's petition and in so doing became the defendant during that action. When the case came up for final judgment the court deliberated upon "the criminal trial . . . pursued before us between Marin Noury, plaintiff and accuser, on the one hand, and Jacques Pommereau, . . . defendant and accused and plaintiff, . . . on the other." [26] Several persons together frequently presented a complaint in common or appeared together for the defense. For instance, the archers of the *maréchaussée* at Provins presented a joint petition asking for the return of their muster rolls which had been entrusted to Jacques Moraut.[27]

As the guardian of the interests of the king the *procureur du roi* often appeared as plaintiff. In criminal cases in the ordinary courts at this period the *procureur du roi* was always a party to the case and the same rule was generally observed in criminal cases tried before the *Connétablie*.[28] Because of various crimes and abuses committed by Jean Barangues in the performance of his duties as *lieutenant* of the *vice-sénéchal* of Armagnac, the *procureur du roi* lodged a complaint against him and caused him

---

25. Z^{1c} 47, f. 88v.
26. Z^{1c} 47, f. 58rv. See also Z^{1c} 47, f. 105v, 108rv, 109rv, 110r, 295r.
27. Z^{1c} 47, f. 196v, 197r. See also Z^{1c} 44, f. 5v, 10r, 21v; Z^{1c} 47, f. 218rv.
28. Esmein, *Procédure*, pp. 139–140.

to be summoned to court.[29] Only occasionally, however, did the *procureur* initiate action in a civil case. He appeared frequently as plaintiff in conjunction with a layman, on the other hand, whereupon the latter retired to a subordinate position known as the *partie civile*. The *Connétablie* had borrowed this practice from the ordinary courts, where it had been in use since the fourteenth and fifteenth centuries.[30] Since litigants thought that the addition of official support lent strength to their complaints, many people petitioned for it. Jean Le Roux disputed the possession of the office of clerk of the *vice-bailli* of Caen with Gilles Rozel, whom the Duchess of Nemours supported. She claimed the position for her candidate on the basis of an agreement made on the occasion of a loan by her ancestor, the Duke of Ferrara, to Francis I. The contract provided that until the loan should have been repaid, any new post created in the *maréchaussée* in the Caen "region" should be filled by a person chosen by the Duke of Ferrara or his descendants. The duchess claimed the right to fill this office of clerk with a man of her choice on the grounds that the post had been created since the loan, that the loan remained unpaid, and that she was a descendant of the Duke of Ferrara. Le Roux petitioned for and received the assistance of the *procureur du roi*.[31] This case dealt with the right of appointment to office. Since appointments were one of the most important interests of the king, the *procureur* intervened, as guardian of those interests.

The record of the trial between Philippe du Resnel and Adrien Barat summarizes the proceedings that had taken place "between the said parties or attorneys for them."[32] Except in the case of testimony by witnesses, of direct questioning, and in the administration of the oath of office, there was no requirement for the presence of parties in the courtroom during sessions of the *Connétablie*. Whether litigants appeared in court in person or were represented there solely by an attorney depended on their own desires, unless the judge specifically ordered otherwise. At the beginning of a trial, or at the opening of a new phase, the parties might appear in court without an attorney. Etienne de Furnes, archer in the *maréchaussée* at Provins, for example, presented

---

29. Z^{1c} 47, f. 195v. See also Z^{1c} 47, f. 225r.
30. Esmein, *Procédure,* pp. 111–112.
31. Z^{1c} 47, f. 205v. See also Z^{1c} 44, f. 10r; Z^{1c} 47, f. 57rv, 78rv, 88v, 90r, 200rv, 204v, 268rv, 287r, 288v.
32. Z^{1c} 44, f. 74r.

a petition in person to the court.[33] Litigants at times, however, sent attorneys to act for them. Pierre de Miraulmont, on one occasion, was plaintiff "through Viart, his attorney." [34] Litigants often accompanied their attorneys to court. Nicolas Coquelaire appeared in court "in person and through Berrier, his attorney," for the prosecution of his charges against Jean Sorny.[35] One party sometimes sent his attorney to court, while his opponent appeared in person, alone or with an attorney. François Le Faucheux petitioned for confirmation as counsellor in the court of the *lieutenant* in the *maréchaussée* at Mayenne and appeared in court with his attorney. Gilles Richard, *sénéchal of* Bourgnouvel, personally and without counsel opposed the appointment.[36] Although the judges often ordered parties to come before them, there was still no uniform rule. At the request of Mathurin de Saint-Frais, the court summoned several villagers to appear. Since the defendants had not come, "nor attorneys for them," the judges commanded that an earlier sentence in favor of Saint-Frais be carried out.[37]

In some instances, however, personal appearance was specifically required. The court forbade Nicolas Breton to perform the duties of commissioner for musters of the company of the *prévôt des maréchaux* at Orléans and ordered him to appear and defend himself in court.[38] The judges on some occasions decreed imprisonment in order to have the culprit on hand for questioning and usually handed down this order after a defendant had failed several times to obey judicial commands. Jean Barangues, an official of the *maréchaussée*, had been charged with various crimes in the performance of duty. Summoned before the tribunal, he had failed to appear, whereupon the court ordered his arrest and imprisonment in Fort L'Evêque.[39] The registration of letters patent of appointment to positions in the *maréchaussée*

33. Z^{1c} 44, f. 123v. See also Z^{1c} 44, f. 11v; Z^{1c} 47, f. 110r.
34. Z^{1c} 44, f. 11r. See also Z^{1c} 44, f. 63r, 78v, 79r; Z^{1c} 47, f. 208r, 289v.
35. Z^{1c} 44, f. 11r. See also Z^{1c} 44, f. 13v, 69v, 119v, 120r, 142v, 147v; Z^{1c} 47, f. 52rv, 57r, 246v, 247r.
36. Z^{1c} 46, f. 173v. See also Z^{1c} 44, f. 66r, 79r; Z^{1c} 46, f. 150r; Z^{1c} 47, f. 50v, 51r, 210r, 258v.
37. Z^{1c} 47, f. 224rv. See also Z^{1c} 44, f. 167r; Z^{1c} 46, f. 7r; Z^{1c} 47, f. 60v, 61r, 197r, 207r, 223 bis v, 224r, 266r, 281rv, 283r.
38. Z^{1c} 47, f. 60v. See also Z^{1c} 44, f. 10rv, 66r, 152v, 153r; Z^{1c} 46, f. 2rv, 131v, 132r, 223r; Z^{1c} 47, f. 12v, 13rv, 17r, 55r, 62r, 66r, 79v, 80r, 84r, 88v, 89r, 105r, 199rv, 200r, 215v, 216v, 229r, 233r, 240v, 261r, 267v.
39. Z^{1c} 47, f. 195v. See also Z^{1c} 47, f. 89r, 234r, 288v, 296rv.

usually required presence in person at the clerk's office. Jacob Le Prestre, a paymaster, appeared "in person at the clerk's office of this court" for registration of his letters.[40] The sending of attorneys for this purpose was, however, sometimes permitted. Le Roy, attorney of Nicolas Mauroy, presented for registration his client's letters of appointment as *commissaire des guerres* in Champagne.[41] There was no strict requirement of personal appearance when the decision in a trial was handed down. In general, the party in whose favor the judgment was delivered was present personally or represented by an attorney. The loser of the case and his attorney, on the other hand, were usually absent.[42] This practice was, however, not invariably followed.

There was one requirement of procedure which of necessity demanded the personal appearance of the persons concerned. This was the swearing of the oath. Witnesses took the oath and hence were present in person. When Claude de Fontaynes petitioned for installation as *lieutenant de robe longue* at Alençon, four witnesses testified under oath concerning his character, religion, and ability.[43] Officials were required to appear personally when they were received into office. When all formalities had been completed, the judge administered the oath of office, for which the presence of the candidate was naturally necessary. Claude Collas had for some time been fulfilling the duties of *prévôt des maréchaux* of Orléans. He took the oath and was confirmed by the court in his possession of that post, on condition that he come to court a year later in person and swear the oath.[44]

Two principles governed the procedure in any case on trial before the *Connétablie*. The first was that the court should pos-

---

40. Z^{1c} 44, f. 121v. See also Z^{1c} 44, f. 116v, 126r; Z^{1c} 45, f. 291rv; Z^{1c} 47, f. 121v, 122r.

41. Z^{1c} 44, f. 117r. See also Z^{1c} 44, f. 127rv, 139v, 140r; Z^{1c} 46, f. 147v, 148r, 173r.

42. For example, the Duchess of Nemours and Gilles Rozel lost their case against Jean Le Roux, who was the plaintiff in the dispute. When the decision was handed down it was "pronounced to the said Aimé Salé, attorney of the said plaintiff [Le Roux], in the absence of the said defendants [Nemours and Rozel] and of . . . Doublet and Liesse, their attorneys." Z^{1c} 47, f. 206v. See also Z^{1c} 44, f. 74v, 85r, 110r, 128v, 135v, 141v, 142r, 171r; Z^{1c} 45, f. 53v; Z^{1c} 47, f. 59r, 66r, 79v, 110r, 196r, 200v, 204v, 207r, 216r, 218r, 219v, 224r, 225r, 234r, 244v, 257r, 270r.

43. Z^{1c} 282, Sept. 29, 1594. See also Z^{1c} 282, July 27, Sept. 17, 19, 23, Oct. 11, 24, 27, Nov. 4, 14, 18, Dec. 20, 1594.

44. Z^{1c} 44, f. 129r. See also Z^{1c} 44, f. 124r; Z^{1c} 46, f. 131r; Z^{1c} 282, Sept. 17, 29, Oct. 24, Nov. 14, 18, Dec. 20, 1594.

sess all possible facts concerning the case. The judges could formulate an opinion only if they possessed a complete and accurate picture of the situation. The *Connétablie* used five direct and indirect methods of establishing the facts. Investigation before a trial gave the court considerable knowledge about the case. The investigation enabled the judges to verify the allegations which the plaintiff had made in his petition and to decide whether the matter should come to trial. Witnesses were used both during the investigation and during the trial to assist in the establishment of fact. All who gave evidence or who were questioned were required to take an oath, a third method used to gain information. The oath bound the witnesses and litigants to speak the truth. If further information were deemed essential the judges issued a summons to appear to one or both of the litigants. The summons was another indirect method of establishing fact. By virtue of the summons the defendant or the plaintiff was compelled to come to court and submit under oath to questioning by the judges. Finally, if the court needed more evidence it issued an *appointement* which compelled the parties to conduct further investigations. The second principle governing procedure gave to each party the right to present his side of the case. Each litigant personally or through his attorney presented his arguments and then submitted his demands. Furthermore, each party could present during the trial whatever evidence he felt would help his case and was given an opportunity to try to refute the charges of his opponent. This evidence was of various types. The judges had legal weapons at their disposal, which they employed to put these judicial principles into practice and to ensure obedience to summonses and other court orders. After all the evidence had been presented and all the witnesses heard, and after the court had questioned the litigants if it so desired (which was not always the case) the judges reviewed the evidence, obtained the opinion of the *procureur du roi*, and announced their decision.

In the ordinary courts criminal procedure was guided by the provisions of the great ordinance of 1539. According to that law a layman or the *procureur du roi* might request an investigation or the judge might begin one on his own authority.[45] The *Connétablie* seems to have adopted these principles, for almost the identical procedure is followed. In the *Connétablie* a civilian might demand an investigation; a civilian and the *procureur du*

45. Esmein, *Procédure*, pp. 139–140.

roi jointly might ask for it; the *procureur du roi* alone might demand it; or the judges might require it.[46]

Investigation begun at the request of civilians occurs most frequently. Marin Noury obtained an investigation against Jacques Pommereau and Alexandre Daier. The judges found facts warranting further action, for the accused were then summoned to appear. After they had failed to obey Noury petitioned for their arrest. A few days later, therefore, the court questioned Daier concerning the content of the investigation "undertaken against him at the petition of Marin Noury."[47] Investigations were also begun at the request of a civilian plaintiff, to whom the *procureur du roi* was joined as co-petitioner. In connection with the trial of François Baudry, accused by François Le Peigné of armed violence, a supplementary investigation against several soldiers was begun at the request of both Le Peigné and of the *procureur du roi*.[48]

If the *procureur* felt that the interests of the king were involved he intervened of his own accord. When it was discovered that a *maréchaussée* official in Guyenne had been embezzling funds and committing various other crimes the investigation for more facts on the case was "done at the petition of the *procureur du roi*."[49] The conduct of a royal officer was of course one of the concerns of the representative of the crown. The most common example of official intervention was induction into office. The prospective office-holder, bearing his royal letters of appointment and other documents, appeared before the court and petitioned that they be registered. In order to determine the petitioner's fitness for office, the *procureur du roi* always requested an investigation of his habits, religion, character, and ability.[50]

In the ordinary courts the witnesses heard in the investigation were called singly either before the judge, before special inspectors,[51] or before ordinary bailiffs.[52] Here again the practice of the *Connétablie* conformed to the general character of ordinary

---

46. See Z[1c] 282. In each case the judge initiates the investigation of applicants for office in the *maréchaussée* by referring their petitions to the *procureur du roi*.

47. Z[1c] 47, f. 51r, 56r. See also Z[1c] 44, f. 68rv; Z[1c] 46, f. 210rv, 223r; Z[1c] 47, f. 66r, 295rv.

48. Z[1c] 47, f. 244v. See also Z[1c] 47, f. 204v, 287r.

49. Z[1c] 47, f. 269v, 270r.

50. Z[1c] 282. See this series of cases. Intervention by the *procureur du roi* is found in every instance.

51. *Enquêteurs*.

52. Esmein, *Procédure*, pp. 140–141.

judicial procedure. The court conferred at its own discretion the power to conduct an investigation. Sometimes one of the judges assumed the rôle of investigator. In the case between Georges Nodot and Guillaume and Jacques Rousseau the investigation was done by the chief judge of the *Connétablie*, "at the request of Guillaume and Jacques Rousseau." [53] At other times the judges delegated the conduct of the investigation either to the litigants themselves or to other judicial officials, or they would at times receive for consideration an investigation already completed elsewhere. The charges against the Sieur de Poitrincourt were investigated both by the chief judge of the *Connétablie* and by Etienne de Brye, examiner and commissioner at the Châtelet. In this case, an outside official began the probe and then sent it to the *Connétablie* for further consideration.[54] The court granted the petition of Nicolas Lespoir for additional time in which to complete his investigation against Jean de Montbrun and commanded the chief bailiff of the *Connétablie* to take with him a reliable assistant, conduct the investigation, and then send it "closed and sealed to the office of the clerk" of the *Connétablie*.[55] If Lespoir did not wish to deal with the chief bailiff of the *Connétablie* he was permitted to employ any other royal bailiff.

During the investigation the examining magistrate called before him a number of people alleged to have knowledge relative to the case. These witnesses delivered their testimony, read it over, and signed their names. In its investigations and trials the *Connétablie* employed the same methods as the ordinary criminal courts, whose subsequent procedure was usually, though not always, as follows:[56] The witnesses heard in the original investigation were summoned to court at the time of the trial. The process known as "*recollement et confrontation*" then took place. In the "*recollement*" the judge first administered the oath. The witness repeated his testimony. The transcript of the witness's testimony given during the original investigation was then read to him. He was then given an opportunity to state in what respects he adhered to his original statements and in what respects these should be corrected. The next step was the "*confrontation*" of the ac-

53. Z^{1c} 44, f. 68rv. See also Z^{1c} 44, f. 129r; Z^{1c} 46, f. 121 rv, 122r.
54. Z^{1c} 45, f. 1r. See also Z^{1c} 44, f. 84v, 110r, 136r, 163v, 164r; Z^{1c} 46, f. 8rv; Z^{1c} 47, f. 79v, 200r, 215v.
55. Z^{1c} 47, f. 243v, 244r. See also Z^{1c} 47, f. 244rv, 265r, 268v, 272v, 273r, 284r, 295v.
56. Esmein, *Procédure,* pp. 140–141.

cused and the witnesses. This gave to the defendant an opportunity to try to disprove the witnesses' statements and to produce any objections he might have concerning the character or reliability of the witnesses.[57] Etienne Guichard, archer of the *prévôt des maréchaux* at Meaux protested the withholding of his salary and demanded that the money be released to him. The *prévôt* was summoned to testify. The court asked him whether it was true that Guichard had asked to be excused to go and visit his sick father and whether he (the *prévôt*) had ordered Guichard to appear at the muster of the company. The *prévôt* delivered a verbal broadside against Guichard, saying that the archer had never asked permission to visit his sick father, that he had refused to attend the muster of the company, and that he had been lax in the performance of his duties as archer. The court then confronted Guichard with this testimony. The archer reiterated that he had asked permission of the *prévôt* to go and "attend to the sickness of his father, which he is ready to prove, should it please us to allow him." [58]

The usual procedure in the *Connétablie* was for the person bringing witnesses to send a list of their names to his opponent, who was allowed to make inquiries concerning their general character. Witnesses were not supposed to communicate with the litigants or discuss a case among themselves.[59] These precautions seem to represent an effort by the judicial authorities to ensure reliable testimony and to prevent collusion and perjury. Nicolas Lemaire was disputing the possession of a horse with Nicolas Lefebvre, who claimed that he had bought it from a certain Pierre Auvray. Lemaire contested the validity of the depositions of Lefebvre's witnesses, since they had "come without any summons and without summoning the plaintiff [Lemaire] to see them sworn in and without granting any time for him to inquire into their honesty." [60] When La Macque, the intermediary in the alleged sale of the horse, attempted to bring witnesses, Lemaire's attorney maintained that they too were ineligible, because they had "spoken of and discussed the aspects of the present case and furthermore because they were soldiers and companions of the said La Macque, in whose [*i.e.*, the witnesses'] deposition no faith

---

57. *Ibid.*, p. 145.
58. Z^{1c} 47, f. 210rv. See also Z^{1c} 44, f. 76v; Z^{1c} 45, f. 1v, 2r; Z^{1c} 47, f. 200v, 204v, 270r.
59. Z^{1c} 47, 204v.
60. Z^{1c} 44, f. 91v.

should be placed." [61] Lemaire evidently followed the proper procedure, for the court recorded that it had "seen . . . the act handed to Tallon [attorney of Lefebvre] . . . of the names and surnames of the said witnesses." [62]

Witnesses also played an important part in the investigation of the character and ability of an applicant for a position in the *maréchaussée*. In order to obtain a better idea of the candidate's qualities the court listened to the opinions of several people who knew him well. The procedure employed was as follows. The witness appeared before the presiding judge or the officer conducting the investigation. After taking an oath he delivered his testimony and signed it. The transcript was then handed to the *procureur du roi*, who delivered a written opinion. The judge then deliberated upon all the evidence, announced his decision, and, if his decision was favorable, administered the oath of office.

The preservation of the texts of petitions for admittance to office and the subsequent proceedings makes it possible to learn something about the character of the testimony of witnesses in such cases. Four witnesses testified on behalf of Gabriel Gaulterot, prospective *commissaire ordinaire des guerres*. All gave their names, ages, occupations, and addresses, took the oath, and then delivered their testimony. One thing which all emphasized was that Gaulterot was of noble blood, perhaps a prerequisite for the office. As one of them expressed it, Gaulterot was "of the rank necessary to fill the said office." He then elaborated both on the candidate's experience with the artillery and on his aptitude as *commissaire des guerres* and stated that the witness had seen him as such for the past six months "holding the musters of the regiments and companies of the Sieur de Montbarot, governor of . . . Rennes." The witness signed his deposition after it had been

---

61. Z^{1c} 44, f. 93v. See also Z^{1c} 44, f. 88r.

62. Z^{1c} 44, f. 92v. Marshal Charles de Gontaut de Biron judged in person the case of the Sieur de Tignonville against the Sieur de Badoux. Tignonville alleged that he had captured Badoux as a prisoner of war and that after the latter had promised to pay 1500 écus' ransom he had released his captive on his word of honor. Since then, despite all the plaintiff's efforts, Badoux had refused to pay the debt. After hearing as witnesses "several captains, sieurs, and gentlemen," the marshal condemned Badoux to pay Tignonville 800 écus, to which sum he lowered the ransom which the plaintiff had demanded. Z^{1c} 44, f. 206v, 207r. This case is of interest as one of the very few cases judged by a marshal of France in person. Although the marshals had always retained the right to render judgment personally in the *Connétablie*, they seldom exercised it. See also Z^{1c} 44, f. 11v, 14r, 17v, 22v, 81v, 82r, 87v, 88r, 93v, 110r, 111r, 130r, 207rv; Z^{1c} 45, f. 4v; Z^{1c} 47, f. 207r.

read to him and he had asserted that it was the truth. According to another the candidate had been among the advisers of the king and a member of his council. The third deposed that Gaulterot had been for some time employed in Brittany, both as *commissaire ordinaire des guerres* and as comptroller of the artillery and that he had performed his duties "very faithfully and to the satisfaction of His said Majesty." In addition to Gaulterot's religion and character, one of the others cited his ability in matters pertaining to war.[63] Analysis of the testimony by witnesses in such cases makes it evident that information on certain specific points was expected.[64] Every witness was expected to tell his name, age, occupation, and residence. A fairly intimate acquaintance with the applicant was required, for the witness always told the length of time during which he had known him. Information on the Catholicism of the candidate was expected, since each testified that he had seen the prospective office-holder in church or in the act of receiving the Catholic communion. Evidence as to his character and good repute was sought. If noble blood was a requirement for the office, as in the case of *commissaires des guerres*, the witness gave information on that subject. Finally, evidence of the applicant's loyalty to the king and of his ability and experience in the job was sought.

In order to assist the establishment of facts the judge administered an oath in various situations. Persons testifying in an investigation or trial were compelled to submit to it.[65] Suspects were always required, in an effort to arrive as nearly as possible at truthful testimony, to take the oath before beginning to answer the queries of the judges. Suspects already in prison were sometimes released, usually in order to confront the prosecution witnesses. As this was often done in provincial courts, the prisoner was allowed to proceed thither for the ceremony. Release might follow a decision that the evidence was insufficient to justify continued incarceration. If one of the numerous decrees of

---

63. Z^{1c} 282, Oct. 27, 1594. See also Z^{1c} 282, July 27, Sept. 17, 19, 20, 23, 29, Oct. 11, 12, 24, Nov. 4, 14, 18, Dec. 20, 1594.

64. Perusal of the cases cited will reveal this, as will study of the remaining cases in Z^{1c} 282.

65. Séverin and André Dumont "swore and affirmed before us that they had paid for the . . . ransom of the said defendant." Z^{1c} 44, f. 46v. See also Z^{1c} 44, f. 48r. Jean Viard, "after oath taken by him," asserted that Claude Pingray was of good character, loyalty, religion, and ability. Z^{1c} 282, Nov. 14, 1594. See also Z^{1c} 44, f. 74v, 82r, 87v, 88r, 110r, 120r; Z^{1c} 47, f. 210rv; Z^{1c} 282, July 27, Sept. 17, 19, 20, 23, Oct. 4, 24, 27, Nov. 4, 18, Dec. 20, 1594.

amnesty had annulled the crime for which imprisonment had originally been ordered, the prisoner was freed. Prior to his release he was always required to swear that he would appear at the place and time ordered by the court's decision.[66] Finally, the oath was required of new officials of the *maréchaussée* after their acceptance by the court.[67]

Although it is impossible to determine the text of the various types of oath which the *Connétablie* used in its procedure, it has proven feasible in some cases to reconstruct the framework and general content. With regard to witnesses, the register says only that before testimony was taken the witness took an oath to tell the truth. A bit more is revealed by the records of the oath taken by suspects. Apparently each was required to raise his hand and swear in some fashion to tell the truth.[68] Defendants released from jail were compelled to swear that they would appear at any time the court thought it necessary, but the exact form of the oath is not given. The oath taken by newly inducted officials was designed to give assurance to the *Connétablie* that the candidate fulfilled the basic requirements: the Catholic religion and loyalty to the king. The importance of the oath is that it represents one more effort by the court to arrive at a truthful, impartial, and definite establishment of fact.

If, after an investigation, the judges and the *procureur du roi* decided that the case merited further attention, they summoned the accused to appear in court for questioning on the charges

66. Nicolas Baguet was released temporarily, so that he might proceed to the court of the ordinary royal judge in the "region" of Alg. There he was to be confronted with the witnesses heard in the investigation against him. Baguet was released, after he had "promised and sworn to appear at any time it should be required." Z^{1c} 47, f. 204v. See also Z^{1c} 47, f. 225r, 234r, 244v, 270r.

67. Z^{1c} 46, f. 127r. See also Z^{1c} 44, f. 18v, 111r, 124r, 136r, 142v, 143r; Z^{1c} 46, f. 131r, 234rv; Z^{1c} 47, f. 21rv, 121v, 122r, 206v; Z^{1c} 282, July 23, Aug. 17, Sept. 17, 19, 27, 29, Oct. 10, 12, 24, 26, Nov. 14, 18, Dec. 20, 1594.

68. François Taverny, chief judge of the *Connétablie*, descended into the dungeons of the Conciergerie, caused a prisoner (a certain Sieur de Mosny) to be brought before him, and ordered him "to raise his hand" to take the oath. Mosny refused, saying that by virtue of a recent royal edict his alleged crime had been annulled and "begging us to excuse him on this occasion from raising his hand." Taverny insisted, but Mosny refused a second time and asserted that his case was to be transferred and was to be tried by the marshals of France in person. After some argument Taverny became impatient and "for the third time . . . ordered him to raise his hand without regard to the transfer that he says he has obtained, unless he can now show it." Mosny again refused, after which Taverny finally gave up the attempt and "sent the said Sieur de Mosny back to the said Conciergerie after he wished to say nothing more." Z^{1c} 45, f. 39rv. See also Z^{1c} 45, f. 272rv; Z^{1c} 46, f. 121rv, 122r; Z^{1c} 47, f. 20v, 84r, 288v.

PROCEDURE 81

formulated against him in the preliminary investigation. A document was thereupon issued to the plaintiff giving him permission to order his opponent to come to court. In accordance with the provisions of an ordinance of the fourteenth century, the warrant indicated in clear fashion the reasons for the summons. The duty of serving it upon the accused was among the functions of the royal bailiffs, attached either to the *Connétablie* or to other courts.[69]

The summons of personal appearance required the party to appear in court. The summons of arrest provided that the party be arrested by the authorities and brought to court.[70] François de La Verdure, accompanied by his attorney, appeared in person for questioning according to the terms of the personal summons "served on him at the request of the *procureur du roi*."[71] The summons of arrest was used only for serious offenses or after repeated failure to answer a personal summons. On occasion it was issued immediately after the court's decision to undertake further action in a case. Sometimes, as added inducement to the defendant to surrender himself, a simultaneous order was issued to seize the suspect's property and to make an inventory of it by commissioners chosen for this purpose. The order for arrest was always proclaimed publicly on three successive days. If the suspect was then still at large, the property was ordered seized. At the request of the *procureur du roi* and of Louis Vazet, after investigation of the murder of François de La Vergne, the tribunal decreed that Jonathan Petit should be arrested. If arrest proved impossible, the decree was to be proclaimed publicly on three successive days. Petit's property was then to be seized and inventoried by honest commissioners who were to render an account of their labors whenever the court should order it.[72] On other occasions the decree of arrest was issued as a penalty for attempts to delay the trial. Nicolas Noblet protested that he had complied with a summons to appear for questioning, but that Jacques Bataille, his opponent, had failed to do so. Instead, solely

69. Orgeval, *Connétablie*, pp. 218–219.
70. Compare this with the procedure in the ordinary courts and note the similarity. See Esmein, *Procédure*, pp. 141–142.
71. Z¹ᶜ 47, f. 17r. See also Z¹ᶜ 44, f. 22r, 80r, 89v, 109v, 170v; Z¹ᶜ 46, f. 149r, 150r, 210rv, 223r; Z¹ᶜ 47, f. 12v, 20v, 55rv, 60v, 61r, 62r, 66r, 79r, 80v, 84r, 216v, 217r, 225r, 244v, 246v, 247r, 265r, 267v, 283r.
72. Z¹ᶜ 47, f. 287r. See also Z¹ᶜ 47, f. 88v, 89r, 90rv, 195v, 196r, 199v, 200r, 204v, 215rv, 216r, 269v, 270r, 295r.

to postpone the final judgment as long as possible or to avoid it altogether, Bataille had filed an appeal against the order for appearance. Since there was as yet no question of a judgment, Noblet petitioned that Bataille should be compelled within a day to submit to questioning or else be taken as a prisoner to the Conciergerie.[73]

The entire procedure of summonses showed in reality great forbearance for the accused. Except in very serious cases, the decree of arrest was not issued until the defendant had shown himself most inattentive to summonses for personal appearance. Even after arrest was finally decreed, the authorities used great restraint, for often the accused was released simply on his own word that he would re-appear when the exigencies of procedure made it necessary.[74]

The commission put into effect the orders which the judges handed down. It authorized the accomplishment of any action and contained an exposition of the things to be done. The court granted to both Pierre Le Mareschal and Joachim Le Vasseur the right to gather information about each other, to be used in the final decision on their dispute, and ordered that "to do this they shall have a commission addressed to the *sénéchal* of Maine and [the] *bailli* of Perche, . . . *prévôts* and inspectors [*enquêteurs*] of the said regions and [to] every one of them called upon . . . for this."[75] The commission ranged over all fields of endeavor and was an important part of the precedure of the *Connétablie*. Such diversified topics as commands for arrest, the surrender of property, the conduct of investigations, the production in court of evidence, the transfer of cases, and non-interference with officials all were implemented by means of the commission. Furthermore, the commission was addressed either to a single person, to a group of people, or to officials or judges in any part of the kingdom.

The publication of a command by the *Connétablie* and the issuance of a commission were the first steps in its execution. The decrees were delivered by bailiffs, who brought with them documents which bore their own signatures and that of a court officer.

73. Z¹ᶜ 46, f. 8rv.
74. See above, pages 79–80.
75. The French word is *"commission."* Hereafter rendered as "commission." Z¹ᶜ 46, f. 221r. See also Z¹ᶜ 44, f. 6r, 8r; Z¹ᶜ 47, f. 24r, 51rv, 55r, 61r, 66r, 79rv, 82r, 121v, 122r, 206v, 207r, 216v, 217r, 218v, 243v, 244r, 269v, 295v, 297v; Z¹ᶜ 282, Oct. 24, 1594. See Appendix 4 for the text of a commission.

PROCEDURE

In this way they legalized their actions with regard to the person named in the decree. These documents were known by the generic term of *exploit*. *Exploits d'exécution*, or orders for the execution of the sentences of May 10 and May 22, 1590, were delivered to Jacques Bourdin. Later, an *exploit d'assignation*, or an order for personal appearance in court, was handed to him by a bailiff.[76] Just as an *exploit* was required for the execution of a court decree or commission, so was the promulgation of the decree necessary for the existence of the *exploit*. During his action against Eustache de Jouy, Pierre de Miraulmont submitted as part of the evidence "our order for personal appearance and the *exploit* issued by virtue of it." [77] Since the publication of an ordinance on the subject in the fourteenth century, the *exploit* had always stated in full the reasons for the accompanying court order.[78] In order to force Jacques Garègues to rebuild their church, which he had caused to be demolished, the dean and chapter of the collegiate church of Saint-Martin de Montpénard caused him to be summoned to court "for the above reasons, as they showed to us by the *exploit* of . . . La Coste, bailiff." [79]

The *exploit* served a two-fold purpose. Should the person against whom it was issued ignore its commands, he thereby automatically became liable to a decree of default. Furthermore, if the recipient remained at large in defiance of these orders, it furnished documentary proof that the command had been issued by the court and that the person concerned had actually seen and handled it. All excuses of ignorance of the existence of a court order were thereby removed.

When judicial orders were not heeded, the judges used the *défaut* and its counterpart, the *congé*. The mechanism, briefly, operated as follows. If a defendant refused or neglected to obey a court decree, the plaintiff demanded a *défaut*, by virtue of which a penalty would then be issued against the defendant. Conversely, if the plaintiff were negligent, the defendant received a *congé* and the accompanying benefit of a penalty against his opponent.[80] The demands and penalties did not fall into clearly

---

76. Z^{1c} 44, f. 3v.
77. Z^{1c} 44, f. 10r. See also Z^{1c} 44, f. 10v, 19r, 23v, 24r.
78. Orgeval, *Connétablie*, pp. 217–219.
79. Z^{1c} 47, f. 215v. See also Z^{1c} 44, f. 31r, 80r, 109v; Z^{1c} 45, f. 250r; Z^{1c} 46, f. 220v; Z^{1c} 47, f. 55r, 79rv, 89r, 105r, 199v, 200r, 219r, 269v, 295v, 296r.
80. Since the *défaut* and the *congé* were identical in operation, the term "default" will hereafter be used exclusively, except in discussion of a specific case.

defined categories but varied according to the nature and circumstances of the case. In an effort to speed up procedure the judges, when granting a default, often ordered the delinquent to appear in person at once, so that the trial might proceed with no further delay. A default was granted to Josias Martineau, who was requesting transfer of his trial to a different court. By virtue of the decree, his opponents were summoned for the next day, to give their reasons why the case should be retained in the *Connétablie*.[81] A penalty often provided either that a sentence already handed down should be carried out, or that facts alleged against the delinquent in an investigation should be considered as true and so used in the deliberations of the judges. In the ordinary courts this penalty was in common usage.[82] Jean Chitton, newly appointed *lieutenant* at Saumur of the *prévôt des maréchaux* of Anjou, complained that René Bodet and Jean Jarry, also *lieutenants* of the *prévôt des maréchaux* of Anjou, had protested against his reception into office, simply to annoy him. Since they had not obeyed the court order to appear and state their reasons for their opposition to him, Chitton requested that he be granted a default against them, that he be received at once into his new office, and that they be compelled to pay the costs of the litigation. The tribunal granted him a default, but ordered that the delinquents at once appear and state their reasons for opposition.[83] On the stated day Chitton appeared for the hearing, but Bodet and Jarry once again failed to obey the court's commands. The judges thereupon granted a second default to Chitton, by virtue of which he was at once received into office despite the opposition of Bodet and Jarry, who were ordered to pay the costs of the trial.[84]

Punishments also provided for the arrest of the delinquent, or in extreme cases for his execution. Charles de Sonningue was condemned to death by default.[85] Jean Barangues refused to obey the command of the court and appear personally for questioning on the charges lodged against him by the *procureur du roi*. The

Defaults were subdivided into *défaut faute de comparoir* (default for not appearing) and *défaut faute de défendre* (default for not defending). The difference, however, lay merely in the circumstance, the operation remaining the same.

81. Z^{1c} 44, f. 167r. See also Z^{1c} 44, f. 65v, 66r, 69v; Z^{1c} 46, f. 2v, 139rv; Z^{1c} 47, f. 185v, 197r, 257v, 258r, 281rv.

82. Esmein, *Procédure*, pp. 156–157.

83. Z^{1c} 46, f. 148v, 149r.

84. Z^{1c} 46, f. 150v, 151r. See also Z^{1c} 44, f. 7r, 21r, 29v, 30r, 72v, 82rv, 89v; Z^{1c} 47, f. 90r, 224rv, 246v, 247r.

85. Z^{1c} 47, f. 90rv.

judges then granted a default to the *procureur* and ordered the arrest of Barangues. Should it be impossible to arrest him he was to be summoned once more to court and his property was to be seized. In the meantime he was forbidden to continue in his office of *lieutenant* of the *vice-sénéchal* of Armagnac.[86] The practice of seizure of the property of the accused was common with the *Connétablie* and formed a regular part of its procedure. This also was borrowed from the criminal procedure of the ordinary courts.[87] The default sometimes deprived the delinquent of certain rights that he might otherwise have enjoyed during his trial. Herbert Serveuil and several co-defendants failed to obey a court command. The judges thereupon issued a default to the plaintiff, François Canivet. By its terms Serveuil and his friends were debarred from bringing any more witnesses in their favor.[88]

The default was a most effective instrument of compulsion. The relatively drastic penalties inflicted in some circumstances were due to the comparative difficulty of forcing parties to come to court. Noteworthy features in any discussion of the default are that really drastic penalties were inflicted in a minority of the total number of cases and that on many occasions the parties at whom the defaults were aimed obeyed under the mere threat of application of a penalty. Cases like that of Charles de Sonningue were decidedly in the minority. In an age such as the last years of the sixteenth century, when the country was in the midst of pacification after forty years of the wildest upheaval, it is somewhat surprising at first sight to find that severe application of the weapon of the default was relatively so little in use and to learn that litigants usually obeyed court orders. A fundamental respect for and reliance on due process of law by the bulk of the population seemed to be the rule rather than the exception.

A further effort to ensure the establishment of fact was the questioning during the trial of the defendants on the charges brought against them. The *Connétablie* again took the ordinary courts for its model.[89] The judges ordered Claude Guimont, appointed *lieutenant* of the *prévôt des maréchaux* of Orléans in place of Michel du Bois, who had resigned in his favor, to come to court for questioning concerning an irregularity in the trans-

---

86. Z¹ᶜ 47, f. 195v, 196r. See also Z¹ᶜ 47, f. 55rv, 199v, 200r, 216r.
87. Esmein, *Procédure,* pp. 157–158.
88. Z¹ᶜ 44, f. 130r. See also Z¹ᶜ 44, f. 22v, 109v, 110r; Z¹ᶜ 47, f. 266r.
89. Esmein, *Procédure,* pp. 142–143.

fer of title. The court reminded Guimont that du Bois' authorization to resign the office to him was dated June 28, 1597, and that his own appointment bore the date of January 26, 1597. Since the appointment was based on du Bois' authorization to resign the matter of the dates was "an impossible and incompatible thing." The judges therefore wished to know how and by whom the thing was done. Guimont replied that he knew only that the authorization and letters of appointment had been given to him by his widowed mother, who had received them from du Bois, "according to the promise which he had made to the said widow to furnish her with the said letters." The court then asked if he proposed using the documents for his own benefit in their present illegal form. Guimont answered that such was not his intention, but that he intended to summon du Bois to render the letters valid and live up to his promise. The court thereupon issued a summons to du Bois to appear for questioning.[90]

Before admitting applicants to office the judges sometimes questioned them on their duties. Claude Collas, appointed *prévôt des maréchaux* in the *bailliage* of Orléans by the Duke of Mayenne, applied to the *Connétablie* for confirmation. After he had been "questioned by us on some points concerning the exercise" of the duties of his post, the tribunal forthwith confirmed the appointment and ordered the registration of his letters of appointment at the clerk's office.[91] The court also questioned the plaintiffs as well as the defendants, in both civil and in criminal cases. Perrette de Fontenay appealed to the *Connétablie* from a decision handed down against her and in favor of Pierre du Castel. Before rendering the judgment, however, the tribunal considered "the questioning done by us ... both of the said appellant and of the defendant." [92]

If the judges felt that the evidence was insufficient to warrant a sentence, or if they desired further clarification on a point of law, they issued an interlocutory decree. Such a judgment was termed an *appointement* and represented the final effort to establish a complete and accurate picture of the facts in a case. The time limit, or *délai*, granted for the production of the additional evidence was extremely variable, ranging from a few hours up to

90. Z¹ᶜ 46, f. 121rv. See also Z¹ᶜ 44, f. 163v, 164r, 170v; Z¹ᶜ 45, f. 8v, 9r, 272rv; Z¹ᶜ 47, f. 20v, 58v, 66r, 77rv, 84rv, 85r, 105v, 204v, 225r, 244rv, 269v, 270r, 288v, 289v, 296r.
91. Z¹ᶜ 44, f. 129r. See also Z¹ᶜ 282, Sept. 17, 29, 1594.
92. Z¹ᶜ 44, f. 9v. See also Z¹ᶜ 44, f. 6r, 120r, 128r; Z¹ᶜ 47, f. 210rv.

several weeks. The length of the *délai* was entirely dependent upon the will of the judges or on the circumstances of the trial and did not depend upon observance of any fixed rule. *Appointements* were divided into two classes. The *appointement au conseil* and the *appointement à mettre* called for additional evidence and differed from each other only in the amount of time allowed. The *appointement en droit* demanded opinions and evidence concerning a disputed point of law. This distinction between fact and law was the sole determinant of the classification of *appointements*.[93] A definitive judgment might follow after one *appointement*, or might be indefinitely postponed. Here again the will of the judges was the basis for the decision.[94] In every case the responsibility for the production of further evidence rested upon the litigants.

During the trial the attorneys for both sides were given the opportunity to plead their clients' cases. The lawyer for the plaintiff first listed the arguments of his client, referring to the background of the complaint, and then presented his demands for

93. See Orgeval, *Connétablie*, pp. 232–236. He divides *appointements* into three principal categories. The *appointement au conseil* was an interlocutory decree, by virtue of which the tribunal, finding itself insufficiently informed on the matter of a case, ordered the litigants to bring within three days more information in writing on points which seemed obscure to the court. The *appointement à mettre* differed only in that the delay allowed was even shorter, sometimes a matter of only several hours. The preceding two types were concerned merely with facts, whereas the *appointement en droit* was concerned with the interpretation of law. In this case, the parties drew up documents listing fact by fact the points to be proved. A second *appointement* was then issued for the purpose of collating the two sets of facts and of hearing witnesses. A departure from this procedure was for the court to order the litigants at weekly intervals to exchange written contradictions of each other's lists of facts. Only after a considerable period did the case then come before the investigating judge. In practice, however, the *Connétablie* does not seem to have adhered to these time-schedules. For instance, Pierre Le Mareschal and Joachim Le Vasseur were given one month to assemble all their evidence. Z^{1c} 47, f. 102rv. Philippe du Resnel and Adrien Barat were given three days to produce new evidence. Three days later they were to answer each other's new allegations, and one week later were to conduct new investigations. Z^{1c} 44, f. 74v. This arrangement fits none of the foregoing categories. The time-limit of one week excludes the case of Jean Maurault and Gabriel de Montboucher from classification as an *appointement à mettre* or *au conseil*. Since the final judgment was handed down after but one postponement, it cannot be an *appointement en droit*. Z^{1c} 47, f. 218r. Many *appointements* issued by the *Connétablie* conform to Orgeval's description. But so many do not that it is obvious that the court followed no particular rule in the matter of *appointements*. The only sure method of classifying them is therefore that of subject matter.

94. See the following examples: Z^{1c} 44, f. 2v, 8v, 9v, 10r, 25v, 26r, 46rv, 82r, 128v; Z^{1c} 45, f. 125v, 126r; Z^{1c} 46, f. 220v, 221r; Z^{1c} 47, f. 59r, 207r. In all these cases the judge exercises the initiative in the matter of *appointements*.

reparation. After the witnesses had been heard and the evidence of both sides presented, the attorney for the defense stated his arguments and submitted his demands. Pleading in court was oral. Before pronouncing sentence the judges always reviewed the evidence on which the decision was to be based. This review always made a clear distinction between the written pieces produced and the oral pleading of the parties. Pleading was spoken of as "heard," to distinguish it from the rest of the evidence, which was always "seen." Furthermore, when the pleas themselves are reproduced in the record, the use of the word "said" and of other words and phrases indicating speech is universal.[95]

At the end of their pleas the parties always presented their demands for reparation. Both the plaintiff and the defendant presented these demands, which were known as *conclusions*. It is impossible to place *conclusions* into well-defined categories, since each depended upon the particular circumstances of the case. For instance, Michel Le Gallois charged that Thibaut de Vausselles, *lieutenant* of the *prévôt des maréchaux* of Picardy, had acted purely on his own authority and had released some prisoners whom Le Gallois had arrested and whom he was about to send to Paris for trial. The defendant had then stolen a quantity of Le Gallois's property. The latter in his *conclusions* demanded that Vausselles be condemned to return the prisoners to the prisons of the Petit Châtelet. He also demanded the return of all his war equipment and coined and uncoined silver which Vausselles had taken, and asked that Vausselles be compelled to make restitution on pain of imprisonment. He also demanded that the defendant pay the costs of the trial, make reparation for all the inconvenience he had caused Le Gallois to suffer, and pay all the expenses of the plaintiff's stay in Paris during the trial.[96] In addition to the *conclusions* submitted by the litigants there were those which the *procureur du roi* presented. At the end of each case the judges required the *procureur*, as the representative of the crown, to give his opinion on the facts and evidence brought out during the trial. After receiving the *conclusions* of the *procureur* the

---

95. The judges, "after having heard these parties," handed down their decision in favor of Jean Sasserye against François Berland and others. Z¹ᶜ 46, f. 141rv. See also Z¹ᶜ 44, f. 19r, 23r, 25v, 26v, 79r, 120r, 152v, 153r; Z¹ᶜ 45, f. 53r; Z¹ᶜ 47, f. 51r.

96. Z¹ᶜ 47, f. 78rv. See also Z¹ᶜ 44, f. 2rv, 7v, 9v, 15rv, 16r, 20r, 47v, 66r, 133rv, 134r; Z¹ᶜ 47, f. 74rv, 90r.

judges deliberated upon all the documents and handed down their decision.[97]

Conclusions had as basic common characteristics the name, the desire to obtain reparation in sufficient quantity for wrongs and injuries inflicted, and their place in the proceedings immediately following the pleas of the suitors. Demands for monetary damages and for the payment by the opposing party of the costs of the trial were always included.

At the conclusion of a trial the judges gathered together all the evidence which the litigants had submitted. They deliberated upon it and used it as the basis for their decision. One sort of proof which the parties offered was that which may be called oral. This included testimony by witnesses and by the litigants and was obtained through questioning conducted by the judges. A second type employed was written proof, wherein the parties submitted as evidence any documents which they felt would bolster their arguments with facts. Copies of ordinances, contracts, promissory notes, and other items in this manner took their places among the evidence upon which the judges deliberated. Written proof also included the *exploits*, commissions, defaults, and other documents issued by the court during the trial. Such things were often deemed useful both to the litigants and the judges, for they made it possible to determine easily what the court had done and ordered and whether the parties had complied.

The nature and circumstances of the individual case determined in each instance whether oral or written proof was the more important. Although there was no general rule on the use of evidence, both types of proof were invariably offered. Written proof played the major part in the conviction of Jean Dupuys and Jean Bardin, accused by some merchants of Pithiviers, Boiscommun, and Brouville of stealing sheep. The judges first reviewed and considered the investigations against Dupuys and the statements he had made. The record of the confrontation of witnesses and of the questioning of Bardin was also reviewed. The Sieur de Tignonville Dupuy's former commanding officer, had testified. He stated that in June, 1591, Dupuys had seized some sheep which were being driven "into a city in revolt against His Maj-

97. The *conclusions* of the *procureur du roi* are likewise borrowed from the procedure followed in the ordinary courts. See Esmein, *Procédure,* pp. 147–149. Also see Chapter V for further discussion of the *procureur du roi* and his *conclusions.*

esty." Tignonville said that at the time he had declared the seizure to be legitimate and justified. The plaintiffs first introduced as evidence some copies of certain royal ordinances. These declared that peasants should not be molested by troops unless they were caught within two leagues of cities in rebellion against the crown, or unless they were found on the roads carrying food supplies or other things to be employed against the king. The merchants also brought a copy of a safeguard issued by Marshal Aumont to the inhabitants of Boiscommun. This safeguard forbade all garrisons of the neighborhood to prevent the inhabitants from carrying on their agricultural and commercial activities. The evidence of the plaintiffs also included three copies of receipts from the *receveur extraordinaire des guerres*, which stated that the inhabitants of the three towns had paid 1,000 écus and seven *muids* of wheat as their share of the "levies ordered by His Majesty." The magistrates also reviewed all the additional evidence produced by the parties as a result of an *appointement* and heard the pleas and *conclusions* of Dupuys, Bardin, and the plaintiffs, and the *conclusions* of the *procureur du roi*. Then, having "diligently considered" the whole, they handed down a decision against Dupuys and Bardin.[98]

In this matter the court considered both oral and written proof. Dupuys relied exclusively on testimony and called Tignonville, who asserted that since the sheep were destined for a "rebel city"

---

98. Z^{1c} 45, f. 52v, 53rv. See also Z^{1c} 44, f. 170v; Z^{1c} 45, f. 1r. Charles Lauret had served for a few months as an archer of the *maréchaussée*, then complained to the *Connétablie* that his salary had been attached, and petitioned that it be released. He had succeeded Nicolas Dannerot in the post of archer. In this case the court based its decision almost entirely upon written proof. The judges first deliberated upon "the petition presented by Charles Lauret, by which he protested to us that by contract the late Nicolas Dannerot . . . had ceded to him his position of archer." The agreement provided that after Dannerot's death Lauret would use 20 écus to bury him and would give his widow 66 écus, 40 sols. Dannerot was in return to cede to Lauret the salary which was due to him for the last three months of the year 1597, together with his horse. Lauret brought receipts to show that he had fulfilled his part of the bargain. He then complained that although he had accomplished what he had promised, his commander had stopped payment on the portion of Dannerot's salary which was to be given to Lauret as part of the agreement. Lauret brought as proof of the commander's action a copy of a recent muster roll of the company. Lauret relied almost entirely upon written evidence and brought contracts, receipts, muster rolls, and letters patent as evidence. By means of these documents he convinced the tribunal that he had fulfilled all his obligations and that his commander had acted illegally in attaching his salary. Z^{1c} 46, f. 163rv. See also Z^{1c} 47, f. 218r, 223 bis v, 224r, 295rv, 296rv. See Appendix 5 for further examples of evidence available to the court at the time of pronouncement of decision.

the seizure was justified. The accused also depended on their own answers during the examination. The plaintiffs, however, except for the witnesses heard in the investigation, based their plan of attack entirely upon written proof. By producing the receipts for levies collected, they intended to show that the inhabitants of the town to which the sheep were being taken were loyal citizens and that they had contributed their share to the royal war chest. They then introduced the royal edict, to show that since the city was loyal to the king the seizure was illegal. They strengthened their case by producing the safeguard issued by Aumont. They hoped to recover the sheep and to convict Dupuys and Bardin through three means: proof of their loyalty, proof of faithful payment of the necessary war levies, and proof that a seizure under such circumstances was illegal. Although the fact of the seizure had evidently been established through the use of the oral method, the merchants relied principally upon written proof.

When deciding whether or not to admit a candidate to office, the magistrates were called upon to consider both oral and written evidence which he always submitted. The oral evidence included the opinions offered by witnesses regarding the applicant's character, religion, and aptitude. The written evidence represented the efforts of the candidate to prove that he had complied with all the requirements for admission to office. Invariably submitted were his written petition for induction, his letters of appointment, and the *conclusions* of the *procureur du roi*. For instance, the court considered the petition presented by Charles Lauret, in which he stated that he had been appointed archer in the company of Jacques Moraut, *lieutenant* of the *prévôt des maréchaux* of Meaux, succeeding Nicolas Dannerot in that post. The judges in addition saw the letters of appointment, the investigation of Lauret's life, habits, and religion, and the *conclusions* of the *procureur du roi*.[99]

Analysis of the court records shows the great variety of evidence which the parties in litigation marshalled and submitted for consideration to the judges. While the establishment of facts by the oral method was extremely important, their substantiation by written proof was most useful to procedure in the *Connétablie*. Whereas oral proof was employed usually on the initiative of the court, in the form of ordering investigations and questioning of principals and witnesses, the written method was used chiefly by

99. Z^{1c} 46, f. 131r. See also Z^{1c} 46, f. 6v, 7r.

the litigants, who were naturally anxious to obtain copies of letters, contracts, and other documents likely to strengthen their arguments. The constant reference to *exploits*, summonses, and other court orders served to determine what steps had been taken towards settlement of the cases. But these documents served especially to keep a record of obedience to judicial decrees, a factor which frequently had considerable influence on the outcome of a trial. Each type of proof thus had its place in the evidence, though the circumstances of the particular case alone dictated whether oral or written proof was to be the more important in the arrival at a decision.

The *Connétablie* used various methods to determine the true history of the cases brought before its judges. The investigation was an attempt to establish at least a presumption of guilt by the means of the testimony of people other than the principals. The use of witnesses in trials was characteristic of efforts to arrive fairly at the establishment of subsidiary fact and of guilt or innocence. The oath attempted to bind the persons under questioning to the relation of nothing but the truth. The summons to court implemented the desire of the tribunal to question directly the defendant as a means of striving from a different angle for the establishment of fact. The questioning of plaintiffs was another attack on the problem of establishing just what had happened. Finally, by the use of the *appointement* the judges called for more facts to complete the picture or to supply material for an interpretation of law.

The defendant had every opportunity to be heard. He could testify. He could select witnesses to speak in his favor. He could force his accuser to take the stand and be questioned in his turn. Finally, the defendant had the right to be confronted with the witnesses who had spoken against him during the investigation and to attempt to force them to retract their stories. In the case of applications for induction into office, the *Connétablie* endeavored to determine the competence of the candidate by hearing witnesses and by questioning the man himself on his prospective duties. In almost every phase of this procedure the *Connétablie* took the ordinary courts for its models.

The final phases of the trial were the rendering of the sentence, the assessment of the costs of the trial, and the collection of the fees due to the judges. The judges deliberated on the evidence, announced their decision in court to the parties or their attorneys and then imposed sentence. The costs of a trial were considerable, since they included all expenses incurred by both parties, a formidable array. They included the expenses of delivery by bailiffs of all *exploits* used during the trial, the services of the attorneys, the fees due to the clerk of the court, the fees due to the judges, the tax levied on the trial, and even the wine consumed by the messengers.[100] It was therefore natural for each party to attempt to rid himself of the burden. After a case had been decided, the attorney of the victor listed all the expenses of his client and submitted it to the judges. The loser then submitted his opinions on the list and his suggestions for reductions. The final step was the concordance of the two expense lists by the judges, who possessed the power of final decision.[101]

Under some circumstances the court required one or both of the litigants to furnish bond.[102] This obligation had long been an established practice in criminal trials in the ordinary courts, and was used by the *Connétablie* for its civil, criminal, administrative, and disciplinary cases.[103] The purpose of the bond was to guarantee good behavior or to ensure obedience to court decrees. Pierre Massicot, archer of the *prévôt des maréchaux* of Étampes, Dourdan, and La Ferté-Alain, protested the stoppage of his salary and brought witnesses to certify that royal business had compelled his absence from the last muster. The court released his salary to him and ordered him to furnish "good and sufficient bond before the judge of Étampes." [104]

Officeholders who had been received into office after a dispute with a rival claimant were frequently required to furnish bond. Should some contingency thereafter alter the circumstances of the case the incumbent would still be responsible to the court. In the case of Denis Mahon, who had been installed as an officer of the *maréchaussée* over the vigorous protests of his displaced rival, it was decreed that "the said Mahon will pass onto the muster rolls of the said *prévôt*" and that he should receive the salary attached to the position. But because of the circumstances of the case the

---

100. Orgeval, *Connétablie*, p. 279.
101. *Ibid.*, pp. 279–283.
102. The French term is *caution* and hereafter will be rendered as "bond."
103. Esmein, *Procédure*, pp. 119–120.
104. Z^{1c} 45, f. 5r. See also Z^{1c} 44, f. 2r, 7v, 18rv, 24v, 25r; Z^{1c} 46, f. 169rv; Z^{1c} 47, f. 224r.

tribunal compelled Mahon to furnish "good and sufficient bond." [105] Mathieu Chastenier, a lawyer in the *parlement* of Paris, became Mahon's guarantor and was in his turn certified as solvent by a colleague, Jean Prévost.[106]

The judges often required bond as a guarantee of the payment of costs or damages. Pierre Ollivier was condemned to pay 50 écus to Séverin and André Dumont, and as guarantee of payment was given the choice of remaining in the custody of a bailiff or of furnishing bond. Jean Dumont furnished bond as guarantor that the debt would be paid and saved him from jail.[107] Ollivier's troubles were not yet over, however, for very soon the bailiff under whose guard he had previously been held brought suit against him for failing to pay his fee. Consequently, although Ollivier was already at liberty under bond, the tribunal ordered that he should be returned to the custody of the bailiff, unless he could post a second bond.[108] When the judges pronounced the final sentence they increased Ollivier's obligation to the Dumonts to the sum of 260 écus, ordered that he should pay one-third in cash and the remainder in monthly instalments, and as guarantee of payment commanded him to furnish "good and sufficient bond." [109] In order to guarantee that a suspect provisionally released from custody should appear in court when required, the *Connétablie* sometimes decreed that the prisoner should furnish bond. François Baudry, for example, was at his request released after posting bond to appear at any time "that it shall prove necessary." [110]

The procedure for furnishing bond was, in its main features, the same as that employed by the ordinary courts.[111] Hubert Charpentier presented to the court "as bond for the contents of the said sentence" Pierre Rétif, a Paris wine merchant and hotel-keeper. Rétif constituted himself "pledge and guarantor for the said Charpentier" for the sum of 50 écus, which the court had condemned Charpentier to pay to Marin Lefebvre. Rétif then declared that he owned two houses, courts, gardens with about five and one-half *arpents* of vines, and 3 *arpents* of arable land,

105. Z¹ᶜ 44, f. 69r.
106. Z¹ᶜ 44, f. 70r. See also Z¹ᶜ 44, f. 116v.
107. Z¹ᶜ 44, f. 29rv.
108. Z¹ᶜ 44, f. 46v.
109. Z¹ᶜ 44, f. 49rv.
110. Z¹ᶜ 47, f. 244v.
111. Esmein, *Procédure*, pp. 119–120.

all located at Vaux-sur-Seine. He also had a small annual income derived from other sources. Joachim Texier, a bailiff in the *chambre des comptes* in Paris, certified that Rétif was "sufficient and solvent" and hence a good risk. Texier declared that he himself owned a house, court, garden, and stables located in the village of Rueil-en-Parisis, together with 25 livres of annual income. Rétif and Texier both swore that if necessary they would pay the 50 écus. Charpentier then promised to reimburse both Rétif and Texier for "all penalty, loss, expense, damage, which they might have on account of the said pledge, bond, and certification." [112] The court then ratified the bond.

The principal characteristic of bonds is that the warrantor guaranteed that his charge would comply with the terms of the court's decision. If the sentence was not carried out, the warrantor was then open to punishment. If the litigant were condemned to the payment of costs or damages and failed to comply, the guarantor was compelled to pay them and then to collect from his charge as best he could. The function of the certifier was to swear to the solvency of the guarantor and thus to provide a second line of defense. If there were more than one warrantor all then became collectively and individually responsible for the execution of the terms of the judgment. If one or more defaulted, the others were therefore still held responsible. The bonded individual, for his part, assumed the obligation personally to make good any loss or inconvenience suffered by his guarantor.

Fines were often imposed as penalties in criminal cases. The majority of the fines which the *Connétablie* imposed were for administrative offenses, in which the culprit had violated the ordinances governing the administration of the *maréchaussée*. Ordinary criminal cases between civilians, or between a civilian and the *procureur du roi*, are relatively rare. This fact emphasizes again both the diminishing importance of the criminal jurisdiction of the *Connétablie* and the simultaneous increase in the importance of its administrative jurisdiction.[113]

The origin of *épices* in judicial affairs lies in the Middle

---

112. Z^{1c} 44, f. 24v, 25r. See also Z^{1c} 44, f. 3r, 21v, 74v, 116v; Z^{1c} 46, f. 173r.

113. Charles de Sonningue was convicted by default of murder and sentenced to be beheaded in the main square of Angers. He was also fined 500 écus. Z^{1c} 47, f. 90v. Eustache de Jouy was convicted of embezzling funds of the *maréchaussée*. He was fined 20 écus. Z^{1c} 44, f. 18r. The *prévôt des maréchaux* of the Ile de France was fined 20 écus for having punished his archers by illegal methods. Z^{1c} 47, f. 77rv. See also Z^{1c} 44, f. 196r.

Ages.[114] At that time parties who had just won a case gave spices to the judges, in order to show their gratitude. Although the law ordered magistrates to dispense justice without charge to the litigants, they deemed it legal to accept these gifts. Philip IV tried to restrain them and forbade them to accept any more spices than they could consume in one day in their homes. Money soon replaced spices. Judges finally came to regard these gifts as their due, and in 1402 an edict obliged them and made compulsory the presentation of fees.[115] Like the other courts of the realm, the *Connétablie* also had its fees, which the litigants paid to the judges at any session during the trial or at the final hearing. A survey of a number of typical cases in which fees are recorded shows that in trials of some importance at the end of the sixteenth century the fee usually averaged about 6 écus.[116] The receipt of fees served to offset the price which the judges paid for the purchase of their offices, to augment their insufficient salaries, and to help meet the various expenses of operating the court.[117] Because of abuses, the payment of fees soon became highly unpopular. This unpopularity is reflected in a popular verse written after the great fire of 1618 which gutted the *Palais de Justice* in Paris:[118]

> "Certes ce fut un triste jeu
> Quand à Paris dame Justice
> Pour avoir mangé trop d'épice
> Se mit tout le palais en feu."

The *Connétablie* began its existence as a military court, whose chief function was to administer military discipline and justice and to settle the civil and criminal cases of the soldiery. In the early days the military commanders dispensed this justice in person, but by the end of the fourteenth century began to delegate this power. A court with such responsibilities and administered by military commanders or their henchmen was at the outset a body whose procedure was informal and summary. Speed was the chief

---

114. *Épices:* literally, "spices;" hereafter rendered as "fees."
115. Chéruel, *Dictionnaire*, I, 359.
116. See Appendix 6 for a table of these representative trials.
117. See Orgeval, *Connétablie,* pp. 97–104, for a discussion of the finances of the court and its officers. *Ibid.*, pp. 104–118, outlines the financial privileges and other rights enjoyed by the magistrates.
118. *Ibid.,* p. 26, note 2.

interest. Furthermore, the early judges and administrators were men who knew little or no law and who had little idea of the technicalities of procedure. The effects of the events and constitutional developments of the sixteenth century on the jurisdiction of the *Connétablie* have already been noted. An analysis of the court records has shown also that these developments had a profound effect on the court's procedure. Professional lawyers and court personnel, who had received their training and impressions in the ordinary courts, replaced the military commanders and their early deputies. These men brought with them and introduced wholesale into the *Connétablie* the complete and complex procedure of the ordinary courts. In procedure as well as in jurisdiction the *Connétablie* completed a profound change in the years between 1500 and 1600. All vestiges of the original, military court with its summary methods of procedure had disappeared by the end of the Wars of Religion.

V

THE OFFICES OF THE COURT

THE sixteenth century witnessed a fundamental change in the character and composition of the *Connétablie*. This transformation began when the *connétable* and the *maréchaux* ceased to render judgment in person and left that duty to a delegate. The great constitutional developments of the latter part of the fifteenth century and the entire sixteenth century speeded and greatly influenced this change. These constitutional developments were characterized by a great increase in the influence and strength of the ordinary law courts and by the consequent increase in the numbers and prestige of lawyers and judges trained in their methods and law. When the *connétable* and the *maréchaux* ceased performing their judicial duties in person these professional lawyers and clerks began to be appointed to positions in the *Connétablie* and by 1600 held them all. The modification in the jurisdiction of the tribunal assisted this trend. The court began to change before 1500 from a military court to a primarily administrative tribunal. This administrative jurisdiction and the remaining civil, criminal, and disciplinary duties of the *Connétablie* were much more closely related in character to the work of the ordinary courts than was its original, almost purely military, work. The introduction of the procedure of the ordinary courts and especially of personnel trained in their methods was therefore facilitated. The three elements in the change—the new jurisdiction of the *Connétablie*, the new procedure, and the new personnel—were interdependent and cannot be considered separately. Finally, it must be emphasized that the transformation in personnel, as in jurisdiction and procedure, was the result of a gradual and natural historical evolution, was not brought about by any single royal edict, and was completed before the end of the Wars of Religion.

During the reign of Henry IV the judges were the most important members of the *Connétablie's* staff. They investigated cases, heard trials, received *maréchaussée* officials and some army administrative officers into office, supervised the *maréchaussée*, and pronounced decisions. The *procureur du roi* represented the interests of the king. His duties were to intervene in trials which he felt concerned those interests, to maintain a watch over the operation of the *maréchaussée*, to take part in the investigations of candidates for offices in the *maréchaussée*, and to deliver an opinion on every trial. The clerk and his assistant handled the administrative and financial records and details. The bailiffs maintained order in the courtroom. Their most important task was, however, to enforce the decisions of the magistrates by serving on the litigants the documents issued by the clerk following those decisions.

The personnel of the *Connétablie* was not spared the effects of the Wars of Religion. One of the first acts of Henry IV after his entry into Paris in 1594 was the reinstatement of the court, which had been under royal ban since 1588. Following the "Day of Barricades" in the latter year and his flight from Paris Henry III forbade the *Connétablie* to continue to function in the capital. This order, like so many issued by the last Valois, fell upon deaf ears. Upon his accession to the throne in 1589 Henry IV therefore declared null and void all actions of the recalcitrant court since 1588. The marshals of France loyal to the king then organized a *Connétablie* in the provisional royal capital of Tours. This court was the rival of the body which remained in Paris under the domination of the Catholic League.

After the entry of Henry IV into Paris on March 22, 1594, royal pardons were distributed in profusion. This procedure was in accordance with Henry's policy of making the welfare of the state and the authority of the crown supreme over other considerations. In letters patent issued on March 28, 1594, the king pardoned the Paris *Connétablie*.[1] By his "special grace, full power, and royal authority" he reinstated the officers in their positions. He did this because he considered it necessary for "the good of our service and of the public." A few days later the letters were registered by the *Connétablie*. At the same time the officers of the tribunal swore an oath of loyalty to the crown and repudiated all associations and leagues to which they might have

1. Z^{1c} 92, f. 6rv, 7r. The *maréchaussée* officers who supported the Catholic League refused to deal with the group at Tours. When the triumph of Henry IV appeared imminent, however, many of them rushed to have their appointments confirmed by the Paris body, in the apparent hope of benefiting by a royal pardon. See Chapter IV above for examples. Also see Orgeval, *Connétablie,* pp. 121–123.

been parties, "on occasion of the evils of the times." [2] There is no specific royal declaration regarding the decrees of the Paris *Connétablie* from 1588 to 1594. The legalizing of these actions is, however, implicit in the royal pardon of 1594. That document recalls that Henry III forbade the officers of the *Connétablie* to continue in office and that upon his accession to the throne Henry IV issued a declaration annulling all actions which the court might perform. Henry IV eventually deemed it necessary to forgive the court for its defiance of authority and issued the pardon, which raised the ban imposed both "by the late king and by us." Consequently, the pardon not only reinstated the officers, but also confirmed all their actions during the six-year period of legal suppression.

The edict of forgiveness and the oath of renewed loyalty are excellent examples of the moderate policy pursued by Henry IV after he had overcome the major forces of dissension. It will be recalled that his policy was characterized by what appeared to some extreme leniency. Many who had openly and vigorously opposed the king were freely pardoned. Many others had their debts paid and received in addition gifts of money and lucrative crown posts. Such a policy was bitterly resented by many, particularly (in the appropriate cases) by Catholic and Huguenot extremists and by some of those who had stood by Henry in the days when his fortunes were at their lowest. The king realized, however, that should he adopt a vigorous policy of extermination of all who had opposed him the civil wars might well last for many years longer and might permanently destroy the authority of the crown, the governmental machinery, and the material welfare of the country. He therefore thought that a policy of leniency in return for peace and submission to the crown was preferable to further years of strife. The progress made during the balance of his reign amply demonstrates the soundness of his ideal of unity and the welfare of the state at almost any price. In the case of the *Connétablie*, as in all such cases, both parties affected to ignore the realities of the situation. The pardon states that Paris was occupied by Spanish troops and that some of the inhabitants were obliged to remain there. No mention is made of the dissident elements within the city, but only of those who were supposedly unable to leave because of family or business reasons. In this pardon Henry threw

2. Z^{1c} 92, f. 7v. The above oath and royal edict of pardon immediately preceding it are reproduced in part in Orgeval, *op. cit.*, p. 123.

the major blame for the troubles of France on the Spaniards and other foreigners and lastly on a turbulent minority of Frenchmen. When the officers of the *Connétablie* took their new oath of loyalty they stated that they had been compelled to remain in Paris in defiance of royal orders to leave! They then repudiated any past or future connection with those who had taken up arms against the king. The unfortunate tribunal and its officers had evidently been the playthings of the Spaniards and of fate and had defied their sovereign only under duress! The method of forgiveness was, however, made perfectly clear. The king stated, and the officers agreed, that they owed their reinstatement solely to his special grace and mercy and royal authority. The motive behind the decision of the king was not mentioned, beyond the general reference to the "good of our service and of the public." The king was aware that, although he had virtually accomplished the military defeat of his enemies, the moral and spiritual conquest of his realm was as yet unfinished. These facts were, however, ignored in the document. Both sides thus attained their goals. The king obtained acknowledgment of his sovereign powers, including suspension and reinstatement of the court. The *Connétablie* obtained reinstatement and complete forgiveness for past conduct. The incident is typical of the policy of Henry IV and shows the wisdom of his refusal to act in an unduly vindictive fashion towards his late enemies. By the use of moderation he virtually obtained his two principal aims: the acknowledgment of his authority and the establishment of unity within the kingdom. Such was his interpretation of "the good of our service and of the public."

The lieutenant general was the responsible head of the personnel of the *Connétablie* and was assisted by a *lieutenant particulier*. Their powers were wide and varied and included the right to hear trials, investigate charges, perform various administrative duties, and mete out sentences. Since the lieutenant general was the chief judge of the *Connétablie* and since he was as such the delegate of the military commanders he was also the active administrative head of the *maréchaussée*. The judges purchased their offices and after an examination of their ability and investigation of their character received letters patent of appointment from the king. The lieutenant general was allowed to hold other offices besides his place as chief judge of the *Connétablie*.

After the king had chosen a lieutenant general he issued letters patent addressed to the *parlement* of Paris. On March 23, 1596, that court received letters patent stating that the king had chosen Guillaume Joly, a lawyer connected with the *parlement*, as lieutenant general of the *Connétablie*, to succeed François Taverny, who had resigned in his favor. Following the notification of appointment, and always contained within the same letters patent, was a royal order to the *parlement* requesting that it install the appointee into office at once. On May 3, 1596, Joly professed the Catholic faith, gave the required pledge of loyalty to the king, and was formally installed by the *parlement*.[3] The only other official of the *Connétablie* to be inducted by the *parlement* was the *lieutenant particulier*, whose appointment and induction followed the identical pattern.[4]

Since the *parlement* of Paris was, after the king, at the head of the judicial hierarchy in about half of France, the judges of the lower courts within its territory were installed theoretically subject to its approval. In this connection the incidents attendant upon the appointment of Joly are of considerable interest. According to the rules prior to 1604 for the succession to judicial offices, an office vacated by resignation or death fell to the king, who could then dispose of it as he wished.[5] During the sixteenth century, at the time when to the principle of venality was being added that of hereditary transmission of judicial offices, the socalled rule of forty days was established. By this, if an officeholder died within forty days of his transmission of the office to another person, the resignation was annulled and the office returned to the king.[6] The *parlement* established the practice that at the time of induction into office the candidate should swear that neither directly nor indirectly had he purchased his office. By this

3. Z^{1c} 93, f. 49v, 50rv. See Appendix 7. Orgeval, *Connétablie*, p. 304, states that Taverny was lieutenant general of the *Connétablie* from January 23, 1595, to March 23, 1596, when he was succeeded by Guillaume Joly. This is an error, for the court records of 1591 speak on numerous occasions of Taverny as the lieutenant general. See Z^{1c} 44, f. 3r, 10r, 13r, 18v, 20v, 22v, 23rv, 63r, 68r, and others. As the records prior to 1591 are not at present available, the exact date of Taverny's appointment cannot be determined. The lieutenant general and the *lieutenant particulier* were respectively the chief and assistant judge of the *Connétablie*. Hereafter cited as lieutenant general and *lieutenant particulier*.

4. The royal letters patent of appointment of March 18, 1609, and the documents of July 27 and July 30, 1609, deal with the induction by the *parlement* of Paris of Claude Chrestien as *lieutenant particulier* of the *Connétablie*. See Appendix 8.

5. Esmein, *Cours*, p. 396. Since the king was the fountainhead of justice, all offices were at his disposal.

6. *Ibid.*, p. 396; Chéruel, *Dictionnaire*, II, 959.

means, therefore, the rule of forty days was in theory circumvented. This rule applied also to all other members of the *maréchaussée*, who took a similar oath for the identical purpose. When Joly appeared for his installation, he refused to fall in with the customary practice. The resultant conflict between Joly and the *parlement* reached the attention of the king. At an assembly of notables held in Rouen Henry IV upheld Joly, overruling the *parlement* and abolishing the oath. Joly thereupon took office.[7]

The king could force the acceptance of a candidate fundamentally opposed by the *parlement*. Although the king had delegated the exercise of his judicial powers to what became the *parlement* of Paris and to the other ordinary courts, he could at any time constitutionally intervene and act personally in judicial affairs.[8] Furthermore, although in the sixteenth century the practice of venality and hereditary transmission of judicial offices was the general rule, the operation of both of these could at any time be terminated by royal decree. No candidate could legally take office without royal approval manifested by letters patent.[9] Consequently, there is no doubt that the king had the legal weapons at his disposal to prevail over any resistance on the part of the *parlement*. Joly's refusal to take the oath concerning the purchase of his office is a case in point. A candidate who had refused to conform to the practices established by the *parlement* was sustained in his position by the king and accepted as lieutenant general by the *parlement*.

The lieutenant general was allowed to hold more than one office, but it is uncertain whether the *lieutenant particulier* also enjoyed that right. In 1607 Guillaume Joly was appointed commissioner for the musters of all the *prévôts des maréchaux* in the Ile de France. The king permitted Joly to occupy his new post "concurrently with his [office] of lieutenant general . . . or separately."[10] By 1592, if not before, the lieutenant general bore the title "Councillor of the King." In the early part of 1592 "François Taverny, councillor of the king and lieutenant general" of the *Connétablie*, presided over a trial.[11] Taverny's successor also possessed the title. Accompanied by some of the members of his

---

7. Orgeval, *Connétablie*, p. 79.
8. See Esmein, *Cours*, pp. 421–429, for examples of direct royal action.
9. *Ibid.*, p. 398.
10. Z^{1c} 97, f. 106v, 107r.
11. Z^{1c} 44, f. 68r. See also Z^{1c} 282, July 27, Sept. 17, Nov. 4, 1594; Z^{1c} 45, f. 9v, 10r.

official family, Guillaume Joly, "councillor of the king and lieutenant general at the court of the *Connétablie*," went to Argenteuil and partook of a banquet which a number of the municipal officers and inhabitants had prepared for them.[12] While it is impossible to make a general statement on the subject, it is certain that at least during part of his carer Guillaume Bessaut, *lieutenant particulier* from 1584 to 1606, was a councillor of the king.[13] The register records a session on October 19, 1596, presided over by "Guillaume Bessaut, councillor of the king and *lieutenant particulier*." [14]

The two lieutenants formed the normal complement of judges in the *Connétablie* and in the majority of cases themselves conducted the trials and handed down decisions. At times, however, they used to obtain the assistance of judges or lawyers from other courts or officials from administrative bureaus for certain trials. These temporary assistants were known as *juges bénévoles*. The *Connétablie* often called in as supplementary judges one or more experts in a particular field, who would give the court the benefit of their specialized knowledge.[15] The *juges bénévoles* would occasionally replace the judges on the bench and possessed the right to render judgment in the absence of both regular magistrates. For instance, Claude Collas appeared "before us, Jean du Marche, lawyer in [the] *parlement* [of Paris], occupying the bench of the *Connétablie* . . . during the absence of . . . [the] lieutenant general in the said court." [16]

As the chief responsible officials of the *Connétablie* the two magistrates acted either in the capacity of trial judges, in that of investigating officials, or in that of chief administrative officials of the *maréchaussée*. One or both could render decisions, with or without the help of *juges bénévoles*. They had at their disposal sufficient general powers to enable them to prescribe action in a given case and to reach a decision and possessed many particular powers to implement their general prerogatives. The judges could make what was termed an award "by provision." [17] Such a settle-

12. Z^{1c} 45, f. 247v, 248r.
13. Orgeval, *Connétablie*, p. 304.
14. Z^{1c} 45, f. 283rv. Claude Chrestien in 1609 was appointed by Henry IV "our councillor, and *lieutenant particulier*" of the *Connétablie*. See Z^{1c} 97, f. 188v.
15. Guichard, *Prévôts*, pp. 144–145; Orgeval, *Connétablie*, pp. 75, 77.
16. Z^{1c} 44, f. 129r. See also Z^{1c} 44, f. 125v, 126r, 127r, 132r, 135v; Z^{1c} 46, f. 2v, 3v, 7r.
17. The following discussion of the offices of the *Connétablie* will differ in character from that of Orgeval. See the section dealing with secondary works in the **Bibliographical Note**.

ment was, as the name implies, a temporary arrangement and remained valid only until a final decision was reached. In a financial case, for instance, the provisional award was sometimes made if one of the parties was in financial difficulties. The party who benefited in this manner from the award "by provision" was usually required to furnish bond for the amount. It was also imposed as an indirect disciplinary measure. And when a position in the *maréchaussée* became vacant, the judges had the right to choose "by provision" someone to fill it until a permanent royal appointment should have been made. At the end of one of the sessions of the trial between Philippe du Resnel and Adrien Barat the court condemned Barat to pay to his opponent six and one half écus "by provision" and ordered Resnel to furnish bond to the court for the sum awarded in this manner to him.[18] Marc-Antoine Froment, *lieutenant criminel de robe courte* at Amboise, complained that since he had no clerk the business of justice was being retarded and asked for permission to fill the position. The judge, "for the good of justice, by provision," permitted him to select an experienced clerk, pending a permanent appointment.[19] The judges also decided who was to pay costs and fines and had the right to determine the amount.[20] They sentenced Pierre Ollivier to pay the costs of his trial and reserved for themselves the right to determine the amount.[21] They fined Jean Dupuys, convicted of sheep-stealing, 6 écus, to be paid to the king, 6 écus more to be given to the Penitent Daughters of Paris and the nuns of Sainte-Claire of Decize, and sentenced his accomplice, Jean Bardin, to "2 écus fine to the king." [22]

The magistrates possessed the right to exact guarantees for the execution of the sentences which they handed down. Their prerogatives also included the power to stipulate that a judgment should be carried out "notwithstanding the appeal." If the loser filed his appeal at once, the clause was thereupon inscribed in the sentence; if, on the other hand, he waited until later, the winner could petition at that time for the addition of the clause. The court's decision remained in force until such time as the appeal

---

18. Z^{1c} 44, f. 74v. See also Z^{1c} 44, f. 110v.
19. Z^{1c} 44, f. 142v.
20. See Orgeval, *Connétablie,* pp. 392–400, 415–419, 419–423, 426–428. In those pages are reproduced in full the accounts of the costs of four trials. Therein the action of the judges in modifying the amounts presented as costs by the litigants may be seen in operation.
21. Z^{1c} 44, f. 49v. See also Z^{1c} 44, f. 85r.
22. Z^{1c} 45, f. 53r. See also Z^{1c} 44, f. 6v, 18rv, 196r; Z^{1c} 47, f. 77v. The *Filles Pénitentes* were an order of nuns. See Chéruel, *Dictionnaire,* I, 427.

was accepted by the *parlement* of Paris. When the appeal was accepted by the *parlement* the operation of the original sentence was suspended until it handed down the final decision. The power to stipulate that a decision was to be respected "notwithstanding the appeal" was a partial guarantee that appeals would not unduly delay the machinery of justice. When he learned that the *Connétablie* had fined him 20 écus for misconduct in office and had ordered him to produce at once the money for the salaries of his archers Eustache de Jouy "declared that he appealed from the present sentence." The court felt, however, that Jouy's appeal was not warranted by the facts, decided in favor of the archers, and decreed that the sentence should stand "notwithstanding the appeal." [23]

One of the chief duties of the judges, as the administrative heads of the *maréchaussée*, was to hold the musters of the companies stationed in the Ile de France and adjacent territories. The *prévôt des maréchaux* of Etampes, south of Paris, held the muster of his men in the presence of the magistrates of the *Connétablie*.[24] Originally the lieutenants of the *connétable* and the *maréchaux* had been accustomed to hold the musters of all the armed forces and of all the *prévôts des maréchaux* as well. After the feudal levies had been replaced by a standing army stationed in different localities and after the *prévôts des maréchaux* had likewise become permanently located throughout the kingdom, the lieutenants were manifestly unable to perform this duty as before. Furthermore, after the *Connétablie* was located in Paris the magistrates were restricted to that area. The power to hold the musters of the *maréchaussée* of the Ile de France and neighboring regions therefore represents the remnant of the original wide powers of muster at one time exercised by the delegated representatives of the *connétable* and the *maréchaux*. And it was a power which was not used regularly and systematically. The judges of the *Connétablie* clung to the right, although they held these musters in person only occasionally.

Since the members of the *maréchaussée* were legally the delegates of the marshals of France in the provinces and since the lieutenant general and *lieutenant particulier* were the personal representatives of the *connétable* and *maréchaux*, to the chiefs of the *Connétablie* fell the duty of general supervision over the per-

---

23. Z^{1c} 44, f. 18rv. See also Z^{1c} 44, f. 29r, 80r, 89v.
24. Z^{1c} 45, f. 4v. See also Z^{1c} 44, f. 123r, 149v; Z^{1c} 45, f. 1v, 2r; Z^{1c} 97, f. 106v.

sonnel of the court itself and of the entire *maréchaussée*. When candidates for positions in the *maréchaussée* appeared before the *Connétablie* for induction into office, the lieutenant general or the *lieutenant particulier* formally received them as new members of the hierarchy. Aimé Dumont presented a petition stating that he had been appointed by the *lieutenant* at Meaux of the *prévôt des maréchaux* of Champagne and Brie, to work during the indisposition of Adrien Cochard. The court received him, listened to his affirmations concerning his service, and permitted him to fill the position as long as Cochard should be incapacitated, or "until it should be otherwise ordered by us." [25]

Just as the judges had general supervision over the officers and men of the *maréchaussée* so did they have absolute power over their income, including the right both to seize and to release salaries. The judges reprimanded the *prévôt des maréchaux* of the Ile de France for excessively cruel treatment of his archers and forbade him to punish them by methods other than those prescribed by the ordinances, i.e., "suspension of their salaries and dismissal." [26] Since these rights were granted to the *prévôts des maréchaux*, so were they prerogatives of the judges of the *Connétablie*. The *procureur du roi* had discovered that some officials of the *maréchaussée* in the *généralité* of Paris had been consistently failing to attend their musters. The judges ordered that their salaries should not be paid to them until they should have complied fully with the law.[27] A number of *vice-baillis* had appointed clerks on their own authority, had not compelled them to obtain the necessary letters of appointment, and had failed to have them received by the *Connétablie*. Such actions and omissions violated the royal ordinances on the subject. The lieutenant general therefore forbade all such clerks to continue in office and ordered their salaries stopped at once.[28] The judges could also release a salary that had been seized by virtue of an earlier decree. Quantin Bernard protested that he had been crippled while serving in line of duty and that the action of the court in suspending his salary as archer of the *prévôt des maréchaux* at Meaux was at least unjust, especially on the grounds that he had neglected his duties. He therefore asked for restora-

25. Z^{1c} 46, f. 127r. See also Z^{1c} 282, Sept. 23, Sept. 29, Nov. 18, 1594.
26. Z^{1c} 47, f. 77rv.
27. Z^{1c} 46, f. 72v, 73r. See also Z^{1c} 46, f. 94r.
28. Z^{1c} 47, f. 121v, 122r. See also Z^{1c} 47, f. 199r.

tion of his full income.[29] The court released his salary, "withheld from the said suppliant by act of July 1, 1593," and ordered him to appear at the next muster.[30] Etienne Guichard swore in court that he had missed but one muster and that through no fault of his own. The judges released half his impounded salary and ordered him to attend the musters of his company regularly in the future, under threat of total confiscation of his salary.[31]

The judges could send a trial before another tribunal,[32] or they might deny a petition to that effect and decree that the case should be continued before the *Connétablie*. Marin Noury and the *procureur du roi* protested against Alexandre Daier's petition for a *renvoi*. After listening to the opinion of the *procureur*, the judges denied Daier's petition and ordered the trial to continue before them.[33] The attorney for the women of the Turcault family, who by force of arms had rescued a relative of theirs from the clutches of the law, appeared before the judges and, stressing the difficulties of travel, petitioned for a *renvoi* to the court of the ordinary royal judge in Poitou.[34] The court finally "sent them before the *sénéchal* of Poitiers," but reserved for itself the final disposition of the case. After the *sénéchal* had heard the witnesses and assembled the evidence he was to send the case back to the *Connétablie* for the final decision.[35] The judges had the power to order that a trial in progress before the lower courts of the *maréchaussée* should be brought to the *Connétablie*. They decreed that the case of Silvestre Chareau, *prévôt des maréchaux* of Montfort-L'Amaury, who had illegally punished an archer, should be brought before the *Connétablie* for re-trial.[36] The court commanded the clerk of the *prévôt des maréchaux* at Orléans to send within two weeks to the office of the *Connétablie* the documents in the case of Piart and Fleury, archers in the *maréchaussée* at Orléans.[37]

The powers of the judges of the *Connétablie* endowed them with a quadruple legal personality. First, they were judges. All trials held in the *Connétablie* were argued in their presence. They delib-

29. Z^{1c} 44, f. 125rv.
30. Z^{1c} 44, f. 125v. See also Z^{1c} 45, f. 5r.
31. Z^{1c} 47, f. 210rv.
32. This procedure was called the *renvoi*.
33. Z^{1c} 47, f. 57r.
34. Z^{1c} 47, f. 282v.
35. Z^{1c} 47, f. 283r.
36. Z^{1c} 47, f. 62r.
37. Z^{1c} 47, f. 61r.

erated upon the evidence and handed down the decision, the terms of which they alone decided. Second, they were inquisitors. When an accused person was brought into court, the judges always questioned him concerning the charges against him. They also interrogated witnesses directly. Third, they were investigators and as such ordered new or additional investigations when necessary. Although they did not exercise it frequently, the judges had the right to assume personal direction of investigations.[38] Lastly, they were administrators. As the peak of the hierarchy of the *maréchaussée* the judges had much work of an administrative nature to do, notably in connection with salaries, illegal tenure of office, and disputes over offices. The handling of musters and inductions into office also constituted part of their duties as administrators. They had the power in that capacity to issue interpretative decrees concerning the administration of the offices under their jurisdiction.[39]

They also possessed many single rights and power, which helped them to implement their broad prerogatives. These enabled them to keep a firm hand on the course of a trial and included the decree "notwithstanding the appeal," the provisional award, the summons, the commission, the *exploit*, the power of imposing costs, fines, and bonds, the *renvoi*, and the interlocutory decree.[40] Some of their rights, such as the summons, the commission, and the interlocutory decree, they used primarily in their capacity of investigators and inquisitors. They used the commission to command that an investigation be begun. They used the summons to order suspects and witnesses to appear in court and the interlocutory decree to prolong the time allotted for an investigation. The remainder of these special powers they employed chiefly in their capacity as judges and thereby were able to keep control of the trial and to provide for the enforcement of the decisions which they handed down.

The most important auxiliary of the judges was the *procureur du roi*, who was the permanent representative of the king at the court of the *Connétablie*. The principal reason for the existence of the *procureur* was the necessity for supervision of the king's

38. See Chapter IV for an account of the judges as investigators and inquisitors.
39. See the decree regulating the duties and powers of the *contrôleurs généraux* and the *contrôleurs provinciaux des guerres*. Z¹ᶜ 45, f. 47rv, 48rv.
40. See Chapter IV for the operation of these rights and powers.

interests in the *maréchaussée* and its affairs. This meant not only the protection against encroachment on those interests, but in a broader sense the responsibility for seeing that all ran smoothly in the *maréchaussée*, that disputes over offices were adjusted, and that anything tending to disturb the peace was settled. In fulfilling these duties the *procureur* assumed from time to time three different aspects. He was an investigator and prosecutor. He carried on investigations of conditions in the *maréchaussée*. When he discovered abuses or crimes he came before the court and submitted a petition demanding judicial action. Thereafter he assumed the guiding rôle in the prosecution. He was also a plaintiff. By means of this legal concept the *procureur* was enabled to intervene at any time in any trial which he might deem worthy of official attention. He then virtually replaced the original plaintiff. His third aspect was that of co-ordinator. At the end of every trial he gave his opinion of the validity of the arguments which the parties had presented and submitted his recommendations for action by the court.

From 1578 to 1597 Gilles de Saint-Yon was the *procureur du roi;* from 1597 to 1638 Edmé du Chesne.[41] By letters patent of April 18, 1597, the king granted to the latter "the rank and office of our *procureur* in the *Connétablie* . . . at Paris, which Me Gilles de Saint-Yon, last . . . possessor of it, used to hold and exercise, vacant at present by the pure and simple resignation that he has today made of it into our hands." [42] The *procureur du roi* was installed into office by the judges of the *Connétablie*.[43] On June 25, 1597, du Chesne took the oath and after the usual investigation of his background was admitted into office.[44] The *procureur* was permitted to hold two offices simultaneously. The record for March 14, 1595, refers to Saint-Yon as "*procureur du roi* in the treasury and *maréchaussée*." [45] Barely six weeks after the confirmation of his appointment to the *Connétablie* du Chesne was selected as *procureur du roi* in the *maréchaussée* of the Ile de France. In this position he succeeded Gilles de Saint-Yon, who had also been his predecessor in the *Connétablie*. The letters of appointment stipulated that du Chesne was to fill the new position

---

41. Orgeval, *Connétablie,* p. 305. See Appendix 9 for the text of du Chesne's appointment.
42. Z^{1c} 93, f. 178v.
43. Z^{1c} 93, f. 178v, 179r.
44. Z^{1c} 93, f. 179rv.
45. Z^{1c} 45, f. 37v.

"concurrently or separately from his . . . office of our *procureur* in the said *Connétablie*." [46]

The *procureur's* most important duty was to guard the king's interests in the affairs of the *maréchaussée*. He consequently spent the greatest portion of his time investigating conditions there and frequently came before the judges and demanded action on various problems. Edmé du Chesne recalled that by law the officials of the *maréchaussée* in the *généralité* of Paris were required to have their musters done by the *Connétablie* and commented on the general indifference to the decree. He then demanded that the salaries of those officials who for the past year had not appeared for muster should be withheld until they should have complied with the law.[47] On another occasion du Chesne deposed that "with contempt and disregard for our authority" many *prévôts des maréchaux* and other officers had usurped their positions. They had obtained no letters of appointment from the king; no investigation of their life and habits had been made; nor had they taken the oath of office before the *Connétablie*. He therefore requested authority to summon to court all who were delinquent in these respects.[48] Du Chesne later discovered trials which were not being heard in their proper courts and "requested us to grant him a commission" so that he might bring all cases dealing with military affairs before the *Connétablie* for trial.[49] In this instance the *procureur* was watching over the jurisdictional interests of the *Connétablie* and attempting to prevent encroachment by other tribunals.

There were many cases in which the *procureur* had not begun the prosecution but in which he was nevertheless interested. Under such circumstances he became the actual plaintiff and managed the conduct of the case. The original plaintiff then became the *partie civile*.[50] Those cases in which the *procureur* intervened and became co-plaintiff usually dealt with phases of *maréchaussée* affairs. On one occasion the judges addressed letters patent to royal bailiffs and commanded them to put into effect a sentence

---

46. Z^{1c} 93, f. 198v, 199rv.
47. Z^{1c} 46, f. 72rv, 73r. See also Z^{1c} 44, f. 6r, 110v, 123r, 149v, 152v, 153r, 163v, 164r; Z^{1c} 45, f. 1v, 2r, 52v, 78r.
48. Z^{1c} 46, f. 94r. See also Z^{1c} 46, f. 125v, 126r, 173r, 234rv; Z^{1c} 47, f. 17r, 20v, 21rv, 60rv, 61r, 80rv, 84r, 121v, 122r.
49. Z^{1c} 47, f. 297rv. See also Z^{1c} 47, f. 195v, 225r, 244rv, 267v, 269v, 270r.
50. Parties often petitioned for the intervention of the *procureur du roi*. See Chapter IV.

which the court had handed down. The trial had taken place "at the request" of a certain Jacquart, "with the collaboration of the *procureur du roi*." [51] The judges deliberated upon investigations done at the request of Jean Guytard, a captain of infantry, against Guyot Berthélemy and Gabriel La Combe and, "at the request of the said Guytard, with the collaboration of the *procureur du roi*," ordered Berthélemy and La Combe to appear for questioning.[52]

The third rôle of the *procureur* was to deliver a *conclusion*, or opinion, on every case.[53] When a trial had reached the point where a judgment was in order, the court always commanded that all the evidence be communicated to the *procureur*, who would then analyze it and deliver his opinion. In most cases the record simply states that he delivered an opinion, but does not record its details. A few of these analyses have, however, been preserved. There is no record of the judges' deliberations, which makes it impossible to determine the amount of consideration given to the *conclusions* of the *procureur*. In the cases where the opinion is reproduced, however, the final judgment conforms to it. The *procureur* occasionally refused to commit himself to an opinion. The king had by an edict erected into purchasable offices all positions of archers in the *maréchaussée*.[54] After deliberating and listening to the opinion of the *procureur* the court refused to register the decree.[55] Some months later, the king sent *lettres de jussion*[56] to the *Connétablie*, by which he ordered the court to register the edict at once. The *procureur* when consulted "said to us that he was unable for the present to submit any opinion." [57] In a delicate situation discretion evidently seemed the better part of valor.

Jean Robbe protested his dismissal as archer by Adrien Char-

51. Z^{1c} 46, f. 210v.
52. Z^{1c} 46, f. 223r. See also Z^{1c} 47, f. 78rv, 88v.
53. The *conclusions* of the *procureur* have been briefly referred to in Chapter IV. The present discussion will serve to illustrate more fully the character of the *procureur's* arguments.
54. All offices in the *Connétablie* itself were purchasable.
55. Z^{1c} 46, f. 140r.
56. *Lettres de jussion:* A royal decree sent to a recalcitrant court ordering the immediate registration, without changes, of an edict. If the *jussion* failed, the *lit de justice* was then employed. It must be remembered that when such practices were used, it was not simply the exercise of an arbitrary power, but was the act of the king, as the fountainhead of justice, constitutionally exercising in direct fashion, rather than by delegation, his judicial powers. See Esmein, *Cours*, p. 513.
57. Z^{1c} 46, f. 187rv.

tier, *prévôt des maréchaux* of Blois and Vendômois. Robbe stated that a royal edict had created a new legal post and in the interests of economy had also provided that one archer of the company of Blois and Vendôme (either the junior member or the least diligent) should be dismissed. He asserted that in fulfilling the terms of this edict Chartier had first dismissed and then reinstated another archer, named Verneuil, and then instead had dismissed the plaintiff. Chartier denied this allegation and said that he had been perfectly within his rights in dropping Robbe, who was lazy, had evil habits, and had been confined in the pillory. The latter indignity apparently debarred a candidate from the ranks of the *maréchaussée*.[58] The *procureur* was called upon as usual for his *conclusions* and said that since the edict was designed to reduce the staffs of the *maréchaussée* in the areas where *assesseurs*[59] were established, Chartier was within his rights in dismissing one of his archers. But the dismissal of Robbe was a thing apart from the edict, which had been put into effect by the defendant by his dismissal of Verneuil and which could not be revoked to the prejudice of Robbe. Chartier had in his defense claimed that the archers at Blois and those at Vendôme formed two companies and that therefore he might under the terms of the edict dismiss one archer from each group. This interpretation the *procureur* denied and pointed out that the two groups formed only one company. Chartier had also conducted an investigation into Robbe's character and had uncovered certain facts which he used as justification for his dismissal of Robbe. The *procureur* asserted that the investigation had nothing to do with the question of the dismissal, since the dismissal had occurred nearly two weeks before the start of the investigation. In view of these facts the *procureur* stated that in his opinion the original dismissal should stand and that Robbe should be reinstated.[60]

The *conclusions* of the *procureur du roi*, therefore, served to sum up the case with regard to the validity of the arguments presented by the parties. Therein lies the difference between the *conclusions* of the litigants and those of the *procureur*. The suitors presented their arguments and then stated their demands in the form of *conclusions*. The *procureur*, on the other hand,

58. Z^{1c} 47, f. 268rv. See also Z^{1c} 46, f. 173v, 174r; Z^{1c} 47, f. 84r, 206r.
59. *Assesseurs:* in the Old Régime *assesseurs* most often denoted councillors to a *juge d'épée*. Thus, *baillis* had *assesseurs* who were law graduates. See Chéruel, *Dictionnaire*, I, 51.
60. Z^{1c} 47, f. 268v, 269r.

reviewed and analyzed their contentions and then stated his opinion and recommendations as *conclusions*.

The *procureur's* rôle as the defender of the king's interests necessitated his intervention in the matter of appointments to office in the *maréchaussée*. In every case the judges turned over to the *procureur* the petition for installation into office. The latter always ordered an investigation of the character and ability of the candidate. After the completion of the investigation the *procureur* examined the documents and then delivered his opinion in the form of *conclusions* as to whether or not the applicant should be received.[61]

The clerk of the *Connétablie* had three principal duties. He recorded the proceedings of the court when it sat in judgment and on occasion assisted with investigations. He had certain financial responsibilities and was in a sense the court treasurer as well as its clerk. Finally, he was the keeper of the records, principally those of court proceedings and of the registers of court acts. The clerk was appointed in the same fashion as the *procureur du roi*. The king issued letters patent announcing the appointment, after which the judges of the *Connétablie* inducted the new incumbent into office. On January 17, 1595, Henry IV confirmed François de Bourges as clerk. Claude de Bourges, former owner of the post, had died in December, 1589, and had willed it to François, who was his sole heir. The latter had been received into office, had stayed in Paris, and was included in the amnesty of 1594. He then obtained official confirmation of his inheritance and possession of the office.[62]

The clerk was occasionally called upon to assist in the conduct of investigations and the hearing of testimony. During the trial of Nicolas Lemaire the court at one juncture took from some witnesses brought by Lemaire "the oath required in such a case, in the presence of our clerk, whom we have taken as an assistant." Bourges swore that he knew nothing of the case and that he had not been counsel to either of the litigants.[63]

All official funds were the clerk's responsibility until they had reached those for whom they were destined. Léon Habert had caused several summonses to be served on Jean de Vallencourt, in

61. See Chapter IV. See also Appendix 10 for examples of these *conclusions*.
62. See Appendix 11. As there is no record of the death, resignation, or dismissal of Bourges, it may be assumed that he was still in office in 1610. His tenure of office was therefore at least concurrent with the reign of Henry IV.
63. Z¹ᶜ 44, f. 88r. See also Z¹ᶜ 282, Nov. 4, 5, 14, 18, 26, Dec. 20, 1594.

order to force him to come and show why an obligation for 25 sols, made out by Vallencourt in favor of Habert, and at the time deposited in the clerk's office, should not be paid. Vallencourt had refused to appear and Habert demanded that the note should be handed over to him. The judges granted the petition and discharged the clerk from further responsibility in the matter.[64] The *procureur du roi* reminded the court that by an edict of 1575 the king had assigned an annual sum of 200 livres to the *Connétablie* to supplement its income. This sum was to come from fines and money due to the king from forfeited salaries and was to be "employed by the clerk." [65] This order indicates that the clerk was in general personally responsible for the distribution and administration of funds. When litigants were obliged to furnish bond they deposited the money with the court clerk. Jean Ysambert, a lawyer in the *parlement* of Paris, "appeared at the clerk's office of this court" and furnished bond for Jean Le Roy, *prévôt des maréchaux* of Brie and Champagne.[66]

The clerk registered the letters of appointment of all members of the *maréchaussée* and those administrative officers of the army responsible to the *Connétablie*. Quantin Pillon deposited in the clerk's office his letters of appointment to the rank of *conseiller contrôleur . . . des guerres* of the province of Picardy and the Ile de France, to be enregistered there according to the ordinance of the king of January 15, 1573." [67] When a litigant appeared in answer to a summons he was obliged to register with the clerk. Mere presence in the courtroom was not sufficient in the case of a personal summons. Josias Martineau, a member of the staff of the royal court of Fontenay, presented himself at the clerk's office in order to fulfil the requirements of a personal summons served on him after actions of his had been investigated.[68] The clerk also had to register complaints regarding tenure of office. René Bodet, *lieutenant de robe longue* of the *prévôt des maréchaux* of Anjou, appeared at the clerk's office to register his opposition to the creation of another judge to help the *prévôt*.[69] Gilles Richard, *sé-*

64. Z^{1c} 44, f. 31r. See also Z^{1c} 44, f. 196r.
65. Z^{1c} 44, f. 149v.
66. Z^{1c} 46, f. 173r. See also Z^{1c} 44, f. 70r, 116v.
67. Z^{1c} 44, f. 116v. See also Z^{1c} 44, f. 117r, 121v, 139v; Z^{1c} 47, f, 80rv; Z^{1c} 282, Sept. 17, 27, Oct. 10, 27, Dec. 20, 1594.
68. Z^{1c} 44, f. 163v, 164r. See also Z^{1c} 44, f. 10r; Z^{1c} 45, f. 9v; Z^{1c} 47, f. 13r, 17r, 55r, 79v, 105r, 229r, 261r.
69. Z^{1c} 46, f. 131v, 132r.

néchal of Bourgnouvel, sent his attorney to the clerk's office in order to oppose the induction of François Le Faucheux as assistant judge to the *prévôt des maréchaux* of Mayenne.[70] When the court ordered litigants to produce new evidence they were compelled to deposit it with the clerk. After discovering an irregularity in the resignation as *lieutenant* of the *prévôt des maréchaux* of Orléans by Michel du Bois in favor of Claude Guimont, the judge ordered the pertinent documents to be deposited in the clerk's office and countersigned by the clerk.[71] After the court had issued a default or any other order the clerk made out and delivered the actual document. Included in the evidence in the trial of Jacques Bataille was "the default obtained at the clerk's office" of the *Connétablie* by Jean Lambert, Bataille's attorney.[72]

The low-ranking officers of the *Connétablie* were the bailiffs. In the early years of the sixteenth century there was a single bailiff.[73] In the seventeenth century there were eight bailiffs, and in the eighteenth century three. The single original officer was represented in the later period by a "first" bailiff. It is impossible to tell from the records the number of bailiffs attached to the court during the reign of Henry IV. Like the *procureur du roi* and the clerk, the bailiffs were appointed by the king. After an investigation of their character and religion the judges of the *Connétablie* admitted them into office.[74] The chief duty of the bailiffs was to maintain order in the courtroom during sessions and to perform any necessary errands.[75] Their second principal task was to put into execution, through the use of the *exploit*, the decrees of the tribunal.[76] Gilles de Bray, bailiff in the *Connétablie*, served a court decree on Alexandre de Berthuier in the presence of Robert Pyneau, Mathieu Misles, and several other people, "so that he may not claim the reason of ignorance and may be required to comply with its contents."[77] The tribunal ordered "the first bailiff-in-ordinary of our court" to summon Silvestre Chareau to

70. Z^{1c} 46, f. 173r.
71. Z^{1c} 46, f. 121v. See also Z^{1c} 45, f. 9r, 53v; Z^{1c} 47, f. 62r.
72. Z^{1c} 46, f. 7r. See also Z^{1c} 47, f. 196r, 224r.
73. Orgeval, *Connétablie*, pp. 74–75.
74. See the following letters of appointment: Z^{1c} 92, f. 74v, 75rv, 85rv; Z^{1c} 95, f. 22rv, 23rv, 24r, 45rv, 46r, 54v, 55rv, 129rv, 130r; Z^{1c} 96, f. 118v, 119rv, 120r; Z^{1c} 97, f. 55v, 56rv; Z^{1c} 98, f. 38rv, 39r, 53rv, 54rv. Some examples are reproduced in Appendix 12.
75. Orgeval, *Connétablie*, p. 74.
76. See Chapter IV for a discussion of the operation of the *exploit*.
77. Z^{1c} 44, f. 184v. See also Z^{1c} 44, f. 10v, 30r, 31r, 79r, 89v.

appear in court.[78] When the court pronounced sentence it sometimes provided that the bailiffs should put it into effect. Having settled the dispute between Claude Bédault and Pierre Massicot, the judges commanded the first bailiff of the *Connétablie* to enforce the decree of the court "point by point, according to its form and content." [79]

In its personnel the *Connétablie* by the end of the sixteenth century resembled the ordinary courts of the realm. For the military personnel of the original body and their early, non-professional delegates had been gradually substituted a staff of lawyers and men trained in the practices and customs of the legal profession. These men brought their training and background to the *Connétablie* and during the fifteenth and sixteenth centuries brought about the transformation of its procedure and the character of its personnel. All vestiges of the military court of the fourteenth century had disappeared.

78. Z^{1c} 47, f. 61v, 62r. See also Z^{1c} 47, f. 20v, 79v.
79. Z^{1c} 45, f. 5r. See also Z^{1c} 44, f. 150r; Z^{1c} 45, f. 1v, 78r; Z^{1c} 46, f. 210v; Z^{1c} 47, f. 80v.

VI

GENERAL CONCLUSIONS AND SUMMARY

THE *Connétablie*, like so many institutions, had its period of glory, which was followed by a decline and a transformation. Its brilliant period as a military court was probably between 1450 and about 1510. In the Middle Ages the right of military command carried with it the right to dispense military justice. Since the purely military duties of the *connétable* were numerous and burdensome, the post of *lieutenant* was established to assist in the discharge of his judicial duties. To the *maréchaux de France,* in addition to their military work, fell various administrative and some judicial functions, especially the administration of the relations of the military with the public. The *connétable* and the *maréchaux* both established various deputies and a tribunal to assist them. In the judicial sphere there arose two courts, which relieved the *connétable* and the *maréchaux* of their judicial duties. Besides discipline over the troops both tribunals also handled the civil and criminal cases of the soldiers.

By the late fifteenth century the process which had been operating for so long had finally arrived at its logical conclusion. The work of the *connétable* and that of the *maréchaux* was so similar in character that duplication, conflicts, and confusion were inevitable. The two tribunals therefore finally joined into one body under a single judge. As the new court combined in itself all the prerogatives of its two component parts, it was indeed powerful at the outset of its career. Its sway extended over the disciplinary and administrative phases of army life and included both the responsibility for the maintenance of public order between the army and the civilian population and the majority of the civil and criminal suits of soldiers. Since the army was as yet not very large nor organized on a permanent basis the *Connétablie* could by itself handle military affairs with relative ease.

The first years of the sixteenth century marked the beginning of the decline of the military aspects of the *Connétablie* and its transformation into what was principally an administrative tribunal. The chief factors in this change were the great increase in the size of the army and its organization into a permanent standing force, the establishment of the *Connétablie* as a court permanently located in Paris, and the general constitutional development of the period. The new size of the army and the fact that it was stationed in small groups all over France made it impossible for a single body in Paris to supervise directly its discipline, administration, and relations with the general public. During the sixteenth century, therefore, the *Connétablie* lost completely the power of military discipline to the *prévôts des bandes*. The *commissaires des guerres* were also created and handled the administrative duties of the army and the greater part of the court's former civil and criminal jurisdiction. Finally, the *prévôts des maréchaux* now managed the maintenance of public order almost independently of their parent body. These officers were thus transformed from temporary delegates of the *connétable* and the *maréchaux* into permanent, quasi-independent agents.

Virtually the sole original right which the *Connétablie* retained with respect to the foregoing was the power to register the letters patent of appointment of all members of the *maréchaussée*, including the *prévôts des maréchaux*, and of the *commissaires* and *contrôleurs des guerres*. These officials had originated as the temporary delegates of the *maréchaux* in charge of administrative affairs and of the relations of the troops with the civilian population. They were in theory subject to direction from the *Connétablie*, which was the direct representative of the *maréchaux*. The tribunal therefore registered their appointments and swore them into office.

Although the administrative officials had become in their daily activities virtually independent of the *Connétablie*, the court retained extensive disciplinary power over the *prévôts des maréchaux* with regard to their general conduct and their specific actions both towards the public and their own subordinates. This administrative and disciplinary activity formed by 1600 the most important element of the jurisdiction of the *Connétablie*, which remained in fact, as well as in theory, the head of the *maréchaussée*.

In place of its former jurisdiction over the civil and criminal suits of soldiers the tribunal had acquired a unique jurisdiction, which was exercised chiefly in the Paris area. Cases which dealt however remotely with military affairs were brought increasingly to the *Connétablie* for settlement, under the principle of *faits de guerre*. In most instances the litigants were civilians. The most frequent examples of this new jurisdiction were ransom cases, breaches of contract for supply of the armed forces, and suits involving the plunder of country estates. This reflects the decline of the *Connétablie* as a military tribunal, for such cases had little to do with military affairs and were in any event not numerous. The *Connétablie* used the principle of *faits de guerre* in an effort to make up for the losses it had suffered through the rise of new officials and through its chronic struggle for cases with the ordinary courts.

The *Connétablie* in 1600 therefore had almost nothing in common with the administration and discipline of the army save its name and the right to register the appointments of the *commissaires des guerres* and similar officers. Instead, an entirely new field of work had fallen to it. Most important was the active supervision of the personnel, policy, and actions of the *maréchaussée*. This work comprised the bulk of the administrative and disciplinary jurisdiction of the court. The *Connétablie* was an important indirect factor in the maintenance of public order. Just as the *maréchaussée* had been transformed from a military body into a police force, so had the *Connétablie* undergone a like change. The civil and criminal work of the court was quite small and was confined largely to ransom and plunder trials, in which the participants were usually civilians.

In physical appearance the tribunal had also lost all resemblance to its fourteenth century forebear. Whereas in the earlier period the *connétable* and the *maréchaux* had sat personally in judgment and had been assisted by their *lieutenants*, in 1600 the military officials almost never came to court, except on ceremonial occasions. In their stead presided the lieutenant general, assisted by a *lieutenant particulier*, and on occasion by special supplementary judges known as *juges bénévoles*. Grouped around them were a *procureur du roi*, who watched over the king's interest in the *maréchaussée* and who acted as prosecuting attorney, a clerk, and several bailiffs, who respectively kept the records and performed errands. The new judges, professional lawyers, had brought with them almost the complete procedure employed in the regular courts of the realm. Investigations, questionings, summonses, interlocutory judgments, and other features of ordinary legal procedure were found in the *Connétablie*. In its procedure also, therefore, the tribunal had lost its character as a military court. By the reign of Henry IV the tribunal in no way resembled the military court it once had been. It had metamorphosed into a body directed by professional lawyers and employing highly technical rules of procedure. These changes were part of the general transformation in all the courts of the realm. More and more professional lawyers were replacing the old *juges d'épée*, such as the *baillis* and the *prévôts*, in their active rôles. The original *juges d'épée* appeared in their courts hardly at all and became little more than titular magistrates. The *Connétablie* was no exception to this general trend of fifteenth- and sixteenth-century constitutional development.

While the *Connétablie* had changed a great deal and had lost many of its original powers, it was not, as is sometimes asserted, a complete anachronism during the last three centuries of its existence. The *maréchaussée* was a most important factor in the national life, for to it fell the responsibility of maintaining order in the countryside. As the active supervising head of that organization, therefore, the *Connétablie* had a duty of the most significant sort to fulfil, and had a definite and useful place in the royal administration. The disturbed state of the country after the Wars of Religion and the turbulent and lawless nature of so many of the *maréchaussée* officials and subordinates created a dire need for an administrative tribunal to manage and discipline the *maréchaussée*. The *Connétablie*, because of its origins and history, suited the purpose admirably. It must be noted that there is some question as to the effectiveness of the court. The bulk of the cases originated in Paris itself and most of the remainder in the various provinces north of the Loire. It is doubtful that the influence of the court extended effectively much beyond that river. But the *Connétablie* did work at its administrative tasks with a fair degree of success. The large numbers of cases testify alike to the disturbed state of France, to the industry of the magistrates, and to the regard in which many people held the tribunal.

Like many institutions, the court had outlived the purpose for which it had originally been created. Other offices had been established more specifically for the handling of military administrative and disciplinary problems. But unlike many institutions the *Connétablie* had, while preserving its name and theoretical attributes, changed in character and had found new and useful work to do. While it is true that insofar as the army and military affairs in general were concerned the court was definitely of no importance, it is incorrect to brand as useless the entire work of the *Connétablie et Maréchaussée de France* after it ceased effectively to be a military tribunal.

APPENDIX 1

Letters patent of Henry IV appointing Henry, Duke of Montmorency *connétable de France*. December 8, 1593. Oath of loyalty to the king taken by Montmorency on July 2, 1595. Registration of the letters by the *parlement* of Paris on November 21, 1595. Copy. Z^{1e} 93, f. 14rv, 15r.

Henri, par la grace de Dieu Roi de France et de Navarre, à tous ceux qui ces présentes lettres verront, salut. Considérant que les grandes affaires desquelles nous sommes chargés en l'administration et gouvernement de cestuy notre royaume au moyen des guerres, divisions, et désordres dont nous l'avons à notre avènement trouvé rempli, et qui y continuent encore, requièrent plus que jamais qu'entre les grands et dignes personnages qui nous y assistent et font services en charges particulières qui leur sont départies, il y en ait un d'excellente vertu et suffisance qui ait et embrasse sous nous le sein et la direction générale de nosdites affaires, pour nous y aider et soulager au travail continuel qu'il nous y faut prendre, afin qu'ils puissent tant plus facilement et promptement être expédiés pour le bien de notre service et de nos sujets, en quoi il est aussi nécessaire que celui qui y sera par nous appellé soit autorisé de titre et qualité convenables à ladite charge, nous avons à cette occasion délibéré, conclu, et arrêté de pourvoir à l'état de connétable de France quelque bon, grand, et notable personnage, suffisant, capable, et expérimenté au fait de la guerre et autres affaires de notredit royaume, ayant singulière amour, vrai zèle, et parfaite affection à nous et au bien de la chose publique, et connaissant par effet les très-grandes, claires, louables, et recommandables moeurs et vertus qui sont en la personne de notre très-cher et bien aimé cousin Henri, Duc de Montmorency, pair, premier baron, et maréchal de France, gouverneur et notre lieutenant en notre pays de Languedoc, la longue expérience qu'il a au fait des armes, la bonne, sincère, et ardente amour et affection que de long temps il a toujours eues au service de cette couronne, auquel de ses jeunes et premiers ans il a été nourri près les rois nos prédécesseurs et en plusieurs grandes et importantes charges où il avait été par eux et nous employé comme il est encore à présent, èsquelles il a donné et donne continuellement très-évident témoignage des excellentes vertus qui sont en lui de ses sens, suffisance, intégrité, prud'homie, loyauté, et bonne diligence, au moyen de quoi nosdits prédécesseurs rois se seraient reposés sur lui comme nous avons pareillement fait et faisons encore de plusieurs grands secrets et importantes affaires, lesquels il a si bien et prudemment conduits et administrés en temps de paix et de guerre qu'il en a acquis envers nous et le public de notre royaume un très-grand mérite et perpétuelle louange, et s'est rendu digne d'être exalté, élévé, et constitué en état, charge, et honneur où il ait moyen de faire de plus en plus valoir les grandes et vertueuses qualités qui reluisent en lui au bien de notredit service et de nos sujets. Pour ces causes et autres bonnes et grandes considérations à ce nous mouvantes, avons icelui notre cousin le Duc de Montmorency fait, constitué, établi, faisons, constituons, et établissons par ces présentes connétable de France, et ledit état et office lui avons donné, octroyé, donnons et octroyons pour l'avoir et tenir en hommage de nous et dorénavant exercer par lui aux honneurs, autorités, prérogatives, prééminences, privilèges, franchises, libertés, droits, profits, et émoluments qui y appartiennent et aux gages et état de huit mille écus sol par an que nous lui avons pour ce ordonné et ordonnons par cesdites présentes contre et par-dessus les autres charges, pensions, dons, et bienfaits qu'il a et pourra encore avoir de nous ci-après, lesquelles gages de huit mille écus lui seront dorénavant paiées par chacun an sur nos finances et employées ès états de notre épargne, et afin que notredit cousin puisse mieux donner ordre à toutes et chacunes les choses dépendantes dudit état et office, nous voulons et entendons qu'en tous les lieux, provinces, et endroits, tant en notre royaume que dehors, où il sera et se trouvera il soit et demeure notre lieutenant général représentant notre personne, et en ce faisant nous lui avons donné et donnons plein pouvoir, puissance, et autorité par cesdites présentes de faire vivre nos gens de guerre, tant de nos ordonnances que autres, en un ordre, police, et discipline, au bien et soulagement de nos sujets, leur commander et ordonner ce qu'ils auront à faire pour notre service, taxer et mettre prix à leurs vivres et victuailles, punir et faire punir les transgresseurs, délinquants, ou malfaiteurs, donner leurs amendes, confiscations, et forfaitures, leur remettre et pardonner de par nous les crimes et maléfices qui seront par eux commis et perpétrés ainsi que bon lui semblera et verra être à faire, commettre et députer de par nous un ou plusieurs commissaires ordinaires ou autres personnages capables qu'il avisera pour faire les montres et revues desdits gens de guerre toutefois et quantes que le cas y écherra et qu'il verra bon être, leur faire faire paiement suivant les rôles desdites montres et des deniers qui seront ordonnés pour cet effet, signer et expédier tous états, mandements, et ordonnances qui seront pour ce requis et nécessaires, que voulons servir et valoir à l'acquit et décharge des trésoriers et paieurs de nos gens de guerre et autres qu'il appartiendra par tout où besoin sera, et généralement faire ès choses dessusdites, leurs circonstances et dépendances, et en toutes autres qui peuvent dépendre de l'autorité de notredit lieutenant général et desdites prérogatives, autorités, et prééminences dudit office de connétable, jouir par notredit cousin tout ainsi que nous-mêmes ferions et faire pourrions si présents en personne y étions, hors qu'il y eût chose qui requît mandement plus spécial. Si donnons en mandement à nos aimés et féaux les gens tenants et qui prendront nos cours de parlement et de nos comptes que le contenu en cesdites présentes il fassent lire, publier, et enrégistrer, entretenir, garder, et observer chacuns en leurs égards, et à notredit cousin, duquel nous prendrons le serment et hommage en tel cas requis et accoutumé, icelui mis et institué en possession et saisine dudit état et office ils fassent obéir et entendre de tous ceux et ainsi qu'il appartiendra, et à tous nos lieutenants-généraux, gouverneurs, maréchaux, amiraux de France, colonels, mestres de camp, capitaines, chefs, et conducteurs de nos gens de guerre, grand maître de notre artillerie, capitaines et gouverneurs de nos villes, châteaux, et forteresses, et à tous nos autres justiciers, officiers, et sujets que tous et chacun d'eux respectivement lui obéissent et entendent et fassent obéir et entendre diligemment, et au surplus tous généralement le fassent, souffrent et laissent jouir et user dudit office de connétable de France pleinement et paisiblement, ensemble des honneurs, autorités, prérogatives, prééminences, privilèges, franchises, libertés, pouvoirs, puissances, facultés, gages, droits, profits, et émoluments dessusdits en la propre forme et manière qu'ont joui par le passé dudit état et office de connétable ses prédécesseurs en icelui. Mandons en outre à nos aimés et féaux les trésoriers de notre èpargne présents et à venir que lesdits gages et état ils paient à notredit cousin dorénavant par chacun an et rapportant lesdites présentes ou le vidimus d'icelles dûment collationné pour une fois et quittance de notredit cousin surce suffisante tant seulement nous voulons tout ce que paié, baillé, délivré aura été à cette cause être passé et alloué en la dépense de leurs comptes et rabatu de leurs trésoriers par nos aimés et féaux les gens de nosdites comptes sans difficulté. Car tel est notre plaisir. Et parce que de ces présentes l'on pourra avoir affaire et besoin en plusieurs et divers lieux nous voulons qu'au vidimus d'icelles, fait sous scel royal ou collationné par un de nos aimés et féaux notaires et secrétaires, foi soit ajoutée comme au présent original, lequel nous avons en témoin d'icelles signé de notre main et à icelles fait mettre notre scel. Donné à Vernon le 8e jour de décembre, l'an de grace mil cinq cents quatre vingts treize, et de notre règne le cinquième. Signé HENRY et sur le repli 'par le roi, Revol,' et scellé du grand scel en cire jaune sur double queue. Et sur le repli est écrit 'Aujourd'hui 2e jour de juillet mil cinq cents quatre vingts quinze, le roi étant à Dijon, monsieur le Duc de Montmorency, pair de France, a fait et prêté le serment et hommage qu'il était tenu faire entre les mains de sa majesté à cause de l'état et office de connétable de France, duquel sadit majesté le pourvoit, moi conseiller en son conseil d'état et secrétaire de ses commandements présent. Signé De Neufville.' Plus sur ledit repli est écrit 'La cour a ordonné et ordonne que sur le repli des lettres sera mis 'lues, publiées, et régistrées, et consentant le procureur général du roi pour jouir par l'impétrant de l'état et office de connétable de France comme ses prédécesseurs en ont bien joui et usé. A Paris en parlement le 21e novembre, mil cinq cents quatre vingts quinze.'

APPENDIX 2

Letters patent of Henry IV appointing Charles de Cossé, Count of Brissac, *maréchal de France*. March 30, 1594. Oath of loyalty to the king taken by Brissac on April 2, 1594. Registration of the appointment by the *parlement* of Paris on April 5, 1594. Registration by the *Connétablie* on September 3, 1594. Copy. Z^{1c} 92, f. 73v, 74rv.

Henri, par la grace de Dieu roi de France et de Navarre, à tous ceux qui ces présentes lettres verront, salut. Comme pour dignement administrer la justice et par le moyen d'icelle établir un ferme et assuré repos en toute monarchie la punition des méchants est très requise et nécessaire, aussi tenons nous pour maxime infaillable et certaine que l'une des choses qui plus fait prospérer les royaumes est la reconnaissance des bienfaits et mérites des hommes signalés et la distribution des charges, états, et dignités entre les mains des plus vertueux et gens de bien, car encore que la vertu soit la salaire de soi-même et qu'elle fasse assez connaître ceux qui en sont ornés, sans qu'il leur soit besoin de quelque autre signal pour les illustrer davantage, et que les honneurs qui leur sont octroyés ne les incitent pas plus à bien faire que la vertu qui reluit en eux, cela sert néanmoins pour éveiller les esprits des autres qui sont attirés au même chemin par l'espoir de semblable recompense, s'efforçant par ce moyen de tout leur pouvoir de servir dignement leur prince et profiter sans cesse à sa couronne. C'est pourquoi, voulant reconnaître les bons, agréables, et recommandables services qui ont été faits aux feux rois et bien général de ce royaume par les feux sieurs de Brissac et de Cossé, maréchaux de France, père et oncle de notre aimé et féal Charles de Cossé, comte dudit Brissac, et autres ses prédécesseurs, ceux que ledit sieur comte a rendus auxdits défunts rois et même le signal qu'il nous a fait et à cet état et couronne par la prise et réduction de notre bonne ville de Paris en notre obéissance, dont il est le principal motif et occasion, où il a baillé certaine connaissance et témoignage de sa fidélité, affection à notredit service et au bien de cedit royaume, et de ses moeurs, vertus, intégrité, sens, prud'homie, suffisance, diligence, et loyauté, et pour le décorer des charges et honneurs dont il s'est rendu à ces occasions digne, et qu'ont eues ses prédécesseurs, pour l'espérance que nous avons qu'à leur imitation il continuera de bien en mieux, pour ces causes et autres bonnes et grandes considérations à ce nous mouvantes, icelui sieur Comte de Brissac avons fait, créé, ordonné, et établi, faisons, créons, ordonnons, et établissons par ces présentes maréchal de France, pour icelui état et charge avoir, tenir, et dorénavant exercer, en jouir et user aux honneurs, autorités, prérogatives, prééminences, pouvoirs, puissances, facultés, gages, pensions, droits, profits, et émoluments qui y appartiennent, tels et semblables que les ont et prennent les autres maréchaux de France, suivant l'ancienne création et institution, sans qu'il soit besoin d'iceux spécifier ni déclarer, et lesquels nous tenons pour tous spécifiés et declarés. Si donnons en mandement par ces mêmes présentes signées de notre main à tous nos lieutenants-généraux, gouverneurs de nos provinces, à nos aimés et féaux conseillers les gens tenants nos cours de parlement et à tous capitaines, chefs, et conducteurs de nos gens de guerre, tant de cheval que de pied, de quelque langue et nation qu'ils soient, et autres nos officiers et sujets qu'il appartiendra que ledit sieur comte de Brissac, duquel nous avons pris et reçu le serment en tel cas requis et accoûtumé, et icelui mis et institué en possession et saisine dudit état ils fassent, souffrent, et laissent jouir et user pleinement et paisiblement d'icelui, ensemble des honneurs, autorités, prérogatives, prééminences, pouvoirs, puissances, facultés, gages, pensions, droits, profits, et émoluments dessusdits, et à lui obéir et entendre de tous ceux et ainsi qu'il appartiendra en choses touchantes et concernantes ledit état. Mandons en outre à nos aimés et féaux conseillers les trésoriers de notre épargne présents et à venir que audit sieur comte de Brissac ils paient, baillent, et délivrent ou fassent paier, bailler, et délivrer lesdites gages et pensions audit état appartenantes dorénavant par chacun an selon et en ensuivant les états qui en seront par nous faits et qu'il est accoûtumé en semblable, lesquels, en rapportant cesdites présentes ou vidimus d'icelles dûment collationné pour une fois avec quittance dudit sieur comte de Brissac sur ce suffisants, seront passés et alloués en la dépense de leurs comptes, déduits et rabatus de leurs recettes par nos aimés et féaux les gens de nos comptes, auxquels mandons ainsi le faire sans difficulté. Car tel est notre plaisir. En témoin de quoi nous avons fait mettre notre scel à cesdites présentes. Donné audit Paris le trentième jour de mars, l'an de grace mil cinq cents quatre vingts quatorze, et de notre règne le cinquième. Signé HENRY. Et sur le repli 'Par le roi, RUZE.' Et scellées sur double queue de cire jaune. Et à côté est écrit

'Aujourd'hui deuxième avril mil cinq cents quatre vingts quatorze ledit sieur comte de Brissac a fait et prêté le serment dû et accoûtumé ès mains du roi à cause dudit état de maréchal de France, et lui a pour cet effet sa majesté mis en main le bâton, monsieur le chancelier et moi, conseiller et secrétaire d'état de sadite majesté et de ses commandements, présents. Signé Ruze.

Lues, publiées, et régistrées, ouï sur ce le procureur général du roi, pour jouir par ledit sieur comte de Brissac de l'effet et contenu en icelles, et lequel a judiciairement fait et prêté le serment à l'état et charge mentionnés de l'autre part requis et appartenant, et y a été reçu, fait profession de foi et de la religion catholique, apostolique, et romaine, et l'a juré à Paris en parlement le cinquième jour d'avril, l'an mil cinq cents quatre vingts quatorze. Signé De Villontreye.'

Enregistrées au greffe de la maréchaussée de France, au siège de la Table de Marbre du palais à Paris, ce requérant le procureur du roi en icelle, le 3ᵉ jour de septembre 1594.

Petition of Brissac to the court of the *Connétablie* with reference to the above appointment, and the action of the tribunal. Original. Z^{1c} 282, August 3, 1594.

A Monsieur le lieutenant général de la
maréchaussée de France.

Supplie Charles de Cossé, comte de Brissac, disant qu'il aurait plû au roi par ses lettres patentes données à Paris le trentième jour de mars, l'an mil cinq cents quatre vingts quatorze, signées 'HENRY' et sur le repli 'par le roi, Ruze' et scellées sur double queue de cire jaune, le pourvoir de l'état d'un des maréchaux de France, requérant qu'il nous plût ordonner icelles être enregistrées au greffe de céans en la manière accoûtumée et vous ferez bien.

Goddert . . .

Soit montré au procureur du roi. Fait le 3 d'août 1594.

F. Taverny

Je consens et requiers pour le roi.

De Saint Yon

Soit fait ainsi qu'il est requis. Fait ledit an et jour comme dessus.

F. Taverny

APPENDIX 3

Several types of petitions submitted to the *Connétablie*. Originals. All are found in Z^{1e} 282. See also the petition of the Count of Brissac (Appendix 2).

1. September 19, 1594.

        Messieurs de la maréchaussée.

Vous rémontre Louis Morel, sieur de la Tour, qu'il est pourvu par le roi de l'état de prévôt provincial en Normandie et reçu, tant par feu Monsieur le maréchal de Biron que les trésoriers de France, comme il appert par les provision et réceptions y attachées. Ce considéré vous plaise entériner lesdites lettres, ordonner qu'elles seront régistrées et fera le serment en tel cas requis. Et ferez bien.
    Morel

2. October 24, 1594.

        A Nosseigneurs les maréchaux de France, ou leur lieutenant au siège de la maréchaussée.

Supplie humblement Pierre Hersard, sieur de la Mollière, comme il aurait plû au roi le pourvoir de l'état et office de greffier de monsieur le prévôt des maréchaux de France au pays et duché de Bretagne, suivant la résignation faite dudit office audit suppliant par Maître François Basiouc, dernier paisible possesseur d'icelui, comme se voit par les lettres de provision ci-attachées. Ce considéré,

Qu'il vous plaise, nosdits seigneurs, voir lesdites lettres de provision du sixième jour d'octobre, présent mois et an, et quittances de la finance paiée par ledit suppliant et la résignation dudit Basiouc, le tout à la présente attaché, et en conséquence de ce recevoir à l'exercice dudit état et office, et faire défense à toutes personnes de le troubler ni empêcher, lui et ses commis qu'il nommera sur l'exercice et possession dudit état et office. Et ferez bien.
    P. Hersard

APPENDIXES

3. October 11, 1594.

A Messieurs les maréchaux de France
ou monsieur le lieutenant de la Table de Marbre
au palais de Paris.

Supplie humblement Michel Crestot, sire de la Russillière, lieutenant du prévôt des maréchaux de Perche, disant qu'il a obtenu du roi notre sire les lettres de provision de l'état et office de lieutenant de robe longue en la prévôté de la maréchaussée de France au pays et comté de Perche, châtellénie de Nogent-le-Rotrou, Châteauneuf-en-Thiméraie, anciens ressorts et lieux circonvoisins ci-attachées et autres lettres d'attache et à vous, messieurs, addressées pour les causes y contenues. Ce considéré, il vous plaise les entériner selon leur forme et teneur. Et vous ferez bien.

BILLET

4. November 14, 1594.

A Monsieur le lieutenant général de la
maréchaussée de France.

Supplie humblement Pierre Foucault, disant qu'il avait plû au roi le pourvoir de l'état et office de lieutenant du vice-bailli de messieurs les maréchaux de France à Gisors, que naguère soullait tenir et exercer Maître François Le Forestier, dernier paisible possesseur d'icelui, vacant par son décès, comme il apparaissait par lettres de provision de sa majesté, données à Chartres le dernier jour d'octobre, l'an mil cinq cents quatre vingts douze, ci-attachées. Ce considéré, mondit sieur, il vous plaise mettre et instituer ledit suppliant en possession et saisine dudit état et office, et à faire et prêter le serment en tel cas requis et accoûtumé. Et vous ferez bien.

FOUCAULT

5. August 3, 1594.

A Messeigneurs les maréchaux de France ou leurs
lieutenants au siège de la Table de Marbre.

Supplie humblement Maître Thibaut de Vausselles, pourvu de l'état et office de lieutenant particulier du prévôt des maréchaux de la province de Picardie, résidence d'Amiens, comme il vous appert par les lettres de provision dudit état ci-attachées. Ce considéré, nosdits sieurs, il vous plaise le reçevoir audit état et office, après in-

formation faite de sa vie et moeurs et religion catholique, apostolique, et romaine. Et vous ferez bien.
    Bourse

6. August 25, 1594.

    A Monsieur le lieutenant général de la
        maréchaussée de France.

Supplie humblement Pierre Reboure, prévôt de messieurs les maréchaux de France en l'élection de Châteaudun et Bonneval, disant qu'il aurait plû au roi par ses lettres patentes à vous addressantes, données à Paris le neufième jour d'août, mil cinq cents quatre vingts quatorze, signées par le roi en son conseil, faites et scellées sur simple queue de cire jaune, et pour plusieurs considérations contenues en icelles lui faire augmentation de quatre archers et cinquante écus de gages d'augmentation. Ce considéré, mondit sieur, et attendu que lesdites lettres sont à vous addressantes, il vous plaise ordonner qu'elles seront lues et publiées en cedit siège et régistrées au greffe d'icelui, et que le suppliant jouira de l'effet et contenu d'icelles, selon le bon plaisir de sa majesté. Et vous ferez bien.
    Reboure

7. February 12, 1599.

    A Messieurs les connétable et
        maréchaux de France.

Supplie humblement Thibaut Langlois, armurier du roi, disant qu'il a fait appeler pardevant vous dame Marguerite Hurault, veuve du feu sieur de Givry, pour reconnaître, confesser, ou nier certaine cédule et promesse écrite et signée de la main dudit défunt. Les parties étant comparantes, ladite défendeure a requis ladite promesse lui être montrée, pour icelle reconnaître ou nier. Ce considéré, messieurs, il vous plaise ordonner que ladite promesse et cédule sera montrée à ladite dame défendeure, pour la connaître, confesser, ou nier, et en case de dénégation permettre audit suppliant icelle vérifier tant par comparaison de sein et écriture que témoins, partie présente ou appelée, et ce par l'un de vos huissiers que vous commettrez à cette fin. Et ferez bien.
    J. Marchant

APPENDIX 4

Commission issued by the tribunal of the *Connétablie*. June 10, 1600. Copy. Z^{1c} 47, f. 243v, 244r.

Du dixième jour de juin mil six cents.

Les connétable et maréchaux au premier . . . huissier-sergent ordinaire de notredit siège à la Table de Marbre du palais à Paris, ou autre huissier ou sergent royal sur ce requis, salut. Comme par appointement de nous donné par défaut le sixième jour du présent mois de juin, obtenu par Nicolas Lespoir, enseigne d'une compagnie de gens de pied étant en garnison au château de Marle, demandeur selon une commission du 5e octobre, mil cinq cents quatre vingts dix-neuf, et en exécution de sentence du 10e février dernier, contre Jean de Montbrun, écuier, défendeur d'autre, par lequel aurions renouvellé le délai aux parties de faire leur enquête, suivant le jugement dudit 10e février jusqu'à six semaines, pendant lequel temps elles pourraient faire et parfaire leurs enquêtes par vertu des commissions ja levées ou à lever, et par les commissaires à ce commis avec adjoint, et sauf à recuser si y échet, et outre par le premier juge royal plus proche des lieux, premier des huissiers de la cour de céans, ou autre huissier ou sergent sur ce requis, se pourront les parties faire interroger l'une d'elles l'autre sur faits et articles pertinents, et vaudront les exploits qui seraient faits aux domiciles des procureurs des parties comme si faits étaient aux mêmes parties, jusqu'à ce qu'ils aient élu autres domiciles, suivant l'ordonnance. Pour ce est-il que nous vous mandons et commettons par ces présentes que à la requête dudit exposant, pris avec vous un prud'homme pour adjoint, vous procédiez au fait de l'enquête dudit demandeur, et icelle faite envoyer close et scellée au greffe de notredit siège. De ce faire vous donnons pouvoir.

APPENDIX 5

Examples of the use of evidence by the tribunal of the *Connétablie*. Examination will reveal the various kinds of proof employed, as described in the text. Copies.

1. January 2, 1595. Z^{1e} 45, f. 1r.

Vu par nous ou notre lieutenant général au siège de la maréchaussée de France à la Table de Marbre du palais à Paris les informations faites tant par nous que par Etienne de Brye, examinateur et commissaire au Châtelet de Paris à la requête de Denis Boullé, sieur de La Pointe-Le Comte, conseiller du roi, secrétaire, et contrôleur-général des guerres en Bretagne, à l'encontre du sieur de Poitrincourt, un appellé le capitaine La Chapelle, naguère capitaine d'une compagnie de chevaux-légers sous la charge dudit sieur de Poitrincourt, le capitaine Tiphanie, et un nommé La Ramée, leurs alliés et complices. Vu aussi les passeports obtenus par ledit sieur Boullé tant du roi en cour de Roanne que du duc de Mayenne et autres, et lettres étantes avec lesdites charges et passeports, ensemble les conclusions du procureur du roi en notredit siège, auquel le tout de notre ordonnance a été communiqué.

2. January 28, 1597. Z^{1e} 46, f. 6v, 7r.

Vu le procès criminel d'entre Jacques Bataille, demandeur et respectivement défendeur en crimes et délits, et accusateur d'une part, et Nicolas Noblet, archer du grand prévôt de Normandie, défendeur et aussi respectivement demandeur èsdit cas d'autre part, les lettres d'institution dudit Noblet en une place d'archer dudit grand prévôt de Normandie, du 10ᵉ jour d'avril, mil cinq cents quatre vingts quatorze, signé 'CLAUDE GOBE,' un décret en papier du 10ᵉ jour de mai audit an mil cinq cents quatre vingts quatorze, signé 'LE COUSTELLIER,' . . . certaines copies de deux lettres missives dudit sieur grand prévôt de Normandie et de son lieutenant, l'acte de prestation de serment fait pardevant nous par ledit Noblet sur le cas de l'ordonnance, du 26ᵉ jour d'octobre, quatre vingts quatorze, la commission de nous obtenue par ledit Noblet, par laquelle, entre autres choses, aurions ordonné que les y-dénommés seraient appellés pardevant nous pour répondre aux conclusions dudit Noblet, avec défense de faire poursuite des faits y contenus ailleurs que pardevant nous, ni . . . attenter pour le fait d'iceux cas par ledit Noblet, et à lui permis d'informer des voies de fait et évasion y mentionnés en partie du 24ᵉ jour de janvier, mil cinq cents quatre vingts seize, l'exploit d'assignation donné audit Bataille et autres y dénommés en vertu de notredite commission, certaines pièces et procédures faites par ledit Bataille contre ledit Noblet pardevant le bailli de Villedieu, sur lesquelles serait intervenue sentence dudit bailli donnée par contumace le 18ᵉ jour d'août 1594, l'arrêt du Grand Conseil donné le 4ᵉ jour de novembre dernier, entre ledit Bataille, demandeur en règlement de juges, ledit Noblet défendeur, par lequel les parties auraient été envoyés au siège de la cour de céans, le défaut obtenu au greffe des présentations de cedit siège par Maître Jean Lambert, procureur dudit Bataille demandeur, . . . les actes de comparution personnelles faits par lesdites parties au greffe de cedit siège, les charges et informations réspectivement icelles faites, le jugement de nous donné entre lesdites parties le 14ᵉ jour du présent mois, par lequel aurions ordonné que les parties mettraient respectivement leurs informations, pièces, et procédures concernantes le fait de question, pour, icelles communiquées au procureur du roi et par nous vues, leur être fait droit sur le tout, ainsi que de raison, à quoi elles auraient satisfait. Partant savoir faisons que vus par nous notredit appointement, pièces, procédures, productions, lesdites informations, ensemble les conclusions dudit procureur du roi, auquel le tout a été communiqué . . .

3. March 23, 1600. Z^{1c} 47, f. 223 bis rv, 224r.

Vu le défaut obtenu par Clément Girard, marchand de l'Ile de Ré, demandeur suivant la requête du 6ᵉ jour du présent mois de mars, et requérant le profit et adjudication dudit défaut, contre Messire Henri de Bourbon, duc de Montpensier, défendeur et défaillant. Sur ce que ledit demandeur disait que au mois de juin mil cinq cents quatre vingts dix ledit sieur duc de Montpensier, ayant son armée au pays de Bretagne pour le service du roi, le sieur de Mercoeur voulant assiéger Sainebon [also rendered below as "Hennebon"], où commandait le sieur du Pré, il aurait désiré pourvoir à la place et icelle munir de munitions de guerre pour soutenir le siège, s'il se présentait. Comme il a été ledit demandeur, qui est un pauvre marchand, et qui fait grand trafic avec Jean Huet, l'un des pairs de ladite ville de La Rochelle, il lui aurait été commandé et requis par ledit sieur duc de Montpensier de lui fournir quantité de poudre à canon, piques ferrées, barils de goudron, pain . . . , et vins, et que ledit demandeur, sous le prix commencé avec ledit seigneur duc de Montpensier desdites marchandises avec promesse d'icelle paier, se montant à la somme de six cents soixante écus, deux tiers d'écu, suivant laquelle promesse et marché accordé aurait ledit demandeur délivré et fait délivrer ladite marchandise audit sieur du Pré, et ce suivant la réception dudit seigneur de Montpensier, comme il nous a fait apparoir par la décharge dudit sieur du Pré du premier décembre audit an mil cinq cents quatre vingts dix, et reconnaissance même dudit seigneur de Montpensier du 20e décembre mil cinq cents quatre vingts dix-neuf, aurait mené et livré lesdites marchandises tellement que pour être paié de cette somme de six cents soixante écus, deux tiers, ledit demandeur serait venu en cette ville de Paris où il aurait séjourné trois mois entiers, ayant recherché ledit seigneur de Montpensier pour être paié, ce qu'il n'a pu obtenir, en quoi faisant il se serait consommé en frais, tant à cause des précedants voyages qui lui a convenu faire au pays de Bretagne, Rouen, qu'en cette ville de Paris. C'est pourquoi icelui demandeur nous aurait présenté sa requête narrante de ce que dessus, et attendu que le prêt et délivrance de la marchandise susdite est avenu pendant la guerre, lorsque ledit seigneur défendeur et défaillant avait son armée au pays de Bretagne, et que nous sommes les vrais juges pour connaître de la présente cause, il nous aurait requis qu'il nous plût lui permettre faire ledit seigneur duc de Montpensier en reconnaissance dessusdits réscriptions, promesses, fins, et signatures pour l'effet de la délivrance et reconnaissance sur ce faite, et en ce faisant soi voir condamner paier audit demandeur la somme de six cents soixante écus, deux tiers, et en tous les dépenses, dommages, et intérêts soufferts et à souffrir par ledit demandeur pour le remboursement de ladite somme de six cents soixante écus, deux tiers, jusqu'à ce qu'il soit actuellement paié d'icelle, et ès dépenses, sur laquelle nous aurions mis 'soit ledit seigneur appellé aux fins d'icelle requête,' et sur ce aurait ledit demandeur fait assigner ledit défendeur pardevant nous le 10e mars, aux fins de ladite requête, auquel jour . . . ledit demandeur se serait dûment comparu par Maître Pierre Fortin, son procureur, et au regard dudit seigneur défendeur ne se serait nullement présenté ni comparu, ni procureur pour lui, et aurait ledit demandeur pris et levé son défaut contre ledit défendeur, le profit, utilité, et adjudication duquel est à présent question, et lequel ledit demandeur requiert lui être fait et ajugé. Vu la requête dudit demandeur ci-dessus datée, certaine missive du dernier juin quatre vingts dix, souscrit 'le bien votre, HENRY DE BOURBON,' commençant par ces mots: 'Sieur Girard,' autre missive commençant: 'Maître Girard' du douzième juillet quatre vingts dix, signée 'Du Pre,' un état de vin et ammunition signé au bas 'Romanet,' décharge du sieur de Pré, sieur dudit lieu, gentilhomme ordinaire de la chambre du roi, mestre de camp de douze compagnies de gens de pied, et gouverneur de Hennebond [see above, Sainebon], du premier jour de décembre mil cinq cents quatre vingts dix, signé 'Du Pre,' et plus bas 'par ledit sieur du Pré, Lardet,' reconnaissance dudit seigneur de Montpensier défendeur du 20e décembre mil cinq cents quatre vingts dix-neuf, signé 'HENRY DE BOURBON,' et plus bas 'Lomeron,' et scellée en placard de cire rouge des armes dudit seigneur, ledit défaut obtenu par ledit demandeur au greffe des présentations de notredit siège le 9e jour du présent mois de mars, à lui délivré à faute de comparoir contre ledit défendeur et défaillant le treizième jour dudit mois, la demande pour avoir le profit dudit défaut . . .

APPENDIX 6

Table of trials representative of the payment of fees. Copies.

1. Perrette de Fontenay vs. Pierre du Castel........ 10 écus.
   Z^{1c} 44, f. 3r, 10r.
2. François Tavernier vs. Marie de Rogres.......... 2 écus.
   Z^{1c} 44, f. 13r.
3. Eustache de Jouy vs. Pierre de Miraulmont, Denis Mahon, and others.......................... 14 écus.
   Z^{1c} 44, f. 18v, 69r.
4. Pierre de Miraulmont vs. Arnoul Citart .... 8 écus.
   Z^{1c} 44, f. 20v.
5. Jean Dumoulin vs. Charlotte de Luppe .... 00 écus, ½ écu.
   Z^{1c} 44, f. 22v.
6. Hubert Charpentier vs. Marin Lefebvre......... 3 écus.
   Z^{1c} 44, f. 24v, 27r.
7. Séverin and André Dumont vs. Pierre Ollivier ...... 4 écus.
   Z^{1c} 44, f. 49v.
8. Adrien Barat vs. Philippe du Resnel .... 5 écus.
   Z^{1c} 44, f. 74v, 85r.
9. Nicolas Lemaire vs. Nicolas Lefebvre .... 3 écus.
   Z^{1c} 44, f. 86r, 92v.
10. Herbert Serveuil vs. François Canivet .... 4 écus.
    Z^{1c} 44, f. 135v.
11. Jean Dupuys and Jean Bardin vs. the merchants of Boiscommun, etc. .... 10 écus.
    Z^{1c} 45, f. 53v.
12. Nicolas Noblet vs. Jacques Bataille .... 1 écu, ½ écu.
    Z^{1c} 46, f. 7r.
13. Marin Noury vs. Alexandre Daier and Jacques Pommereau .... 7 écus.
    Z^{1c} 46, f. 55v, 59v, 110r.
14. Michel Le Gallois vs. Thibaut de Vausselles........ 6 écus.
    Z^{1c} 47, f. 79v.
15. Jean Chaudet vs. Charles de Sonningue........... 12 écus.
    Z^{1c} 47, f. 90v.
16. Jean Barangues .... 1 écu.
    Z^{1c} 47, f. 196r.

17. Jean Bigot vs. Nicolas Baguet .... 1 écu.
    Z^{1c} 47, f. 204v.
18. The Duchess of Nemours vs. Jean Le Roux .... 3 écus.
    Z^{1c} 47, f. 206v.
19. The dean and chapter of the collegiate church of Montpénard vs. Jacques Garègues .... 1 écu.
    Z^{1c} 47, f. 216r.
20. Jean Maurault vs. Gabriel de Montboucher........ 10 écus.
    Z^{1c} 47, f. 218r.
21. Pierre Le Mareschal vs. Joachim Le Vasseur ...... 25 écus.
    Z^{1c} 47, f. 257r.

Average fee is six and one-quarter écus.

APPENDIX 7

Letters patent of Henry IV appointing Guillaume Joly lieutenant general of the tribunal of the *Connétablie*. March 23, 1596. Order of the *parlement* of Paris for Joly to take the oath of office. April 30, 1596. Reception of Joly by the *parlement* of Paris on May 3, 1596. Copies. Z^{lc} 93, f. 49v, 50rv.

Henri, par la grace de Dieu roi de France et de Navarre, à tous ceux qui ces présentes lettres verront, salut. Savoir faisons que pour le bon et louable rapport qui fait nous a été de la personne de notre cher et bien aimé Maître Guillaume Joly, avocat en parlement, et de ses sens, suffisance, loyauté prud'homie, expérience au fait de judicature et bonne diligence à icelui, pour ces causes et autres à ce nous mouvantes avons donné et octroyé, donnons et octroyons par ces présentes l'état et office de lieutenant-général de la Connétablie et Maréchaussée de France au siège de la Table de Marbre de notre palais à Paris, que naguère soulait tenir et exercer notre aimé et féal conseiller Maître François Taverny, dernier paisible possesseur d'icelui, vacant à présent par la pure et simple résignation qu'il en a faite en nos mains au profit dudit Joly, par son procureur suffisamment fondé de lettres de procuration quand à ce cy attachées, sous le contrescel de notre chancellerie, pour ledit office avoir, tenir, et dorénavant exercer et en jouir et user par ledit Joly, aux honneurs, autorités, prérogatives, privilèges, prééminences, franchises, libertés, droits, profits, revenus, et émoluments accoûtumés et qui y appartiennent, tout ainsi que faisait et en jouissait ledit Maître François Taverny, tant qu'il nous plaira, pourvu que le résignant vive quarante jours après la date de ces présentes. Par lesquelles donnons en mandement à nos aimés et féaux conseillers les gens tenants notre cour de parlement à Paris qu'après qu'il leur sera apparu des bonnes vies, moeurs, conversation, et religion catholique dudit Maître Guillaume Joly, et de lui pris et reçu le serment en tel cas requis et accoûtumé icelui mettent et instituent ou fassent mettre et instituer de par nous en possession et saisine dudit office, et icelui ensemble des honneurs, autorités, prérogatives, prééminences, privilèges, franchises, libertés, droits, profits, revenus, et émoluments dessusdits, le fassent, souffrent, et laissent jouir et user pleinement et paisiblement, et à lui obéir et entendre de tous ceux et ainsi qu'il appartiendra ès choses touchantes et concernantes ledit office, ôter et débouter d'icelui tout autre illicite détenteur non ayant sur ce ni lettres de provision précédentes en date cesdites présentes. Car tel est notre plaisir. En témoin de quoi nous avons en icelle fait mettre notre scel. Donné à Paris le 23ᵉ jour de mars, l'an de grace mil cinq cents quatre vingts seize, et de notre règne le septième. Signé sur le repli 'par le roi, MÉLIAND' et scellées sur double queue dudit grand scel de cire jaune.

Maître Guillaume Joly, dénommé au blanc a été judiciairement reçu en l'office y mentionné, fait le serment pour ce dû, confession de foi, et juré fidélité au roi. A Paris en parlement, le troisième mai mil cinq cents quatre vingts seize. Signé 'VOYSIN.'

Extrait des régistres de parlement.

Ce jour, après avoir vu par la cour l'information faite d'office de l'ordonnance d'icelle à la requête du procureur général du roi sur la vie, moeurs, religion catholique, apostolique, et romaine, et fidélité au service du roi de Maître Guillaume Joly, avocat en ladite cour, pourvu de l'état et office de lieutenant général en la Connétablie et Maréchaussée de France au siège de la Table de Marbre au palais de Paris, conclusions dudit procureur général, la matière mise en délibération, ladite cour a ordonné et ordonne que ledit Joly sera reçu à faire et prêter le serment audit état sans examen, attendu qu'il a fait preuve de sa capacité en ladite charge d'avocat, et sans tirer à conséquence. Fait en parlement le dernier avril, l'an mil cinq cents quatre vingts seize. Signé 'DU TILLET.'

APPENDIX 8

Letters patent of Henry IV appointing Claude Chrestien *lieutenant particulier* of the *Connétablie*. March 18, 1609. Order by the *parlement* of Paris for Chrestien to take the oath of office. July 27, 1609. Reception of Chrestien by the *parlement* of Paris. July 30, 1609. Registration of the letters patent at the clerk's office of the *Connétablie*. August 1, 1609. Copies. Z^{1c} 97, f. 188v, 189rv.

Henri, par la grace de Dieu roi de France et de Navarre, à tous ceux qui ces présentes lettres verront, salut. Savoir faisons que pour le bon et louable rapport qui fait nous a été de la personne de Maître Claude Chrestien, avocat en parlement, fils de défunt notre aimé et féal conseiller et ci-devant notre précepteur, Florent Chrestien, et des sens, suffisance, loyauté, prud'homie, litérature, expérience au fait de judicature, et bonne diligence à icelle, pour ces causes et autres à ce nous mouvantes, avons donné et octroié, donnons et octroyons par ces présentes l'état et office de notre conseiller et lieutenant particulier au siège de la maréchaussée de France à la Table de Marbre du palais à Paris que naguère soulait tenir et exercer notre aimé et féal Maître Guillaume Bessaut, dernier paisible possesseur d'icelle, à présent vacant tant par son décès que par la démission que Maître Papire Masson, qui en aurait naguère été pourvu et n'y a été reçu, en a volontairement faite en nos mains au profit dudit Chrestien par acte ci-attaché sous le contrescel de notre chancellerie, pour ledit office avoir, tenir, et dorénavant exercer, en jouir et user par ledit Chrestien aux honneurs, autorités, prérogatives, prééminences, franchises, libertés, droits, fruits, profits, revenus, et émoluments audit office appartenants, tels et semblables, et dont avait accoûtumé jouir et user ledit Bessaut, tant qu'il nous plaira. Si donnons en mandement à nos aimés et féaux les gens tenants notre cour de parlement à Paris qu'après qu'il leur sera apparu des capacité, bonne vie, et moeurs dudit Chrestien et de lui pris et reçu le serment en tel cas requis et accoûtumé ils le mettent et instituent ou fassent mettre et instituer de par nous en possession et saisine dudit état et office, et d'icelui ensemble des honneurs, autorités, prérogatives, prééminences, franchises, libertés, droits, fruits, profits, revenus, et émoluments dessusdits le fassent, souffrent, et laissent jouir et user pleinement et paisiblement, et à lui obéir et entendre de tous ceux et ainsi qu'il appartiendra en choses touchantes et concernantes ledit état et office. Car tel est notre plaisir. Donné à Paris le 18ᵉ jour de mars, l'an de grace mil six cent neuf et de notre règne le vingtième. Signé sur le repli 'par le roi, Chélanges' et scellées sur double queue du grand scel de cire jaune, et à côté est écrit 'Maître Claude Chrestien, dénommé au blanc des présentes, a été reçu en l'état et office y mentionné, a fait le serment accoûtumé, et juré de garder fidélité au roi. A Paris en parlement le 30ᵉ juillet, l'an 1609. Signé 'Du Tillet.'

Les présentes ont été régistrées au greffe de la Connétablie et Maréchaussée de France siège de la Table de Marbre du palais à Paris le premier jour d'août, 1609.

Extrait des régistres de parlement.

Ce jour, après avoir vu par la cour l'information faite d'office de l'ordonnance d'icelle à la requête du procureur général du roi sur l'âge, vie, moeurs, et fidélité au service du roi de Maître Claude Chrestien, avocat en la cour, pourvu d'un état de lieutenant particulier au siège de la maréchaussée de France, conclusions dudit procureur général, la matière mise en délibération, ladite cour a arrêté et ordonné que ledit Chrestien sera reçu à faire et prêter le serment audit état et office sans examen. Fait en parlement le 27ᵉ juillet mil six cents neuf. Signé 'Du Tillet.'

APPENDIX 9

Letters patent of Henry IV appointing Edmé du Chesne *procureur du roi* in the *Connétablie*. April 18, 1597. Reception by the *Connétablie*. June 26, 1597. Copies. Z^{1c} 93, f. 178v, 179rv.

Henri, par la grace de Dieu roi de France et de Navarre, à tous ceux qui ces présentes lettres verront, salut. Savoir faisons que pour le bon et louable rapport qui nous a été fait de la personne de notre bien aimé Edmé du Chesne et de ses sens, suffisance, loyauté, prud'homie, expérience, et bonne diligence à icelle, pour ces causes et autres à ce nous mouvantes avons donné et octroié, donnons et octroions l'état et office de notre procureur en la Connétablie et Maréchaussée de France au siège de la Table de Marbre de notre palais à Paris, que naguère soulait tenir et exercer Maître Gilles de Saint-Yon, dernier paisible possesseur d'icelle, vacant à présent par la pure et simple résignation qu'il en a cejourd'hui faite en nos mains par sa procuration y attachée sous notre contrescel, pour ledit état avoir, tenir, et exercer, en jouir et user par ledit du Chesne aux honneurs, autorités, prérogatives, prééminences, franchises, libertés, droits, fruits, profits, revenus, et émoluments qui y appartiennent, tels et semblables dont jouissait ledit de Saint-Yon, tant qu'il nous plaira. Si donnons en mandement à nos très-chers cousins les connétable et maréchaux de France, ou leurs lieutenants au siège de ladite Table de Marbre, qu'après qu'il leur sera apparu des bonnes vie, moeurs, conversation, et religion catholique, apostolique, et romaine dudit du Chesne, et de lui pris et reçu le serment requis et accoûtumé icelui mettent et instituent ou fassent mettre et instituer de par nous en possession et saisine dudit état et office et d'icelui ensemble des honneurs, autorités, prérogatives, prééminences, franchises, libertés, droits, profits, revenus, et émoluments dessusdits ils fassent, souffrent, et laissent jouir et user pleinement et paisiblement et à lui obéir et entendre de tous ceux et ainsi qu'il appartiendra en choses touchantes et concernantes ledit office. Car tel est notre plaisir. En témoin de quoi nous avons fait mettre notre scel à cesdites présentes. Donné à Saint-Germain-en-Laye le 18e jour d'avril, l'an de grace mil cinq cents quatre vingts dix-sept et de notre règne le huitième. Signé sur le repli 'par le roi, POTIER' et scellées sur double queue du grand scel de cire jaune.

APPENDIXES

Maître Edmé du Chesne, dénommé ès présentes a été reçu, mis, et institué en possession et saisine de l'état et office de procureur du roi au siège de la Connétablie et Maréchaussée de France et a fait et prêté le serment en tel cas requis et accoûtumé, judiciairement ouï et ce consentant le procureur du roi audit siège, selon qu'il est plus au long contenu au régistre. Fait cejourd'hui 26ᵉ jour de juin mil cinq cents quatre vingts dix-sept.

Vu la requête à nous présentée par Maître Edmé du Chesne, requérant être reçu, mis, et institué en possession et saisine de l'état et office de notre procureur du roi en notre siège de la Table de Marbre du Palais à Paris, dont il avait été pourvu par le roi, comme il apparaissait par ses lettres de provision, données à Saint-Germain-en-Laye le 18ᵉ jour d'avril mil cinq cents quatre vingts dix-sept, signées sur le repli 'par le roi, POTIER' et scellées sur double queue du grand scel de cire jaune. Vu lesdites lettres de provision, l'information faite de notre ordonnance sur la vie, moeurs, conversation, religion catholique, apostolique, et romaine, et fidélité au roi dudit du Chesne, ensemble les conclusions du procureur du roi auquel le tout avait été communiqué, et après avoir pris le serment en tel cas requis et accoûtumé dudit du Chesne, qu'il a fait profession de foi et de fidélité au roi et été par nous interrogé, tant sur la loi que sur l'ordonnance, nous avons icelle reçu, mis, et institué, reçevons, mettons, et instituons en possession et saisine dudit état et office de procureur du roi en notredit siège de la Connétablie et Maréchaussée de France à la Table de Marbre du Palais à Paris, pour en jouir selon la forme et teneur de sesdites lettres de provision, que nous avons fait lire et publier judiciairement et ordonné icelles être régistrées au greffe de notredit siège. Fait le 26ᵉ jour de juin, mil cinq cents quatre vingts dix-sept.

APPENDIX 10

Examples of the *conclusions* of the *procureur du roi*. Originals. All are found in Z^{1c} 282.

1. October 10, 1594. Pierre Vial, *prévôt des maréchaux* at Châteauneuf-en-Thiméraye, asks for registration of royal letters patent granting him an increase of three archers in the force at his disposal.

Vu les lettres patentes mentionnées en la présente y attachées. Je ne peux empêcher les lettres être lues, publiées, et régistrées au greffe de la cour de céans.

DE SAINT-YON.

2. October 11, 1594. Michel Crestot. See Document 3 in Appendix 3.

Information préalablement faite de la vie, moeurs, religion, et conversation catholique, apostolique, et romaine du suppliant, ferez ce qu'il appartiendra.

DE SAINT-YON.

Et depuis, après avoir vu ladite information, je ne peux empêcher que le suppliant ne soit reçu en l'état et office mentionné en la présente, ayant fait le serment en la manière accoûtumée et profession de sa foi.

DE SAINT-YON.

3. November 25, 1594. Léonard Barbot asks confirmation as *vice-sénéchal* of Angoûmois, Aunis, and the government and city of La Rochelle.

Information préalablement faite de la vie, moeurs, religion, et conversation catholique, apostolique, et romaine du suppliant, ferez ce qu'il appartiendra.

DE SAINT-YON.

Et depuis, après avoir vu ladite information, je ne peux empêcher que le suppliant ne soit reçu en l'état et office mentionné en la présente, ayant fait le serment en la manière accoûtumée et profession de sa foi.

DE SAINT-YON.

4. December 13, 1594. Romain Cauvel asks registration of his letters patent of appointment as archer of the *grand prévôt* of the Ile de France.

Information préalablement faite de la vie, moeurs, religion, et conversation catholique, apostolique, et romaine du suppliant, ferez ce qu'il appartiendra.

De Saint-Yon.

Et depuis, après avoir vu ladite information, je ne peux empêcher que le suppliant ne soit reçu en l'état mentionné en la présente, en la manière accoûtumée et suivant l'ordonnance.

De Saint-Yon.

APPENDIX 11

Letters patent of Henry IV confirming François de Bourges as clerk of the *Connétablie*. January 17, 1595. Reception by the *Connétablie*. January 23, 1595. Copies. Z^{1c} 92, f. 127v, 128rv, 129r.

Henri, par la grace de Dieu roi de France et de Navarre, à tous ceux qui ces présentes lettres verront, salut. Notre bien aimé François de Bourges nous a fait rémontrer qu'il se serait au mois de décembre mil cinq cents quatre vingts et neuf retiré au lieutenant général au siège et juridiction de la maréchaussée de France établi à la Table de Marbre de notre palais à Paris et lui aurait fait entendre le décès avenu au même temps de Maître Claude de Bourges, son frère, dernier possesseur paisible de l'office de greffier dudit siège, lequel il tenait et avait en domaine perpétuel et qu'il était son héritier universel et pour ce l'aurait requis le vouloir reçevoir à l'exercice dudit greffe, ensemble du greffe des présentations en icelui, que ès places de clercs et commis èsdits greffes, pour en jouir ainsi que sondit frère avait fait. Sur laquelle requête, après qu'information aurait été faite sur sa vie, religion, et capacité, suivant le réquisitoire de notre procureur et vues les lettres en vertu desquelles icelui défunt de Bourges en jouissait, l'acte de sa réception, les quittances de la finance par lui paiée pour ladite acquisition, avec le testament par lequel ledit François institué héritier universel dudit défunt son frère, ledit lieutenant l'aurait reçu au serment et mis en possession desdits greffes de ladite maréchaussée et des présentations en icelui et des places de clercs et commis, et parce que lors notre ville de Paris était tenue contre notre service, en laquelle ledit François de Bourges a continué de résider et en icelle exercer lesdits greffes et places de clercs et commis, comme plusieurs nos officiers avaient fait, leurs charges et offices dont étaient ensuivies contre eux les interdictions faites par le feu roi dernier, notre très-honoré seigneur et frère, que Dieu absolve, et par nous, par nos lettres patentes du vingt-huitième mars dernier après la réduction de notredite ville de Paris nous aurions remis et réintégré toutes les juridictions particulières de notredite ville et les officers d'icelles qui étaient demeurés en leurs maisons en l'exercice de leurs offices, et levé lesdites interdictions, pour jouir par eux de leursdits offices après la prestation de serment de fidélité qu'ils seraient tenus faire, ainsi qu'ils soulaient paravant, à quoi ceux de ladite maréchaussée, du nombre desquels est ledit de Bourges, auraient obéi et dès le second jour d'avril ensuivant fait les submissions suivant laquelle ils font [sic] rentrés en leursdits offices, même ledit de Bourges en iceux greffes et places de clercs et commis dont il jouit au mois dudit engagement. Lequel partant il nous aurait supplié vouloir ratifier et confirmer pour lever l'empêchement qu'il lui pourrait être mis ou donné à l'avenir s'il n'avait sur ce nos lettres particulières. Pour ces causes, après qu'il nous est apparu en notre conseil des titres et contrats dudit engagement fait audit feu de Bourges, ensemble de nosdites lettres de déclaration portant rétablissement de nosdits officiers de notre grace spéciale et pleine puissance, nous avons ledit François de Bourges, suppliant, en tant que besoin serait, confirmé et confirmons en la propriété et jouissance desdits greffes de ladite maréchaussée de France établie à la Table de Marbre de notredit Palais à Paris et des présentations et clercs et commis en iceux, pour en jouir suivant ledit engagement et ainsi que icelui défunt son frère en jouissait, et que ledit François, suppliant, a fait lequel engagement comme à nous agréable, voulons et nous plaît sortir effet et être entretenu comme s'il avait été ajugé audit François de Bourges, suppliant, depuis notre avènement à la couronne. Si donnons en mandement à nos très-chers et aimés cousins les maréchaux de France, ou leur lieutenant audit siège de la Table de Marbre de notre palais à Paris, et avertissons nos autres officiers qu'il appartiendra que ces présentes nos lettres de confirmation ils fassent lire, publier, et régistrer, souffrent, et laissent ledit Maître François de Bourges, ses hoirs, successeurs, et ayant cause jouir desdits greffes de ladite maréchaussée et des présentations, places de clercs et commis en iceux, pleinement et paisiblement, ensemble des droits, profits, et émoluments qui y appartiennent, tels et semblables que les prenait sondit feu frère et prédécesseur auxdits offices, et qu'il est plus amplement porté par les ordonnances et règlements faits sur l'ordre de la justice, sans souffrir lui être fait, mis, ou donné aucun trouble ni empêchement au contraire, nonobstant oppositions ou appellations quelconques, pour lesquelles, et sans préjudice d'icelle, ne voulons être différé. Car tel est notre plaisir. En témoin de quoi nous avons fait mettre notre scel à cesdites présentes. Donné à Paris le dix-septième jour de janvier, l'an de grace mil cinq cents quatre vingts quinze, et de notre règne le sixième. Signé sur le repli 'par le roi, THOMAS' et scellé sur double queue de cire jaune.

Lues, publiées au siège de la Connétablie et Maréchaussée de

France à la Table de Marbre du palais à Paris, et régistrées au greffe d'icelui, ouï et ce consentant le procureur du roi, pour jouir par l'impétrant de contenu èsdites lettres, selon leur forme et teneur. Le vingt-troisième jour de janvier mil cinq cents quatre vingts quinze.

Cejourd'hui vingt-troisième janvier mil cinq cents quatre vingts quinze serait comparu judiciairement devant nous Maître François de Bourges, greffier en ce siège, assisté de Maître Jean Salle, son procureur, lequel nous auroit rémontré avoir obtenu lettres de confirmation du roi tant de la vendition en domaine dudit greffe de la cour de céans, greffe des présentations, et clercs en iceux, que de la réception ci-devant par nous faite de sa personne èsdits greffes et places, lesquelles il requiert être lues et publiées en cedit siège et régistrées au greffe d'icelui, pour jouir du contenu d'icelles selon leur forme et teneur, dont il aura acte sur le repli d'icelle avec le présent. Surquoi, ouï le procureur du roi en ses conclusions et de son consentement, après qu'il a eu communication desdites lettres de confirmation données à Paris le dix-septième jour du présent mois, signées sur le repli 'Thomas' et scellées du grand sceau sur double queue de cire jaune, la réception par nous faite de la personne dudit de Bourges èsdits greffes et places de clercs du cinquième jour de décembre mil cinq cents quatre vingts neuf, ensemble de la quittance de la finance paiée pour le prix et achat desdits greffes et places de clercs en iceux, du douzième jour de février mil cinq cents quatre vingts deux, signée 'Le Roy,' le tout par nous vu, ensemble le rétablissement fait par Sa Majesté de nous officiers en ce siège, où ledit de Bourges est compris, du deuxième jour d'avril mil cinq cents quatre vingts quatorze, signé 'H. Godefroy,' nous avons ordonné que sur le repli desdites lettres il sera écrit qu'elles ont été lues et publiées en ledit siège et régistrées au greffe d'icelui, pour jouir par l'impétrant du contenu d'icelles, selon leur forme et teneur, et à ce faire, ensemble pour délivrer le présent acte en forme comme Gabriel de Charbonnières. Fait les an et jour dessusdits. Signé 'Taverny, Bessaut, et De Saint-Yon.'

APPENDIX 12

1. Letters patent of Henry IV appointing Gilles de Bray bailiff in the *Connétablie*. May 6, 1594. Reception by the *Connétablie*. September 6, 1594. Copies. Z^{1c} 92, f. 74v, 75rv.

Henri, par la grace de Dieu roi de France et de Navarre, à tous ceux qui ces présentes lettres verront, salut. Comme par notre édit fait sur la réduction de notre bonne ville de Paris ayons ordonné que les provisions des offices faites par le duc de Mayenne demeureront nulles et de nul effet, et néanmoins que ceux qui ont obtenu lesdites provisions par mort ou résignation de ceux de même parti seront conservés èsdits offices par nos lettres de provision qui leur seront sur ce expédiées sans paier finance, pour ce est-il que pour le bon et louable rapport qui fait nous a été de la personne de Gilles de Bray, et de ses sens, suffisance, loyauté, prud'homie, expérience, et bonne diligence, à icelui pour ces causes et autres bonnes considérations à ce nous mouvantes, avons donné et octroié, donnons et octroions, et conservons par ces présentes l'état et office d'huissier-sergent royal en la Connétablie et Maréchaussée de France au siège de la Table de Marbre du palais à Paris, que soulait tenir et exercer Pierre Lechantre, son beau-frère, dernier paisible possesseur d'icelui, vacant par la démission et pure résignation qu'il en a faite en nos mains au profit dudit de Bray, son beau-frère, par son procureur fondé de lettres de procuration spéciale ci-attachées sous notre contrescel, pour ledit office, suivant notre édit, avoir, tenir, et exercer aux mêmes honneurs, autorités, prérogatives, prééminences, franchises, libertés, droits, profits, et émoluments accoûtumés et audit office appartenants, tels et semblables dont jouissait ledit défunt Lechantre, tant qu'il nous plaira. Si donnons en mandement à nos aimés et féaux les maréchaux de France, ou leur lieutenant-général en la Connétablie et Maréchaussée de France au siège de la Table de Marbre du palais à Paris, que pris et reçu dudit de Bray le serment en tel cas requis et accoûtumé, même celui de fidélité et obéissance qu'il nous doit, si ja ne l'a fait, ils le reçoivent, mettent, et instituent de par nous en possession et saisine dudit office, ensemble des honneurs, autorités, prérogatives, prééminences, franchises, libertés, droits, profits, et émoluments dessusdits, le fassent, souffrent, et laissent jouir et user pleinement et paisiblement, et à lui obéir et entendre de tous ceux et ainsi qu'il appartiendra ès choses touchantes et concernantes ledit état et office. Car tel est notre plaisir. Donné à Paris le sixième jour de mai, l'an de grace mil cinq cents quatre vingts quatorze et de notre règne le cinquième. Signé sur le repli 'de par le roi, BAIGNEAULX' et scellées sur double queue de cire jaune.

Gilles de Bray, dénommé ès présentes, a été reçu, mis, et institué en possession et saisine de l'état et office d'huissier-sergent royal en la Connétablie et Maréchaussée de France au siège de la Table de Marbre du palais à Paris. Et a fait et prêté le serment en tel cas requis et accoûtumé, judiciairement ouï et ce consentant le procureur du roi audit siège, selon qu'il est plus à plein contenu aux régistres. Fait cejourd'hui sixième septembre mil cinq cents quatre vingts quatorze.

Vu la requête à nous présentée par Gilles de Bray, requérant être reçu, mis, et institué en possession et saisine de l'état et office d'huissier-sergent royal en notredit siège de la Connétablie et Maréchaussée de France, dont il aurait été pourvu par le roi, comme il nous aurait fait apparoir par ses lettres de provision données à Paris le sixième jour de mai, l'an mil cinq cents quatre vingts quatorze, signées sur le repli de 'BAIGNEAULX' et scellées sur double queue de cire jaune, vu aussi lesdites lettres, l'information faite de notre ordonnance sur la vie, moeurs, conversation, et religion catholique, apostolique, et romaine dudit de Bray, ensemble les conclusions du procureur du roi, auquel le tout a été communiqué, et après que ledit de Bray a prêté le serment en tel cas requis et accoûtumé, qu'il a fait profession de foi et de fidélité au roi, avons icelle reçu, mis, et institué, reçevons, mettons, et instituons en possession et saisine dudit état et office d'huissier-sergent royal en notredit siège, que soulait tenir et exercer Pierre Lechantre, son beau-frère, dernier paisible possesseur d'icelui, vacant par la démission et pure résignation dudit Lechantre, pour en jouir par ledit de Bray, selon et conformément au contenu desdites lettres que nous avons ordonné être lues et publiées en notredit siège et régistrées au greffe d'icelui, à la charge de garder par ledit de Bray les ordonnances. En témoin de quoi . . . Fait pardevant nous FRANÇOIS TAVERNY, conseiller du roi . . . ce sixième jour de septembre mil cinq cents quatre vingts quatorze.

2. Letters patent of Henry IV appointing Jean L'Advocat bailiff in the *Connétablie*. April 22, 1605. Reception by the *Connétablie*. June 3, 1605. Copies. Z^{1c} 96, f. 118v, 119rv, 120r.

APPENDIXES

Henri, par la grace de Dieu roi de France et de Navarre, à tous ceux qui ces présentes lettres verront, salut. Savoir faisons que pour le bon et louable rapport qui fait nous a été de la personne de notre cher et bien aimé Jean L'Advocat et de ses sens, suffisance, loyauté, prud'homie, expérience, et bonne diligence, à icelle, pour ces causes et autres bonnes considérations à ce nous mouvantes, avons donné et octroié, donnons et octroions par ces présentes l'état et office d'huissier-sergent royal en la Connétablie et Maréchaussée de France au siège de la Table de Marbre du palais à Paris, que soulait tenir et exercer Edmé Roger, dernier paisible possesseur d'icelle, vacant à présent par la pure et simple résignation qu'il en a cejourd'hui faite en nos mains par son procureur suffisamment fondé de lettres de procuration quant à ce ci-attachées, sous notre contrescel, pour ledit état et office avoir, tenir, et dorénavant exercer par ledit L'Advocat, et en jouir et user aux honneurs, autorités, prérogatives, prééminences, franchises, libertés, droits, profits, revenus, et émoluments accoûtumés et audit office appartenants, tels et semblables dont jouissait ledit Roger, tant qu'il nous plaira, encore que ledit Roger ne vive les quarante jours portés par nos ordonnances, de la rigeur desquelles, attendu qu'il en a pour ce paié le droit de dispense, nous l'avons relevé et dispensé, relevons et dispensons par ces présentes, par lesquelles donnons en mandement à nos aimés et féaux les maréchaux de France ou leur lieutenant-général en la Connétablie et Maréchaussée de France au siège de la Table de Marbre du palais à Paris, que, pris et reçu dudit L'Advocat le serment en tel cas requis et accoûtumé, ils le reçoivent, mettent, et instituent, ou fassent mettre et instituer de par nous en pleine possession, saisine, et jouissance dudit état et office, ensemble desdits honneurs, autorités, prérogatives, prééminences, franchises, libertés, droits, profits, revenus, et émoluments dessusdits, le fassent, souffrent, et laissent jouir et user pleinement et paisiblement, et à lui obéir et entendre de tous ceux et ainsi qu'il appartiendra ès choses touchantes et concernantes ledit état et office. Car tel est notre plaisir. En témoin de quoi nous avons fait mettre notre scel à cesdites présentes. Données à Paris le vingt-deuxième jour d'avril, l'an de grace mil six cents cinq, et de notre règne le seizième. Signé 'par le roi, Dubois' et scellées sur double queue du grand scel de cire jaune.

Jean L'Advocat, dénommé ès présentes, a été reçu, mis, et institué en possession et saisine de l'état et office d'huissier-sergent royal en ce siège de la Connétablie et Maréchaussée de France, et a fait et prêté le serment en tel cas requis et accoûtumé, judiciairement ouï et ce consentant le procureur du roi audit siège de la Connétablie et Maréchaussée de France à la Table de Marbre du palais à Paris, selon qu'il est plus au long contenu aux régistres. Fait cejourd'hui troisième juin mil six cents cinq.

Vu la requête à nous présentée par Jean L'Advocat, requérant être reçu, mis, et institué en possession et saisine de l'état et office d'huissier-sergent royal en ce siège, dont il aurait été pourvu par le roi par la résignation pure et simple d'Edmé Roger, dernier paisible possesseur dudit état, comme il apparaissait par ses lettres de provision à nous adressantes, données à Paris le 22e jour d'avril mil six cents cinq dernier. Vu lesdites lettres, l'information faite sur la vie, moeurs, conversation, et religion catholique, apostolique, et romaine dudit L'Advocat, ensemble les conclusions du procureur du roi, auquel le tout a été communiqué, et après avoir pris le serment en tel cas requis et accoûtumé dudit L'Advocat, qui a fait profession de foi, avons icelle reçu, mis, et institué, reçevons, mettons, et instituons en possession et saisine dudit état et office d'huissier-sergent royal en cedit siège, pour en jouir selon la forme et teneur desdites lettres, que nous avons fait lire et publier judiciairement, et ordonné icelles être régistrées au greffe dudit siège, le troisième jour de juin, mil six cents cinq.

BIBLIOGRAPHICAL NOTE

I. Sources.

Archives Nationales, Série Z^{1e}, Connétablie et Maréchaussée de France.
1. Volumes 44–47 inclusive. Régistres d'audiences et plumitifs.
   44 — 1591–1594.
   45 — 1595–1596.
   46 — 1597–1598.
   47 — 1599–1600.
2. Volumes 92–98 inclusive. Régistres de lettres patentes, provisions d'office, etc.
   92 — 1594–1595.
   93 — 1594–1597.
   94 — 1598–1599.
   95 — 1599–1604.
   96 — 1603–1607.
   97 — 1607–1609.
   98 — 1609–1613.
3. Volume 282. Sentences rendues à l'audience.
   282 — 1530–1616.

These three groups of volumes are all valuable, each for a different reason. Volumes 44–47 contain the summaries of the trials, written up by the clerk for this permanent record. From these accounts much useful information may be gathered. Statements of the nature of the cases, of the causes of litigation, and of the personal status of the parties involved yield valuable information concerning the various elements of the jurisdiction of the tribunal and the relative importance of these elements. Facts on the powers of the judges and on their number are to be found. The rôle of the *procureur du roi* and of other officials is outlined. Information concerning procedure is to be found by study of the forms and practices observed in the conduct of the trials.

The principal drawback is that since the accounts are merely summaries of what was done very few texts are given. The use of internal evidence is therefore required for the extraction of information. For example, when a petition is presented to the court, only the fact of its presentation is noted, together with a summary of its contents. Little light is thrown on the form or text of the document, beyond what may be learned from the summary. When a summons is issued, only the fact is noted. When the *procureur du roi* gives an opinion on a case, his words and reasons are almost never included. Hence, we can rarely learn what he said, or whether the judge, in pronouncing sentence, agreed or disagreed. Whether the opinion carried any weight or not cannot generally be determined. Only occasionally is the text of a plea in favor of or against an issue included. It is difficult, therefore, to tell what were the arguments put forth.

Volumes 92–98 are of great value. As they contain texts of letters patent installing people into offices of the *maréchaussée* and the record of the court's action, much data on the rights, privileges, powers, and duties of officials can be gained. This group of volumes is valuable for an appreciation of the court as the administrative head of the *maréchaussée* and forms a complete register of the appointments to office from 1594 to 1610.

Volume 282 has a place peculiar unto itself. It is a collection of miscellaneous, but very vital, documents. In this group of papers are some texts. The first part consists of petitions for appointments to office, submitted by persons who have already obtained the necessary royal letters patent. Here are the petitions themselves. The form and text may be noted. At the bottom of each petition are the written comments of the judge and the recommendations of the *procureur du roi*. Enclosed in each case are the texts of the depositions of the witnesses called to testify as to the character and ability of the applicant and the final action of the court. This single volume, therefore, does much to fill the gaps in Volumes 44–47, which are caused by the omission of texts. Furthermore, many facts relative to procedure and to the functions of the various court officials may be gleaned from a careful study of these bundles of petitions. The second part contains numerous other petitions, dealing with various actions during the hearing of cases. In form these petitions are like those requesting induction into office. This part also includes more trial records.

No printed sources have been used. As has already been noted, it was felt that more value could be gained from the records, which tell what the court was like, than from ordinances and treatises specifying what it ought to be or what some of its judges thought it should be.

II. Secondary works.

The four principal secondary authorities for the study of the court of the *Connétablie* are:

    1. Georges Guichard, *La Juridiction des prévôts du connétable et des maréchaux de France*. Lille, Douriez-Bataille (Imprimerie), 1926.

    2. Gabriel Le Barrois d'Orgeval, *Le Tribunal de la Connétablie de France du XIVe siècle à 1790*. Paris, Boccard, 1917.

    3. A. Esmein, *Cours élémentaire d'histoire du droit français*, 15e éd. Paris, Sirey, 1925.

    4. A. Esmein, *Histoire de la procédure criminelle en France*. Paris, L. Larose et Forcel, 1882.

BIBLIOGRAPHICAL NOTE 157

The first two of these treatises were utilized extensively in the preparation of Chapter I, Guichard when discussing the *prévôts des maréchaux* and Orgeval for the origin and early history of the *Connétablie et Maréchaussée*. Both have been referred to numerous times in the subsequent chapters. Each is an excellent work and each has of necessity certain limitations.

Guichard is more concerned with the *prévôts des maréchaux* than with the *Connétablie*, which to him is incidental to the general study of the *maréchaussée*. He relies a great deal upon the writings of the ancient authors. His chief primary sources are the Thoisy and Cangé collections in the Bibliothèque Nationale and the Series AD VI (*maréchaussée*) in the Archives Nationales. He uses also the collections of ordinances by Isambert and Fontanon. This is not said to detract from the value of his work, since there are few primary sources of material on the *prévôts des maréchaux* other than their letters patent of appointment to office. His treatment of the ancient authors is most judicious and removes many of the legends created by them.

Orgeval has done much with manuscript sources. Besides the Series Z^{1c} in the Archives Nationales, he has used Series U and X (*parlement*) and Series AD VI and AD XVII in the same place. He has also consulted many volumes in the manuscript department of the Bibliothèque Nationale, in the Sainte-Geneviève Library, and in the library of Rouen. The history prior to the sixteenth century comprises but a small part of the entire work. Here again, the lack of manuscript records must bear the blame, for the records of the *Connétablie* prior to about 1530 have all disappeared. The greater part of the work is therefore a history of the court from the sixteenth century to 1790. The bulk of the information is drawn from the eighteenth-century records, with occasional bits drawn from those of the earlier period. Much, in addition, is drawn from the works of three men who were officials of the court: Guillaume Joly (1598), Jean Pinson de la Martinière (1661), and Henri de Bauclas (1748). Orgeval also relies considerably upon others of the ancient treatises already discussed. His chief fault in this respect, I believe, is that he does not regard them with sufficient skepticism. As has already been pointed out, these works were written with the aim of glorifying the tribunal and of extending its jurisdiction as much as possible. Hence, their statements must not be taken too literally. They quote ordinances in detail, always, however, with this proselyting aim in mind. Orgeval likewise relies greatly on ordinances, more so, in truth, than on the court records themselves. Since his work covers several centuries, it is naturally impossible for him to go into very great detail when discussing personnel, jurisdiction, and particularly procedure at a particular period in the court's history. When discussing the personnel of the *Connétablie* he devotes the major part of his attention to the prices paid by the officials for their offices, their privileges and exemptions, and their "professional life." Such a comprehensive discussion of these aspects needs no further elaboration in the present work, which is devoted to an analysis of the powers and duties of the officials, as seen through the court records.

Orgeval's work is of immense value as a full and accurate picture of the court during its four-hundred-year existence and is indispensable as a base of orientation for one who is studying it during a particular, far more restricted, period of time. Both Guichard and Orgeval give complete bibliographies of the works on the *Connétablie* written prior to 1791, in addition to those of modern treatises which contain information on the subject.

Esmein's work on procedure has proved invaluable for a comparison of the procedure of the *Connétablie* and that of the ordinary courts. That the *Connétablie* borrowed much from the regular courts can thus be shown. His other work provides a complete and accurate description and analysis of the judicial system of the Old Régime and much information on legal principles and customs. An understanding of the structure of the judicial system of the Old Régime is indispensable to any study of the tribunal of the *Connétablie*.

A list of works from which bits of information may be gathered concerning the *prévôts des maréchaux* and the history of the *Connétablie*, the *sénéchal*, the *maréchaux*, the *connétable*, and related and derived offices is given below. These passages vary but little and are all of a general nature.

    1. Aubert, Félix, *Histoire du parlement de Paris de l'origine à François Ier*. 2 v. Paris, Picard, 1894.

    2. Boutaric, Edgard, *Institutions militaires de la France avant les armées permanentes*. Paris, Plon, 1863.

    3. Chéruel, A., *Dictionnaire historique des institutions, moeurs et coutumes de la France*. 2 v. Paris, Hachette, 1884.

    4. Chéruel, A., *Histoire de l'administration monarchique en France, depuis l'avènement de Philippe-Auguste jusqu'à la mort de Louis XIV*. 2 v. Paris, Dezobry, E. Magdeleine et Cie., Libr.-Editeurs, 1855.

    5. Delachenal, Roland, "Journal des états généraux réunis à Paris au mois d'octobre 1356," *Nouvelle revue historique de droit français et étranger*, XXIV (July–August, 1900).

    6. Ducoudray, Gustave, *Les origines du parlement de Paris et la justice aux XIIIe et XIVe siècles*. Paris, Hachette, 1902.

    7. Flach, Jacques, *Les origines de l'ancienne France: X^e et XIe siècles*. 4 v. Paris, L. Larose et Forcel, 1886–1917.

    8. Fustel de Coulanges, Numa-Denis, *Histoire des institutions politiques de l'ancienne France*. 6 v. Paris, Hachette, 1882–1892.

    9. Glasson, Ernest, *Histoire du droit et des institutions de la France*. 8 v. Paris, Librairie Cotillen, F. Pichon, successeur, Imprimeur-Editeur. Librairie du Conseil d'Etat, 1887–1903.

BIBLIOGRAPHICAL NOTE

10. Guérin, Paul, "Recherches sur l'office de connétable," *Positions des thèses (Ecole des Chartes), 1867–1868*. Paris, 1868.

11. Le Barrois d'Orgeval, Gabriel, *Le maréchalat de France des origines à nos jours*. 2 v. Paris, Editions Occitania, 1932.

12. Luchaire, Achille, *Histoire des institutions monarchiques de la France sous les premiers Capétiens, 987–1180*. 2 v. Paris, Picard, 1884.

13. Luchaire, Achille, *Manuel des institutions françaises: période des Capétiens directs*. Paris, Hachette, 1892.

14. Marion, Marcel, *Dictionnaire des institutions de la France aux XVIIe et XVIIIe siècles*. Paris, Picard, 1923.

15. Maugis, Edouard, *Histoire du parlement de Paris de l'avènement des rois Valois à la mort d'Henri IV*. Paris, v. 1–3, Picard, 1913–1916.

16. Viollet, Paul, *Histoire des institutions politiques et administratives de la France*. 3 v. Paris, Librairie de la Société du Recueil Général des Lois et Arrêts et du Journal du Palais (Ancienne Maison L. Larose et Forcel), 1889–1903.

17. Viollet, Paul, *Le roi et ses ministres pendant les trois derniers siècles de la monarchie*. Paris, Sirey, 1912.

INDEX

ACTS of war. *See* Jurisdiction, civil, and Jurisdiction, criminal
Administrative jurisdiction. *See* Jurisdiction, administrative
Admiralty courts, 19
Appeal jurisdiction. *See* Jurisdiction, appeal
Appeals, judges' rôle in permitting, 105–106
Appearance of parties in court, required, 72–73; penalties for non-appearance, 72. *See also* Defendants, Plaintiffs, Procedure
Appointements. See Interlocutory decrees
Army, command of in medieval period, 1–3
Assistant clerk. *See* Clerk
Attorneys, rôle, 64 n; presentation of arguments, 87–89. *See also* Procedure
Audiencia constabularii Franciae. See Connétablie et Maréchaussée de France

BAILIFFS, origin and duties, 21, 99, 116–117; procedure for appointment, 116. *See also* Offices
Bailliages, origin and powers, 15
Baillis, creation and powers, 16; appeal from to *Connétablie,* 60; supplanted by professional lawyers, 121
Bessaut, Guillaume, *lieutenant particulier* of *Connétablie,* 104. *See also* Judges
Biron, Charles de Gontaut de, *Maréchal,* 78 n
Bonds, influence of ordinary courts, 93; purpose, 93; uses of, 93–94; procedure and requirements, 94–95; summary, 95. *See also* Procedure
Bourbon, Charles, Cardinal of, 54, 54 n
Bourbon, *Connétable* de, 6, 23
Bourges, François de, clerk of *Connétablie,* 114, 114 n. *See also* Clerk
Bouteiller. *See Grands Officiers de la Couronne*

Brissac, Charles de Cossé, Count of, *Maréchal,* 51

CAROLINGIAN dynasty, command of army under, 1–2; and *Connétable,* 4; and *maréchaux,* 6
Cas prévôtaux. See Jurisdiction, criminal, *prévôts des maréchaux*
Catholic League, actions of, 23
Caution. See Bonds
Chambres des comptes, origin and character, 19
Chambrier. See Grands Officiers de la Couronne
Chancelier, supreme head of justice, 3. *See also Grands Officiers de la Couronne*
Charles VII, king of France, 23
Charles IX, king of France, 24
Chesne, Edmé du, *Procureur du Roi,* 110. *See also Procureur du Roi*
Chrestien, Claude, *lieutenant particulier* of *Connétablie,* 102 n; councillor of the king, 104 n. *See also* Judges
Civil jurisdiction. *See* Jurisdiction, civil
Clerk, 21, 114–116; duties, 99, 114, 120; procedure for appointment, 114; assists in investigations, 114; responsibility for funds, 114–115; registration of *maréchaussée* appointments, 115; certificates for appearance in court, 115–116; issues court orders, 116. *See also* Bourges, François de, Offices
Clermont, Raoul de, *Connétable,* 5
Clisson, Olivier de, *Connétable,* 5
Comes stabuli, in command of armies, 2. *See also Connétable*
Commis greffier, assistant clerk of *Connétablie,* 21. *See also* Clerk
Commissaires des guerres, creation and duties, 8; relation with *Connétablie,* 15; powers, 20; registration of appointments of, 50, 51. *See also Connétablie, maréchaux*
Commissions, characteristics, 82. *See also* Procedure

Comte du palais, 3
Conclusions, characteristics, 88–89; of *Procureur du Roi,* 112–114. See also Procedure
Congés, 64 n. See also Defaults
Connétable, origin in domestic service, 4; one of *Grands Officiers,* 4; commands cavalry, 4; rise in prestige, 5; holds post of *lieutenant-général* in provinces, 5; summary of prerogatives, 5–6; later history and suppression, 6; early relation with *maréchaux,* 6; relation with *prévôts des maréchaux,* 9; relation with *Connétablie,* 15; relation with *audiencia,* 20; letters of appointment registered by *Connétablie,* 50–51; end of personal rôle in *Connétablie,* 98, 106, 120. See also Comes Stabuli, Grands Officiers de la Couronne, maréchaux, Bourbon, Connétable de, Clermont, Raoul de, Clisson, Olivier de, Guesclin, du, Mello, Dreux de, Montmorency, Henry, Duke of, Montmorency, Mathieu II de, Richemont, *Connétable de,* Saint-Pol, Connétable de
Connétablie et Maréchaussée de France, tribunal of, jurisdiction of under Henry IV. See Jurisdiction
Connétablie et Maréchaussée de France, tribunal of, offices under Henry IV. See Offices
Connétablie et Maréchaussée de France, tribunal of, procedure under Henry IV. See Procedure
Connétablie et Maréchaussée de France, tribunal of, 4; original principle behind, 1–2; origin, 11; debate concerning age of, 11–12; originally two tribunals, 12–13; consolidation, 13–14; reasons for consolidation, 14; jurisdiction in fifteenth century, 14–15; one of special tribunals, 15, 19; relation with *contrôleurs des guerres,* 15; rivalry with ordinary courts, 19; decline, 19–20; change in character, 21, 63; additions in personnel, 20–21; summary of development, 21, 98, 118–119; relation with *Grand Prévôt de la Connétablie, conseils de guerre,* and *prévôts des bandes,* 55; forbidden to function by Henry III and Henry IV, 99; reinstated, 99–101, 100 n; summary of offices and personnel, 117; judgment on under Henry IV, 121–122. See also *commissaires des guerres,* Connétable, *contrôleurs des guerres, Grand Prévôt de la Connétablie, maréchaussée, maréchaux,* ordinary courts, *prévôts des maréchaux*

Conseils de guerre, origin and powers, 20; relation with *Connétablie,* 55. See also *Connétablie*
Consular courts. See *Juges consuls*
Contrôleurs des guerres, creation and duties, 8; relation with *Connétablie,* 15; powers, 20; registration of appointments of, 50, 52. See also *Connétablie, maréchaux*
Costs, expenses included in, 93; procedure, 93; decided on by judges, 93, 105. See also Procedure
Cours des aides, origin and character, 19
Cours présidiaux. See Presidial courts
Criminal jurisdiction. See Jurisdiction, criminal
Curia marescallorum. See *Connétablie et Maréchaussée de France*
Curia regis, 15; powers, 17; change in character, 17

DE BOURGES. See Bourges, de
Defaults, use of, 64, 68, 83–85; purpose, 83–84; penalties imposed by, 83–85; summary, 85. See also Procedure
Défauts. See Defaults
Defendants, change in designation during trial, 69–70; personal appearance in court, 71–73. See also Plaintiffs, Procedure
Délais. See Interlocutory decrees
De Saint-Yon. See Saint-Yon, de
Disciplinary jurisdiction. See Jurisdiction, disciplinary
Du Chesne. See Chesne, du
Du Guesclin. See Guesclin, du

ELECTIONS, courts of, 19; appeal from to *Connétablie,* 60
Epernon, Duke of, negotiates with Philip II of Spain, 24
Epices. See Fees
Evidence, introduction of, 67; types considered by judges, 89; examples of, 89–90, 90 n, 91; importance of

INDEX

oral and written, 91–92; circumstances under which oral and written used, 91–92. *See also* Procedure
Exploits, 82–83; types, 83; purpose, 83. *See also* Procedure

*F*AITS *de guerre. See* Jurisdiction, civil, and Jurisdiction, criminal
Faits militaires. See Jurisdiction, civil, and Jurisdiction, criminal
Fees, origin, 95-96; development and characteristics, 96; purpose, 96; unpopularity, 96. *See also* Procedure
Fines, 95, 95 n; imposed by judges, 105. *See also* Procedure
France, conditions in at end of Wars of Religion, 22–24; disregard for authority of crown, 24; neglect of duty in *maréchaussée,* 24–25; misconduct in *maréchaussée,* 25–26; disputes, fraud, intimidation in *maréchaussée,* 26–30; rivalry of *Connétablie* and other courts, 30–31; disregard for due process of law, 31–38; violations of contract, 31–32; seizure for ransom, 31–34; theft and violence, 34–36; summary, 36–38; efforts at improvement, 37–38
France, development of, 23
Francis I, king of France, creates more *maréchaux,* 7

*G*ARLANDE, family of, holds post of *Sénéchal,* war with Louis VI, king of France, 4
Governors, royal, usurpations by, 23–24; appeal from to *Connétablie,* 60
Grand Prévôt de la Connétablie, duties and relation with *Connétablie,* 55; appeal from to *Connétablie,* 59
Grands Officiers de la Couronne, 4; divide governmental duties, 2. *See* Chancelier, Connétable, Sénéchal
Greffier. See Clerk
Greniers à sel, 19
Guesclin, du, *Connétable,* 5

*H*ENRY I, king of France, adds to power of *Sénéchal,* 3
Henry II, king of France, reorganizes *prévôts des maréchaux,* 9–10; reorganizes local courts, 16–17
Henry III, king of France, forbids *Connétablie* to function in Paris, 99

Henry IV, king of France, tasks of, 22–23; invokes principle of *faits de guerre,* 48; forbids *Connétablie* to function, 99; reinstates *Connétablie,* 99–101; example of policy of after 1593, 99–101; supports Guillaume Joly as lieutenant general of *Connétablie,* 103; appoints Edmé du Chesne *Procureur du Roi* in *Connétablie,* 110; confirms François de Bourges as clerk of *Connétablie,* 114, 114 n
Huguenots. *See* Protestants in France

*I*NTERLOCUTORY decrees, issued by judges, 86; purpose, 64, 86; types and time-limits, 86–87, 87 n. *See also* Procedure
Investigations. *See* Procedure

*J*OLY, GUILLAUME, lieutenant general of *Connétablie,* 102–103, 102 n; allowed to hold more than one office, 103; supported by Henry IV, 103; councillor of the king, 103–104. *See also* Judges
Judges, functions of, 98–99, 104; inducted into office by *Parlement* of Paris, 101–102; determine costs, 105; impose fines, 105; rôle in permitting appeals, 105–106; rôle in holding musters of *maréchaussée,* 106; supervision of *maréchaussée,* 106–108; power of *renvoi* and *prévention,* 108; summary, 108–109. *See also Juges bénévoles,* lieutenant general, Offices, Procedure, Bessaut, Guillaume, Chrestien, Claude, Joly, Guillaume, Taverny, François
Juges bénévoles, function and relation with *Connétablie,* 104, 120
Juges consuls, 19; effect on civil jurisdiction of *Connétablie,* 61
Juges d'épée. See Baillis, prévôts
Jurisdiction, summary, 39–40, 60–62, 98, 118–120
Jurisdiction, administrative, 50–55; importance of and character under Henry IV, 50, 54–55, 61, 62, 119; relation of *Connétablie* with military administrative officials, *Connétable,* and *maréchaux,* 50; right to register appointments, 50–52; verification of appointments made by Duke of

Mayenne, 51–52; administrative problems of *maréchaussée*, 52–55; supervision of *prévôts des maréchaux*, 53; disputes over *maréchaussée* offices, 53–54

Jurisdiction, appeal, 59–60

Jurisdiction, civil, 40–44; ransom questions, 40–41; money disputes and contracts, 41–43; booty, 43–44; attempts to bolster, 48; decline of and summary, 44, 61

Jurisdiction, criminal, 44–50; *cas prévôtaux*, 44–49; origin of jurisdiction over *cas prévôtaux*, 44–45; methods of entering upon *cas prévôtaux*, 45; exercise of right of *prévention*. 45; determination of, 45–46; murder and robbery, 46; *faits de guerre*, 46–49; attempts to bolster, 47–48, 49; rebellion and resistance to *maréchaussée*, 49; decline of and summary, 49–50, 61

Jurisdiction, disciplinary, 55–59; when exercised, 55; decline of, 55–56; abandonment of original claim to, 55–56; when and where exercised, 56–59; types, 56–57; investigation of fraud, 57–58; complaints against *maréchaussée*, 58–59

Jurisdiction, *faits de guerre*, 119–120. See also Jurisdiction, civil, and Jurisdiction, criminal

Jussion, lettres de. See Lettres de jussion

Justice *prévôtale*, transformation during sixteenth century, 10–11; part of special tribunals, 15; extension and rivalry with ordinary courts, 19. See also *Prévôts des maréchaux*

LEAGUE, Catholic. See Catholic League

Lettres de jussion, 112, 112 n

Lieutenant des maréchaux. See *Prévôts des maréchaux*

Lieutenant-général, chief judge of Connétablie, 20, 21. See also Judges, Lieutenant general, Offices

Lieutenant general, functions, 101, 104–106; allowed to hold other offices, 101, 103; procedure for appointment and installation into office, 101–102. See also Judges, Offices

Lieutenant particulier, 20, 21; procedure for appointment and installation into office, 102, 102 n; functions, 104. See also Judges, Lieutenant general, Offices, Bessaut, Guillaume, Chrestien, Claude

Lieutenants criminels de robe courte, origin, 10, 11; and reorganization of *prévôts des maréchaux*, 10, 11; relation with Connétablie, 15, 20. See also *Prévôts des maréchaux*

Lieutenants criminels de robe longue, 10

Lieutenants-généraux, creation and powers, 5; appeal from to Connétablie, 60. See also Connétable, maréchaux

Louis VI, king of France, war with Sénéchal, 3–4

Louis IX, king of France, creates second maréchal, 8

Louis XI, king of France, 23; executes Connétable de Saint-Pol, 6; consolidation of Connétablie under, 13–14

Louis XIII, king of France, suppresses office of connétable, 6

MARÉCHAUSSÉE, development in sixteenth century, 10–11; supervision by Connétablie, 106–108. See also France, conditions, Jurisdiction, administrative, Jurisdiction, criminal, Jurisdiction, disciplinary, *prévôts des maréchaux*

Maréchaux, origin, 6; under Merovingians and Carolingians, 6; relation with Connétable, 6; number, 6–7; development, 7–8; relation with *commissaires des guerres*, *contrôleurs des guerres*, and *prévôts des maréchaux*, 8, 9; character after sixteenth century, 11; relation with Connétablie, 15; rôle in *curia marescallorum*, 20; letters of appointment registered by Connétablie, 50–51; appearance in court, 78 n; end of personal rôle, 98, 106, 120. See also Connétable, Connétablie, Commissaires des guerres, Contrôleurs des guerres, Prévôts des maréchaux, Biron, Charles de Gontaut de, Brissac, Charles de Cossé, Count of

Maréchaux de camp, creation and duties, 8. See also Maréchaux des logis

INDEX

Maréchaux de France. See Maréchaux
Maréchaux des logis, 8 n. *See also Maréchaux de camp*
Marescallus, in command of armies, 2. *See also Maréchaux*
Mayenne, Duke of, appointments of to offices in *maréchaussée,* 51–52
Mello, Dreux de, *Connétable,* 5
Mercoeur, Duke of, governor of Brittany, 24, 33
Merovingian dynasty, command of army under, 1–2; and *Connétable,* 2; and *maréchaux,* 6
Military justice, exercise of in medieval period, 1–3. *See also Connétablie,* Jurisdiction, disciplinary
Montmorency, family of, governors of Languedoc, 24
Montmorency, Henry, Duke of, *Connétable,* 51
Montmorency, Mathieu II de, *Connétable,* 5
Musters, in *maréchaussée,* 106. *See also* Judges, Jurisdiction, administrative

OATH, 73; types, 80, 80 n. *See also* Procedure
Offices, additions to, 98–99; rules for succession to, 102–103; changes and development in, 120–121. *See also* Bailiffs, Clerk, Judges, *Lieutenant-général,* Lieutenant general, *Lieutenant particulier,* Ordinary courts, *Procureur du Roi*
Ordinary courts, 15; rivalry with special tribunals, 19; influence on *Connétablie,* 63, 65, 70, 71, 74–75, 75–76, 93, 94, 97, 98, 120–121

PALACE officials, character and powers under Merovingians and Carolingians, 2
Parlement of Paris, appeal to, 19; rivalry with *justice prévôtale,* 19; inducts judges of *Connétablie* into office, 101–102; appeals to from *Connétablie,* 105–106. *See also Connétablie, Parlements*
Parlements, origin and powers, 15, 17; character, 17; creation of provincial, 17–18. *See also Parlement* of Paris
Partie civile, 71, 111. *See also* Procedure, *Procureur du Roi*

Petitions. *See* Procedure
Philip II, king of France, 23; leaves office of *Sénéchal* vacant, 4
Philip the Fair, king of France. *See* Philip IV, king of France
Philip IV, king of France, 18, 23; creates *lieutenants-généraux,* 5; appoints *connétable* one of *lieutenants-généraux,* 5; appoints *maréchaux* as *lieutenants-généraux,* 7
Philip II, king of Spain, negotiates with Duke of Epernon, 24
Plaintiffs, begin proceedings in *Connétablie,* 63–64; types of action begun by petition of, 66; change in designation during trial, 69–70; personal appearance in court, 71–73. *See also* Defendants, Procedure
Pleading, characteristics, 87–88. *See also* Procedure
Presidial courts, origin and powers, 15; reasons for creation, 16; powers, 16–17
Prévention, right of, exercised by *Connétablie,* 45, 108
Prévôt à la suite. See Prévôts des maréchaux
Prévôtal jurisdiction. *See* Justice *prévôtale, Prévôts des maréchaux*
Prévôtés, origin and powers, 15
Prévôts, 3; origin and powers, 15–16; supplanted by professional lawyers, 121
Prévôts des bandes, origin and powers, 20; duties and relation with *Connétablie,* 55. *See also Connétablie*
Prévôts des maréchaux, origin and duties, 8; relation with *Connétable* and *maréchaux,* 9; development, 8–9; during sixteenth century, 9–10; relation with *Connétablie,* 14, 15, 20, 53; courts of among special tribunals, 19; registration of appointments, 50–51; appeal from to *Connétablie,* 59–60; effect on criminal jurisdiction of *Connétablie,* 61; effect on administrative and disciplinary jurisdiction of *Connétablie,* 61, 62. *See also Connétablie,* Jurisdiction, Procedure, *Vice-baillis, Vice-sénéchaux*
Prévôts généraux des maréchaux, 10
Prévôts particuliers des maréchaux, 10
Prévôts provinciaux des maréchaux, 10
Procedure, summary of, 63–64; prin-

THE CONNÉTABLIE

ciples of, 73–74; summary and character of, 92; summary and reasons for development, 96–97; characteristics, 96–97; influence of ordinary courts on, 97; modification of, 98; development of, 120–121
Procedure, interlocutory decrees, 67–68, 74
Procedure, investigations, 74; at request of civilians, 75; at request of *Procureur du Roi,* 75; begun by judges, 75, 75 n
Procedure, oath, 74; conditions under which administered, 79–80
Procedure, petitions, uses of, 63–64; characteristics and place of, 64–69; requirements for use of, 64–65; forms of, 65–66; types of action begun by, 66; in disputes over offices, 66; regulate actions during trial, 66–68; in administrative activities, 69
Procedure, summons, 74, 80–82
Procedure, use of evidence, 74
Procedure, witnesses, 74; actions and use of, 75–79; in investigations, 76–77; testimony of, for appointments to office, 78–79
Procedure. *See also* Attorneys, Bond, Commissions, *Conclusions,* Costs, Defaults, Defendants, Evidence, *Exploits,* Fees, Fines, Interlocutory Decrees, Oath, Plaintiffs, Pleading, *Procureur du Roi,* Provisional sentence, Questioning, *Renvoi,* Sentence, Summons, Witnesses
Procureur du Roi, 109–114, 120; origin and development, 20–21; recommendations for action, 64, 64 n; compelled to use petition, 65; use of petitions by, 68; relation with litigants, 69; duties and activities, 70–71, 99, 110–111; and petition for investigation, 75; procedure for induction into office, 110; intervention in cases, 110, 111–112; holds other offices, 110–111; *conclusions* of, 112–114; and appointment to *maréchaussée* offices, 114; summary, 114. *See also Conclusions,* Jurisdiction, Offices, Procedure, Chesne, Edmé du, Saint-Yon, Gilles de
Procureurs. See Attorneys
Protestants in France, actions, 23
Provincial *parlements. See Parlements*

Provisional sentences, rendered by judges, 104–105. *See also* Offices

QUESTIONING, of defendants, 85–86; of applicants for office in *maréchaussée,* 86; of plaintiffs, 86. *See also* Procedure

RENVOI, 108
Richemont, *Connétable,* 13
Rochefort, family of, war with Louis VI, deprived of *Sénéchalat,* 3–4
Royal offices, definition, 8

SAINT-POL, *Connétable,* 14; executed by Louis XI, 6
Saint-Yon, Gilles de, *Procureur du Roi,* 110. *See also Procureur du Roi*
Sénéchal, commands armed forces, 2; origin, 3; military rôle, 3; judicial powers, 3; powers under Henry I, 3; civil war and vacancy of office, 3–4; summary, 4; supervises *prévôts,* 15–16; disappearance of and effects, 16. *See also Grands Officiers de la Couronne,* Garlande, Rochefort
Sénéchaussées, origin and powers, 15, 16
Sénéchaux. See Sénéchaussées
Sentences, pronouncement of, 92–93. *See also* Procedure
Special tribunals, 15; creation of and reasons, 18–19; rivalry with ordinary courts, 19
Summons, of personal appearance, 80–81; of arrest, 81–82. *See also* Procedure

TAVERNY, FRANÇOIS, lieutenant general of *Connétablie,* 102, 102 n; councillor of the king, 103. *See also* Judges
Tribunaux d'exception. See Special tribunals

VICE-BAILLIS, origin, 10, 11; relation with *Connétablie,* 15, 20. *See also Prévôts des maréchaux*
Vice-sénéchaux, origin, 10, 11; relation with *Connétablie,* 15, 20. *See also Prévôts des maréchaux*

WITNESSES, conditions of testimony by, 77–78. *See also* Procedure